D1303382

Showdown at Newport

The Race for the AMERICA'S CUP

by GEOFFREY F. HAMMOND

Walden Publications · 1974 · New York · London

"Dame Pattie" and *"Columbia"* brush before '67 match. Both were admonished by the club

For
Margarita

SHOWDOWN AT NEWPORT by Geoffrey F. Hammond

Contents

Introduction

It seems to me that too often we view the America's Cup on a shallow, two-dimensional plane where the match is little more than a game between nations or yacht clubs or just boats. Because sailboats are such beautiful things and because the America's Cup itself has acquired the quality of a national treasure it is easy to lose sight of the fact that objects and institutions are not what make the America's Cup challenge one of the greatest sporting events in the world. The truly fascinating thing about the America's Cup is that it is a battleground for men's ambitions. It is not the America's Cup which is really at stake, but rather men's dreams. The Cup matches merely provide an archaic format for a far more serious game than boat racing. The dramas that will be played out in Newport this summer will be in deadly earnest. Most of the participants will be out to prove something, or gain something, or protect something and the players' motivations will have little to do with the sanctity of the old Victorian cup. Rather, men will be gathering at Newport to create reputations or to feed pride or to get revenge. That is the three-dimensional aspect the America's Cup summer and one which I believe deserves to be explained.

Another intriguing facet of the America's Cup races are the mediums in which the conflicts are carried out. Some are in sailcloth, some in aluminum, some in design and still others in newspaper lineage. The actual boat-for-boat dueling at the end of the summer is only a short chapter in a lengthy story.

In "Showdown at Newport" I have tried to take an objective and frank look at the history of the America's Cup, the people involved in the sport and their motivations, and some of the techniques that are employed in the spectacle. It is my hope that this book will help explain a few of the mysteries surrounding the America's Cup and give some insight into what really goes on in Newport.

January 1974   GEOFFREY F. HAMMOND

1

The Club and Its Cup

The center of the yachting universe is located at precisely 37 West 44th Street, New York City. That is the address of the New York Yacht Club—and the home of the shrine of yachtsmen the world over. Through the club's doors and up the broad, red-carpeted staircase is the club's special trophy room. There, prominently displayed on an oak table in the center of this high-ceiling Victorian room, sits the America's Cup. This silver cup is 27 inches high and weighs eight pounds six ounces. It is the oldest international sporting trophy in existence, predating the Davis Cup and the modern Olympics. The Cup is the only international prize that, once won, has never again changed hands. An artifact of a sporting age long vanished and symbol of the Victorian era from whence it sprang, it is the most prized sporting honor in the world. None even approach it.

The America's Cup has been won only once—that is the essence of its lure. It has proven more difficult to attain than the pinnacle of Everest. Like the Grail, it has been sought after by lords and knights and barons, and it has been beyond their grasp. Like Excalibur, it is dreamt about by kings who would never seek it for fear of humiliating defeat. The America's Cup has transcended the status of a mere sporting prize. It has become an object symbolizing power and invincibility for the victor. Long ago, the America's Cup contest left the mundane world of petty rivalry. Today the quest has reached nearly mythical proportions.

Probably the single most important reason for the prestige of the America's Cup as an international challenge prize is the name itself—"America's Cup." The Cup got its name from the boat that first won it—the yacht *America.* Had she been called *Mischief* or *Reliance,* there is little doubt that her trophy would appeal to ambitious foreign yachtsmen far less. Who would spend $4 million to win the Mischief Cup? The Cup by any other name would not have been the same.

The Club

Since the turn of the century the New York Yacht Club has been located in the heart of Manhattan on land donated by a former club commodore, J. Pierpont Morgan. In many ways the club is like the Cup it so jealously guards. Both are survivors of a different age when gentlemen yachtsmen rode comfortably in the plush, dry cockpits of their great, luxurious yachts, while paid crews and helmsmen did the actual sailing.

Then, even as today, the New York Yacht Club was the meeting place of the American Establishment. For over a half century, industrial tycoons and the barons of Wall Street have met there daily for lunch and drinks to talk of yachts and business. The bank presidents, stock brokers, financiers, and chairmen of boards who meet in the club's darkened bar are not merely presidents and board chairmen—they are the presidents and board chairmen of the most powerful institutions in the country. Here the wealthiest moguls meet, eat, drink, and discuss the affairs of a nation.

The New York Yacht Club is more than a yacht club. Like the famous Algonquin Hotel just to the west of it and the Harvard Club a door away to the east, the yacht club has become an institution. But unlike the other famous rendezvous on 44th Street, the New York Yacht Club is not easily entered. Not only must one be an accomplished yachtsman with decades of sailing behind him, but he must know the right people. It is an exclusive fraternity, one into which some men are admitted on their 21st birthday while others wait a lifetime in vain.

America's Second Yacht Club

The New York Yacht Club was formed in 1844, eight years after the Detroit Boat Club, by John Cox Stevens, a leading businessman of New York as well as a leading patron of the arts and society. Stevens was an avid sportsman in the pastoral traditions of the day and was president of the famous Jockey Club. He owned race horses, introduced cricket and baseball to New York society, and loved nothing more than to wager on a sporting event. One of his favorite pastimes was the placing of small fortunes on the yacht races held on the Hudson River, and it was his affinity for gambling that set in motion a chain of events that would ultimately lead to the establishment of the America's Cup contest in the United States.

The club's founder grew up in the tradition of the sea. His father was Colonel John Stevens, who in 1807 built the first practical river steamboat in the United States, and the family fortune was based on steamboats—an appropriate source for the headwaters of the New York Yacht Club. Colonel Stevens' youngest son, Edwin Augustus, who was born in 1795, grew up to have a business head and was put in charge

The Model Room of the New York Yacht Club

of the family fortune. In Edwin's hands, the family's holdings were diversified and grew enormously. His brother John was more sporting and was so spirited that he was often willing to place money on races months in advance.

On July 30, 1844, Stevens called eight of his yacht-owning friends together on his 49-foot *Gimcrack*, which was anchored off Manhattan's Battery. The New York Yacht Club was formed. Most of Stevens' friends were gentlemen-sportsmen like himself who enjoyed nothing better than to find new ways in which to indulge their gaming spirit. One member of the circle, George L. Schuyler, was the grandson of Revolutionary War General Philip Schuyler. Another member was John C. Jay, grandson of Chief Justice John Jay. Jay took his yachting seriously and later sailed around Cape Horn in 1850. Unfortunately, it was his last yachting adventure. He went blind during the trip, and his schooner ran aground and was lost on the Chilean coast. A third member of the original nine was Hamilton Wilkes, president of the Bank of New York. Today, the main office of the Bank of New York is located at 44th Street and 5th Avenue—just a few doors east of the club.

For the most part, the founding fathers of the New York Yacht Club were not only wealthy and the descendants of the founders of the young nation, but also sporting men with a thirst for gambling. A number of the members owned race horses, and what came naturally at the race track came to be just as much fun along New York's growing waterfront. In fact, Commodore Stevens and his friends were some of the most zestful promoters of the notorious "sandbagger sloop" races conducted in the Hudson and in New York Harbor. Many of the sloops were owned by waterfront saloon owners and their Saturday races were wild and raucous; Stevens took a major part in the wagering action.

It was Stevens' fondness for racing that resulted in a NYYC syndicate being formed to build a racing schooner in 1850. Christened *America,* she left New York Harbor in the summer of 1851 for a series of races in The Solent. The club's role in yachting history has been the result of the turn of events in England that summer when Stevens won the 100 guineas cup.

A Club with a Conscience

On February 3, 1859, in a general meeting with 31 yacht-owning members present (only members who owned yachts could vote), a resolution was unanimously passed erasing the yacht *Wanderer* from the New York Yacht Club roster of yachts and striking the name of William C. Corrie from the membership rolls. Corrie was expelled from the club ". . . primarily for his deliberate violation of the laws of the U.S., but more specially for his being engaged in a traffic repugnant to humanity and to the moral sense of this association . . ." *Wanderer* was a slaver actively working the West African coast and had been flying the NYYC burgee.

The membership, though, was not always as morally committed as the above incident might imply. In 1865 the club motto was adopted—*Nos Agimur Tumidis Velis*—"We go with swelling sails." It might just as well have been, "We go with swelling purses," for this period of yacht club history was the heyday of yacht wagering. There were enough boats in the yacht club to provide ample racing opportunities and hardly a weekend went by without numerous racers on the Hudson River and in New York Harbor. Bets of the day ranged from $500 to $1,000 per race with some going as high as $5,000. Because of the high sums and the prestigious people involved and the fact that there were simply few other sports to cover, the yacht races and the wagering were well reported in the New York City newspapers. New York residents followed the success of their favorite sloop with much the same enthusiasm that contemporary New Yorkers display for the Mets. In 1866 an article in one of the newspapers complained that although New Yorkers were proud of the NYYC, it was ". . . high time its great schooners raced offshore and not merely over the ridiculous course from Hoboken to the Southwest Spit."

Ocean Racing Is Born over Turtle Soup

At a lively October dinner at the fashionable Union Club, over what was reported to be much "turtle soup," the first Transatlantic Race was conceived. Two yacht club members must certainly have had their share of "turtle soup," for no one in their right mind would have planned a Transatlantic Race to commence on *December 11th!* The two gallant yachtsmen who had responded to the newspaper's challenge were George Osgood, son-in-law of Commodore Vanderbilt and owner of *Fleetwing,* and Pierre Lorillard, Jr., the tobacco magnate and owner of *Vesta.* These two sportsmen agreed to put up $30,000 apiece, winner take all. The ocean race would start off Sandy Hook with the finish line off the Needles, Isle of Wight. Neither Osgood nor Lorillard were foolish enough to actually take part themselves—the North Atlantic can get cold and rough in the dead of winter—but it would be a great race all the same. The newspapers had a field day. Immediately, the son of the owner of the "New York Herald," James Gordon Bennett, Jr., wanted to be permitted to enter. He would race aboard his yacht *Henrietta.* The swashbuckling Bennett was only 21 and his $30,000 brought the race's purse to a tidy $90,000—the largest cash prize ever offered (before or since) in a yacht race.

Surprisingly, the three boats were evenly matched, all approximately 106 feet long overall with not more than five tons weight difference between them. Bennett's *Henrietta* finished on Christmas day after 13 days 21 hours and won the race by a little over eight hours; *Fleetwing* was second, just 40 minutes ahead of *Vesta.* However, tragedy had struck the Lorillard vessel when eight men were swept over the side and six were lost.

In 1869, James Gordon Bennett in *Dauntless* raced the Englishman, James Ashbury, in the second Transatlantic Race and the first from

Newport, Goat Island and Narragansett Bay

east to west. This time Bennett was not so lucky. He finished two hours behind the English *Cambria* at Ambrose Lightship off New York Harbor. Tragedy again took its toll when during a storm in the crossing, two men were lost off the bowsprit of Bennett's boat in mid-Atlantic.

The NYYC's Financial Barons

The early days of the NYYC coincided with the growth of an emerging, young America. Tough-minded industrialists were carving out empires; it was the era of the robber barons. At this time, the notorious Jay Gould owned the luxurious steam yacht *Atalanta* and wished membership in the NYYC. It is recorded in the club's official history that Gould "was not considered eligible for membership" because of "his notorious 'robber baron' tactics in finance; notably the Black Friday gold corner panic of 1869 and the Kansas Pacific Railroad swindle had earned him many enemies among the rich business men of the era"—and, it might be added, of the club. Gould was refused membership in the NYYC and in the Eastern Yacht Club in Marblehead. As a result, he and a number of other wealthy individuals who couldn't get into the NYYC formed the American Yacht Club.

It was during this time that the center of financial power in the United States was conferred upon such New York notables as Cornelius Vanderbilt, J. Pierpont Morgan, and John Jacob Astor—all not only members but also commodores at one time or another of the New York Yacht Club. Although there was great Populist sentiment in the Midwest and in the South against these financial titans, for the most part they had amassed their staggering fortunes within the laws of the day. In fact, often the law was instrumental to the accumulation of their fortunes.

This was the Gilded Age for the American wealthy and the roster of the New York Yacht Club swelled to reflect that prosperity. In 1897 there were 1,400 New York Yacht Club members and a little over a third of them owned large yachts. Ownership was divided according to the following breakdown: 77 schooners, 79 sloops, 4 naphthas, 12 launches, 156 steam power yachts. Many members lived up the Hudson River and along the coasts of Long Island Sound, commuting to and from Wall Street in their luxurious steam-driven vessels.

NYYC Explorers and Heroes

Not all of the New York Yacht Club's members, though, were out trying to conquer Wall Street. Some were engaged in more remote geographical exploration, and no fewer than three expeditions under the NYYC burgee tried to reach the North Pole. The first such attempt was sponsored by James Gordon Bennett. His yacht *Jeannette* struck out for the North Pole in 1879, but she was crushed by ice as she plunged north of the Bering Sea. A number of the wreck's survivors made it back to Siberia only to starve and freeze to death, leaving behind only their grisly log. In 1903, William Ziegler's *America* also attempted to reach the pole, but got only as far as the island of Franz Joseph Land, north of Russia. But a third, more famous expedition, was eminently more successful.

On September 6, 1909, Robert E. Perry, a naval member of the NYYC, sent a cable to the New York Yacht Club via Cape Race, Newfoundland that read "Steam yacht *Roosevelt*, flying club burgee, has enabled me to add North Pole to club's other trophies." Perry officially reported to the world that he had reached the North Pole by dog sledge over the ice on April 6, and was generally credited, until

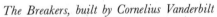

The Breakers, built by Cornelius Vanderbilt

recently, with being the first man to accomplish this feat. Modern scholars now believe that Perry not only did not reach the North Pole, but that he had no idea of exactly where it was.

The Cup Becomes a National Treasure

As the country's sense of manifest destiny forced her boundaries westward, the same sense of national pride gripped NYYC members and the club began to take its international yacht racing even more seriously. Nothing helped the young nation's seafaring pride more than her repeated successful defenses of the America's Cup. It did not take the club and the citizens of New York long to come to the conclusion that there was more at stake during the America's Cup matches than a slender silver cup that originally had been purchased for $500. Americans began thinking of it as a symbol of national honor and with each new triumph over the best from Great Britain, the Cup came to be synonymous with the growth of American power.

During the period after the first World War, the scions of great wealth rose to New York Yacht Club leadership. J. P. Morgan, son of J. Pierpont Morgan, became commodore in 1919. Harold S. (Mike) Vanderbilt was elected commodore in 1921. Harold was the son of William and the grandson of the famous "Commodore" Vanderbilt. In 1927, Vincent Astor, grandson of the John Jacob Astor who came to New York in 1783 and son of the John Jacob Astor who went down with the *Titanic,* took over as commodore.

A Town Near the Wind

It had long been the club's custom to either start or end its annual summer cruise at Newport, Rhode Island. There, far from the hustle of New York City's harbor, was beauty and peace. The waters surrounding Newport are, in fact, the most delightful on the American Eastern Seaboard between the Chesapeake Bay and Maine. The sea there is clean and fresh, the air is crisp and the landscape is exciting and varied. Within a radius of 60 miles there are 15 beautiful islands, hundreds of miles of intriguing coastline, and thousands of enticing coves and inlets, perfect for fishing, swimming, or just enjoying the balmy breezes of a New England afternoon. Most important of all for sailboats, there is usually wind off Newport. In the middle of the summer the air on the western part of Long Island Sound and off Sandy Hook is usually flat, while the weather over Block Island Sound is usually alive with fresh breezes.

Since 1930, the America's Cup has been held in the indigo blue waters of Block Island Sound. The special America's Cup buoy that the Coast Guard sets out at the beginning of each America's Cup summer is exactly nine miles southeast of the Brenton Reef Tower. For each race that 15-foot tall red-and-white buoy marks one end of the starting line and the downwind or leeward mark of the course. (Today, during an America's Cup race the boats will pass it three times. On a clear day, people can sit on their front porches high on the cliffs of lonely Block Island and with binoculars they can watch the tall-masted racing boats more than 15 miles away.) There probably could not be a more historic body of water in which to defend America's honor, for it was through this sound that New England's great whaling fleet sailed to ply the North Atlantic under the press of canvas.

The center of all America's Cup activity is Newport, the legendary summer resort of the American rich. During the country's Gilded Age, which extended from the late 1880's until the enactment of the income tax laws in 1913, Newport was the unrivaled social capital of the United States. Newport was first used as a summer resort by wealthy southerners who sent their families north to escape the summer's swelter, and by the 1830's it had become a popular retreat for many of the prominent families of Charleston, South Carolina. After the New York Yacht Club was founded, its very first order of business was to cruise to Newport in August 1844. It was partly because of the annual NYYC cruises that the town soon became the summer resort and playground for wealthy families of New York, Boston and Philadelphia. By 1890 Newport had become the summer resort of the fabled "400."

The first summer cottages—as the million-dollar mansions were called by their owners—were relatively modest in comparison with those that followed. Fortunes were being made overnight and it wasn't long before each succeeding mansion built at Newport was grander than the last. The golden era saw repeated examples of ostentatious one-upsmanship. Mansions were outdone by chateaus, which were overshadowed by English castles, which were in turn topped by palaces. In 1905 there were no fewer than 100 of these monuments to capitalism and some of the better-remembered last names of their owners were Vanderbilt, Astor, Belmont, Whitney, Auchincloss, Morgan, Grosvenor, Brown, Iselin, Fish and Goelet.

Now, only a few descendents from these 19th-century aristocratic families live on in the mansions of Newport. Most of the cottages are now museums, others have been divided into apartments or have been turned into schools. A number are leased by the America's Cup syndicates to house their crews and rents for the four-month America's Cup summer range from $20,000 to $50,000.

2

"America" Rules the Waves

In 1851 Great Britain seemed truly great. Her empire was at its apex. Europe was living through what has been called the period of *Pax Britannia*. Her fleet had been the undisputed master of the seas for 150 years. Englishmen everywhere rose with throbbing hearts when they heard the stirring strains of "Hail Britannia, Britannia Rules the Waves . . ." And, as blatantly chauvinistic as the song was, it was true. Her Majesty's fleet did indeed rule the oceans.

In the fall of 1850, while England was preparing for what was to be the first World's Fair, the International Exhibition in the Crystal Palace, someone in London wrote to a New York City merchant suggesting that an American show off the speed of the New York pilot schooners the following summer during the yacht races to be held in The Solent. The prospect of crossing the Atlantic to race in England—the home and capital of yachting—against the best of the Queen's fleet appealed to Commodore John C. Stevens and other sporting members of the six-year-old New York Yacht Club. Word of this interest spread quickly along the New York waterfront.

When officials of the Royal Yacht Squadron, then the most prestigious yacht club in the world, learned that a yacht was being built in New York to take part in The Solent races the following year, the commodore of the Squadron sent a letter to Commodore Stevens inviting him to be a guest of the club in Cowes, Isle of Wight. It was a cordial note, the kind one would expect to be exchanged between yacht club commodores, and the Americans prepared for a month of racing—and wagering.

"America" is Born Under Curious Circumstances

There seems to be little doubt that John C. Stevens was the member of the syndicate—the club's very first—to select George Steers

A modern full-size replica of the yacht "America"

as the designer and builder of *America*. Steers initially owned the new boat he had constructed and he offered her to the syndicate with the unique proposal that they would pay him $30,000 for her if she beat every yacht her size in the U.S. and in England and that he would take the yacht back if she did not.

That kind of offer was hard to refuse, even though the boat was overpriced by one-third, and Stevens agreed to the proposal with the stipulation that she be completed by April 1st. The contract was unique and it no doubt amused many observers of the day that the richest men in New York were getting the use of a boat for free that they could reject if she didn't live up to their expectations. Steers was extending quite a bit of cash for the opportunity to expand on his budding design reputation. His highly successful pilot schooner *Mary Taylor* had been launched the year before and had become famous for being the fastest schooner around New York. With another success, Steers would be confirmed as a top naval architect.

The design of *America* rested basically on that of the proved *Mary Taylor,* herself an amalgam of ideas from years of ship design. Much of *America* incorporated features of the famous Baltimore Clippers. Steers duplicated in his design their flat stern quarters and their hollow bow sections to give *America* much of her speed. He was also influenced by American pilot boat design. Large numbers of these boats had been used extensively as slavers and had sailed around the world, spiriting their cargoes of human slaves and opium from market to market and eluding the patrol ships of the law. Not only did they have to be fast to slip by the blockading British fleet off the African coast and move in the light breezes which prevail in the "middle passage" of the Mid-Atlantic's horse latitudes, but they also had to be substantial enough to withstand the fierce tropical storms that often sweep the Caribbean. Steers copied both their low-freeboard and raked-mast features.

America's design had quite a heritage and Steers and the syndicate rightly felt that she would sail with unquestionable speed, especially to windward. Even though the departure from the traditional "cod's-head-and-mackerel's-tail" design was not unique with *America,* designer Steers deserves credit for combining a number of speed-producing factors in one efficient hull. When she was finally launched, everyone could see her long, sleek lines. She was 101 feet overall with a beam 23 feet wide and a draft of 11 feet. She carried 5,263 square feet of canvas. Instead of having full, bluff bows that would push the water, she had a shallow, sharp entry and concave bows that would slice through the water, parting it easily. Her two masts were raked back even more than the pilot schooners of the day, and it was this excessive rake together with her sharp clipper bow that gave *America* the illusion of speed even when she was tied up at the dock.

Long before America was even launched, the English press ran notices of her progress at the Brown yard. The first drawing of *America* to appear anywhere was published in the "Illustrated London News" on March 15, 1851. Trials were held toward the end of May in New York Harbor against the larger centerboard sloop *Maria*. This boat, which was owned by John Stevens, had aboard a crack crew who knew the vessel well and she beat *America* in a number of light-air skirmishes. The New York newspaper "Courier and Enquirer" reported that *America* had won the first two races against *Maria*, losing only the last one because of a gear failure. Commodore Cox disputed the "Enquirer" articles in a letter published in the "New York Herald" that said, "No one of the gentlemen interested in the success of the *America* would more sincerely rejoice at the proofs of her good sailing than myself. But I do not believe that it will serve the interests of her builder . . . to sanction an account so wide of the truth . . ." Because of the late delivery and because *America* had been beaten by *Maria*, the designer-builder was offered $20,000 for her. Steers gave in and accepted the $20,000, and the syndicate immediately fit *America* out for her transatlantic crossing.

"America" Goes Transatlantic

It is a little known fact that the professional crew which had been assembled to cross the Atlantic in such a small craft threatened to desert the vessel before she left for Europe. A couple of days before *America's* scheduled June 21st departure, Captain Dick Brown assembled his men on the dock, gave them a short berating, and then announced, "If there is a white livered dog among you chaps who wants to stay behind, now is the time to bark." No one abandoned ship. On the crew's behalf, it should be noted the *America* was the first pleasure yacht in history to cross the Atlantic. (The first Transatlantic Race was still a decade away.) Despite the confidence exuded by Capt. Brown the crew was understandably fearful as they departed the American shore. It is interesting to note that Commodore Stevens and the NYYC syndicate members chose not to sail across on *America*, taking a commercial steamer, instead.

Thirteen men made the crossing on *America* including designer George Steers, his brother, and a nephew. His brother, James Steers, kept a diary that was published many years later. It is from this source that we learn of the crew's lack of enthusiasm for the North Atlantic crossing and also about the way Commodore Stevens conducted himself during the eventful days on The Solent. According to young Steers, the English landowners were not the only people who displayed an autocratic air at Cowes during the races. Stevens, we are told, was himself guilty of unegalitarian behavior. Indeed, the three Steers only caught sight of the Commodore while he was aboard during the races;

the rest of the time Stevens was off cutting a dashing figure around Cowes and Ryde. There seems to have been some especially hard feelings because Stevens repeatedly locked the door to the cabin which contained his personal supply of whiskey.

America had arrived in Le Havre, France, after an uneventful, 20-day crossing during which time her best run had been 284 miles in a 24-hour period. Stevens and the syndicate boarded at Le Havre, themselves having made the trip on a commercial vessel. *America* crossed the English Channel and proceeded to Cowes but could not arrive before dark. Wisely, the Americans anchored in The Solent six miles east of Cowes as a thick fog set in. The next morning an incident occurred that may well have spoiled Commodore Steven's wagering plans. When the fog lifted, news of the arrival of the "Yankee," as she was called in the English press, spread along the Isle of Wight coast as if sent by telegram. The following is an account of what happened as told in New York the following October by Commodore Stevens at a dinner given in his honor at Astor House:

"... a gentle breeze sprang up, and with it came gliding down the *Laverock,* one of the newest and fastest cutters of her class. The news spread like lightning that the Yankee clipper had arrived, and that the *Laverock* had gone down to show her the way up.

"The yachts and vessels in the harbor, the wharfs, and the windows of all the houses bordering on them, were filled with thousands of spectators, watching with eager eyes the eventful trial they saw we could not escape; for

John Cox Stevens, NYYC founder

George Steers, designer of "America"

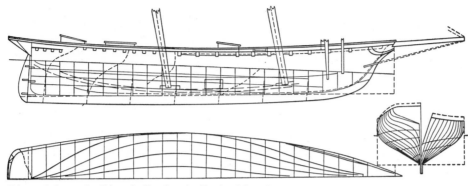

Lines of the yacht "America" taken in England in 1851

the *Laverock* had stuck to us, sometimes laying to, and sometimes tacking, with no intention of quitting us.

"We were loaded with extra sails, with beef and pork, and bread, enough for an East India voyage, and were somewhere between four and five inches too deep in the water. We got up our sails with heavy hearts—the wind had increased to a breeze; and after waiting until we were ashamed to wait any longer, we let her go about 200 yards ahead, then started in her wake.

"I have seen and been engaged in many exciting trials at sea and on shore without suffering one-hundredth part of the trepidation I felt at the thought of being beaten by the *Laverock* in this eventful trial.

"During the first five minutes not a sound was heard, save, perhaps, the beating of our anxious hearts, or the slight ripple of the water upon her sword-like stem. The captain (Dick Brown) was crouched down upon the floor of the cockpit, his seemingly unconscious hand upon the tiller, with his stern, unaltering gaze upon the vessel ahead. The men were motionless as statues, with eager eyes fastened upon the *Laverock* with a fixedness and intensity that seemed almost supernatural. The pencil of an artist might perhaps convey the expression, but no words can describe it.

"It could not, nor did not, last long. We worked quickly and surely to windward of her wake. The crisis was passed; and some dozen of deep-drawn sighs proved that the agony was over. We came to anchor a quarter, or, perhaps a third of a mile ahead."

"America" Arrives to a Mixed Reaction

It was reported in an English journal that first shock and then amusement was the response of Cowes yachtsmen when reports of *America's* arrival reached what is generally considered to be the cradle of the sport. Englishmen had not even known of the existence of yachts in the United States, much less of a yacht club. There was no doubt a great shaking of heads among the fathers of the Royal Yacht Squadron in Cowes when they received a letter from Commodore Stevens before his arrival that read in part: ". . . We propose to avail ourselves of your friendly bidding and take with good grace the sound thrashing we are likely to get by venturing our longshore craft on your rough waters."

Because of the International Exhibition in Hyde Park, the eyes of the world were focused on England that summer. The cream of society had decided to descend on the Isle of Wight for two weeks of regattas in August. More than the usual number of visitors crowded into Cowes, and even Southampton, across The Solent, was filled with visitors. One English newspaper of the day reported, "Cowes is so crammed with people that scarcely a bed is to be had for love or money. Visitors are moving about the streets long after midnight knocking on doors . . ."

"The London Times" reported, ". . . A large part of the peerage and gentry of the United Kingdom left their residences, and forsook the sports on the moors to witness the struggle between yachtsmen in England, hitherto unmatched and unchallenged, and the Americans who crossed the Atlantic to meet them. Until the last few days, no Englishman ever dreamed that any nation could produce a yacht with the least pretentions to match the efforts of White, Camper and Ratsey (Cowes boat builders) . . ." Even Queen Victoria and Prince Albert were on hand for the races.

Amid all of this commotion, Commodore Stevens wrote a letter addressed to all yachtsmen assembled challenging them to a contest of speed and offering to meet all wagers to "a sum not to exceed 10,000 guineas" in a race in any wind above six knots. The letter was posted at the Royal Yacht Squadron. The English lords could hardly believe their eyes when they read the challenge. Never in the history of English yachting had so much money ($50,000) been offered as a wager over a sailboat race. Perhaps the yachtsmen at Cowes considered the amount excessive and beyond the bounds of friendly wagering, perhaps they considered the suggestion of such an amount vulgar, or perhaps they feared the self-confidence that such a sum represented and had been alarmed by *America's* show of force upon her arrival. Whatever the sporting men present were thinking, not one wager was offered to Commodore Stevens. As the days passed, he practically went begging, in the words of one contemporary, for a betting match "that would in some way compensate the owners of the *America* for the big expense of building the *America* and taking her to England." Perhaps the six-mile brush between *America* and *Laverock* had been more than a grandly theatrical announcement of her arrival. Stevens had broken the cardinal rule of the gambling man and had tipped his strong hand too soon.

Stevens' inability to find takers for his wagering was followed by an even greater disappointment. To everyone's surprise, it was soon announced that *America* had been unaccountably denied permission to enter the regatta of the Royal Victoria Yacht Club of Ryde. It seemed inconceivable that a sporting yacht club would not allow a boat that had traveled 3,000 miles across the ocean to engage in a race in The Solent, but that is exactly what happened. Not only could the Yankees not find anyone to bet against, but they wouldn't even be allowed to race.

However, Commodore Stevens wasn't about to let a formality keep him from showing off his boat's speed. After the first race started, *America* tagged along behind and caught up with the English fleet, even though only half of her sails were set. By the time the fleet reached the Needles, Stevens had demonstrated *America's* speed and ordered her back to Cowes. In the next Royal Victoria Yacht Club race, *America* dallied behind the starting line long after the 30-boat fleet had begun racing. When the wind piped up over six knots, Stevens ordered his boat about and took after the finest yachts in England. *America* quickly closed the three-mile gap that separated her from the rest, then passed the English boats as close abeam as safety would allow. By the time the yachts neared the finish line, the Americans were over two miles ahead.

Showdown in The Solent

At length the Royal Yacht Squadron decided that the only race during the whole period of regattas in which the American yacht could officially participate would be the "All Nations Race." The squadron was to award as the prize a 100 guineas cup which had been funded by subscription earlier in the year. The entrants would race around the Isle of Wight, starting and finishing at Cowes. By the time of the announcement, Stevens was thoroughly disgusted with the British and let it be known that he had no intention of entering. He was justifiably upset, considering the fact that the letter he had received during the previous winter from the Earl of Wilton had extended him the hospitality of the club; participation in the August races certainly had been implied. *America's* exclusion from the racing was an unpardonable affront.

The "London Times" had been goading its country's yachtsmen for days for their reluctance to race the Yankees. At the end of one particularly colorful editorial, the "Times" taunted, "She [*America*] has flung down the gauntlet to England, Ireland and Scotland, and not one has been found there to take it up." This type of article played some part, it is certain, in the invitation being extended to *America* to join in the "All Nations Race" on August 22nd. Even Queen Victoria and Prince Albert were interested in seeing *America* race; as the "Times" reported, ". . . her majesty and the court felt the influence of the universal curiosity which was excited to see how the stranger, of whom such great things were said, should acquit herself on the occasion."

When the "Times" got wind of Steven's refusal to race for the Royal Yacht Squadron's 100 guineas cup, it commented, "The course around the Isle of Wight is notoriously one of the most unfair to strangers that can be selected, and indeed, does not appear a good race-ground to anyone, inasmuch as the current and the tides render local knowledge of more value than swift sailing and nautical skill."

This was all Stevens needed to read. Since the race was so heavily weighted in favor of the British, it gave him the perfect chance to quash them—in their own backyard. He accepted the invitation.

The Great Race

The Solent was filled with spectator boats on the morning of August 22nd. The race fleet lined up off Cowes in two rows, cutters anchored in front and schooners anchored about 300 yards behind. Of course, the 15 boats in the race were not all the same size, and there was no doubt that there would be some inequity in the proceedings since no handicaps were to be awarded. But there was a cluster of boats of relatively equal tonnage to *America's,* giving her a number of yachts her own size to compete against. At 10 o'clock the starting gun fired. The Yankee schooner was last to get away, as Capt. Brown customarily preferred not to hoist her sails until after the anchor had been raised.

Spectator boats lined the race course from Cowes four or five miles east to the resort town of Ryde. As in any race of this type, after the first few boats went by, the spectator fleet had a tendency to fill in behind and thus impede the boats that had started behind the pack. In addition to the disrupting influence of the waves created by these attending vessels, the *America* was also handicapped by the addition of six new crew members unfamiliar with her layout. It seems that Capt. Brown had decided that the 12 men in the working crew were not sufficient to handle the ship in an efficient, racing-like fashion, so he had hired six British tars from the Cowes quayside to supplement the crew. Before the start of the race they all ganged together and threatened to be a disruptive influence on the boat, so he assigned crew positions and made sure that not more than two of the "John Bulls" were close together.

The winds were mild and from the west, so the famous race started out as a light run eastward to the Nab, 12 miles away. *America* sliced through the large boats, and nearly four miles before the turn at the Nab, she came up behind the four in the lead. The light breeze had blown the boats with the lowest tonnage ahead (*Volate,* 48 tons; *Freak,* 60 tons; *Aurora,* 47 tons; and *Gypsy Queen,* 160 tons), and as the black Yankee clipper approached, they formed up side-by-side, sailing wing-and-wing with their immense mainsails out to one side and their headsails stuck out on the other. In violation of all accepted protocol, the English boats were conspiring together to keep *America* behind and boxed in. When Captain Brown attempted to pass the English sportsmen to windward, they headed up to prevent him from getting by. When Brown tried to get by to leeward, the four yachts drove off to keep the Yankees in their trap. Finally, Brown yelled in exasperation, "Commodore, should I put the bowsprit into the back of that fellow?"

The yacht "America" at the turn of the century

With gentlemanly restraint, the Commodore wisely responded in the negative.

At No Man's Land buoy *America* was in fifth place, exactly two minutes behind the leader, *Volante*. The rest of the fleet was thundering down on her, just minutes behind, when the wind began to pipe up. As they passed the buoy the Yankee gamblers' luck began to change. One of the four boats behind retired unexplainedly. Then as the leader, *Volante*, rounded the buoy and went onto a reach, she sprung her bowsprit and was forced to strike her jib. As *America* drew alongside, she, too, downed her jib to even the contest. Nevertheless, *Volante* retired. A few minutes later another of the following boats, *Arrow,* went aground and *Alarm* stood by to assist. Four boats had been picked off within minutes and now the odds were ten to one. Once on the reach herself and with the leading boats (now reduced to three) unable to throw up a defensive wall, *America* kicked up her heels and romped by.

As *America* was beginning to head west off Sandown Bay and was coming on the wind, the breeze freshened and carried away the schooner's new jib-boom. This happened off Ventnor with the nearest boat, *Aurora,* over a mile behind. The Americans hauled in the wreckage and kept racing.

Halfway around the 74-mile course off St. Catherine's Point at the southernmost tip of the Isle of Wight, the weather thickened and those aboard *America* lost sight of *Aurora* a mile behind them. With the sea and wind increasing, *America* would chew her way to windward and leave the smaller boat even farther behind. As *America* rounded the world-famous Needles, the westernmost point of the diamond-shaped island, the royal yacht *Victoria and Albert* came into view. It must have been a thrilling sight for the Americans, as they passed close by the towering pinnacles of rock that stab 200 feet sky-ward, to see Her Majesty's own yacht waiting nearby.

"America" Wins the 100 Guineas Cup

As *America* passed the *Victoria and Albert,* Commodore Stevens ordered the American flag dipped and all the crew took off their hats in courtesy. This show of respect for the crown was noted by the press and further helped build Stevens' reputation as America's gentleman-sportsman. As *America* entered The Solent, the wind dropped away and *Aurora* began to close the eight-mile gap that had developed between them. *America* slowed as *Aurora* continued to glide along in the wafting breeze. The American yacht crossed the finish line off the Royal Yacht Squadron Castle first at 8:37 in the evening, having made a respectable average speed of seven knots. The British yacht finished at 8:55, just 19 minutes behind her. As the race was boat-for-boat and there was no handicap system, *America* won the 100 guineas cup.

Had the boats been racing under the British handicap system in vogue at the time, *America* would have won the race by just over two minutes. This was a point that Commodore Stevens made during a regular session of the New York Yacht Club upon his return. But what most histories fail to point out is that had the race around the Isle of Wight been held under the New York Yacht Club's own tonnage handicapping system, the English *Aurora* would have beaten *America* and won the cup by nearly one hour. The fact that the Yankee clipper would have lost under the Americans' own rule, though, should not detract from her victory. Clearly, *America* was significantly faster than any British yacht even approaching her size. Also, this little known fact points out the importance of handicap rules in international yacht races, a point that was not missed by the Americans at Cowes.

A popular saying in yacht-racing circles originated as *America* neared the finish line that evening of August 22nd. It was reported in the next day's "London Times" that spectators in yachts anchored in the Roads and along the squadron's promenade had asked "Who is first?" and the response had been *"America."* In answer to the question, "Who is second?", the reply that foggy evening had come back, "There is no second." Within a matter of days the newspaper account had been repeated so many times that the story had gotten changed around somewhat. When the Americans arrived back in New York, they were telling anyone who would listen that it had been Queen Victoria herself who had asked one of her aids who was second and had been told, "There is no second." The myth is now deeply ingrained in yachting lore.

The popular English magazine character, Mr. Punch, took up the banner of the Americans and chided the RYS with the following ditty:

> "Yankee Doodle had a craft,
>   A rather tidy clipper.
> And he challenged while they laughed
>   The Britishers to whip her.
> Their whole squadron she outsped
>   And that on their own water;

The Solent is between the English coast and the Isle of Wight

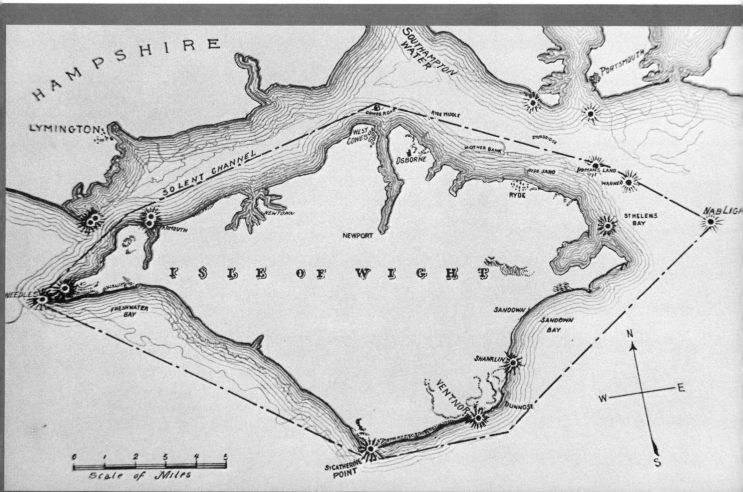

Of all the lot she went ahead
And they came nowhere after."

After winning the squadron's 100 guineas cup, which was also
called the All Nations Cup in reports of the day, Commodore Stevens
continued to ask for a match upon which wagers could be made. The
Royal Yacht Squadron turned a deaf ear to Stevens, and one imagines
that after so many weeks the scene became a bit boorish. On the other
hand, Stevens was getting great delight in driving home the point that
Britannia no longer ruled the waves, at least as far as pleasure yachts
were concerned. He also struck quite a blow to their sporting reputation. As the weeks wore on he fell to giving odds on *America,* offering
to put up 1,000 pounds Sterling for every 200 the British would post;
there was only one taker, and he was easily defeated.

As she lay at anchor in the Roads off Cowes' Medina River, the
low-slung schooner looked like the fastest yacht that had ever been
built. In explaining why *America* was unbeatable, one chronicler of the
day wrote, "No foam but rather a water jet rose from her bows . . .
While the other cutters were thrashing through the water, sending spray
over their bows, and the schooners were wet up to their foremast, the
deck of the *America* was dry as a bone. All her sails were set as flat
as a drumhead. The way her sails were set evidenced a superiority in
cutting which our sailmakers would barely allow; but certain it is, that,
while the jibs and mainsails of her antagonists were bellied out, her
canvas was as flat as a sheet of paper." *America's* sails were obviously
important to her victory, and in the years following, the fashionable
baggy English mainsails went out of style. Also, her sailmaker had used
cotton where the English used flax. The Americans had taught their
hosts yet another lesson.

"America" Lives On

Before returning to the United States, the NYYC syndicate sold
America to the English Lord de Blaquiere for $25,000, which just about
covered her building and racing costs. The next year she lost the race
for the Queen's trophy to *Arrow,* and she never performed particularly
well even after that. While in the service of the English lord, she cruised
the Mediterranean and the European coast before being sold to a
syndicate from Mobile, Alabama, during the American Civil War to
be used as a blockade runner. This kind of work well suited the swift
vessel and she slipped by Union warships for months until a dozen
Northern Men-of-War gave chase in a particularly determined pursuit.
Rather than let her be taken, *America's* owners ran her into the St. Johns
River and scuttled her in 42 feet of water.

She was later found and raised by the Federal Government, and impressed into service of the blockading fleet at Charleston, South Carolina. After the war, she was sent north to be used as a United States Naval Academy training ship. She proved herself as indomitable as ever, when during the first race for the America's Cup in 1870, she finished 14 minutes behind the winning American boat *Magic* and nearly 13 minutes ahead of the British challenger *Cambria*. The 19-year-old vessel still had enough spirit left in her to have successfully defended her own cup.

During the late 1800's *America* appeared from time to time in the spectator fleet that followed after the new challengers and defenders for the America's Cup. After deteriorating in Boston for some years, she was restored by a group of public-spirited citizens and presented again to the U.S. Naval Academy at Annapolis. But the academy had no special fund for her maintenance, and she eventually ran down once more. During World War II she was hauled out of the water and placed under a shed in Trumpy's boatyard in Annapolis. There, during a severe snowstorm in the winter of 1945, the roof of the shed collapsed, destroying her frail and rotting hull. She had lived nearly 100 years.

Local yachtsmen and naval buffs picked over the debris that winter and spring, and within a year most of *America's* wood planking, frames, and spars had been spread far and wide as treasured bits of history from yachting's glorious past. As late as 1970, one Annapolis *America* buff acquired part of one of her spars and carved half models of the famous yacht out of her own wood, selling the ten-inch models for $25 apiece.

3

The Tradition Begins

The impact of *America's* devastating rout of the British fleet had an immediate effect on shipbuilding in the United States. Like the Royal Navy, American shipbuilders were quick to perceive the implications of Steers' design. Now, Americans knew that their New York pilot schooners were not only the fastest boats in the United States, but very likely the swiftest vessels in the world. The shape of American vessels changed almost overnight: clipper bows became popular, bows were hollowed out, the widest part of the boat was moved further aft, and the shapes of the ships' underbody changed. One race had opened the eyes of designers and builders in every important seafaring town in America. The value of *America's* victory was not lost on John Cox Stevens or the other members of the boat's syndicate. They had, in the pursuit of sport, contributed mightily to the art of naval architecture. If one international race could produce so much progress in hull design, Stevens reasoned, possibly an international contest every so often would bring about even further progress.

On July 8, 1857, the four surviving members of the *America* syndicate wrote a letter to the secretary of the New York Yacht Club tendering the Cup to the club with the understanding that it would be held as a permanent challenge trophy, open to the competition of any member of any organized foreign yacht club. The letter, later referred to as the Deed of Gift, stated that any foreign yacht club would always be entitled to challenge for the Cup. In case of a "disagreement" between the parties concerned, it read, "the match shall be sailed over the usual course for the Annual Regatta of the Yacht Club in possession of the Cup, and subject to its rules and sail regulations . . ." A notice of the existence of the challenge trophy including the few basic requirements specified in the letter was mailed out to all of the existing yacht clubs in the world at the time—about twenty. After the American Civil War Mr. James Ashbury, from England, wrote the NYYC in 1868 expressing a desire to race against the champion American schooner.

The First Challenge

With James Ashbury's first letter the curtain was drawn on a Gilbert and Sullivan-type comic opera that would continue far into the next century as the challengers and the New York Yacht Club would haggle and harrumph over the terms of nearly every match until the 12-Meter boats came into play in 1958.

Ashbury, although he was newly bitten by the racing bug, was not a fool. He realized that for there to be a real race at all, the boats would have to be somewhat similar. It would be a ludicrous international racing match, indeed, if one yacht were 190 feet long and the other only 100 feet long. In the interest of a genuine contest, Ashbury asked that the boat that the NYYC selected to defend would not be in excess of 10 percent of his *Cambria's* 188 tons. Ashbury also asked that the winner of the Cup be the boat which won two out of three races, thus eliminating the possibility that a chance windshift or gear failure might determine the outcome. In addition, the English millionaire requested that centerboarders be disallowed and that the boats be sea-going vessels and not "a shell" or a "racing machine." Further, the Englishman invited the American defender to The Solent for a series of races and then proposed a transatlantic ocean race back to the U.S. for a prize of $1,250 before challenging for the Cup. Obviously, Ashbury was trying to make certain that the defender would be a heavy, strong vessel like his own and not a mere "shell."

There is no doubt Ashbury's motivations for challenging for the Cup held by the NYYC were prompted by desires other than pure love of yacht racing. Ashbury was the son of a wheelwright who invented the railroad carriage, thus laying the foundation of a fortune. Though possessed of great wealth, his social standing was considerably below that of men far less wealthy than he. Ashbury's entry into the sport of yachting in the first place was probably in large part inspired by his ambition to pick his way into the incredibly tight-knit British society. It is nowhere recorded whether Ashbury was the first person to employ a yacht as a vehicle of social mobility, but he certainly wasn't the last. The Cup that Stevens had put up to help advance naval architecture was being sought to advance social position. It is a recurring aspect of America's Cup history.

The Club Responds

The NYYC officers stated that if Ashbury wanted to challenge for the Cup, he would have to do it against the entire NYYC fleet—a flotilla that would include small centerboard boats in case the weather was light and large deep-draft vessels on the off chance that the weather was blustery. And since *America* had won the Cup sailing in The Solent with its tricky currents and strong tides where local knowledge was important, the club would have its race from New York's inner harbor down to Sandy Hook and back. The NYYC couldn't have picked another place within 100 miles that would have been more difficult for an outsider. This was a medieval kind of sportsmanship which was in large measure the result of the treatment *America* had received in 1851 in Cowes.

In the winter of 1869–70 Ashbury agreed to the NYYC's terms. The club, in turn, threw him a bone of accommodation by helping to set up a Transatlantic Race between *Cambria* and James Gordon Bennett's new schooner *Dauntless,* which was in England at the time.

The First Challenge Race

On August 8, 1870 history was made as the first challenge for the America's Cup got underway. It was *Cambria* against 17 American defenders including the 19-year-old *America* herself which had just been refitted by the Navy at a cost of $25,000. The boats started from anchor and the club had graciously given the challenger the windward, and therefore favored, berth. But just before the gun fired the wind shifted, making *Cambria's* starting position one of the most unfavorable. The schooner *Magic* was the first to get away with *Cambria* not far behind. *America* was living up to her lethargic starting tradition and was nearly the last boat to weigh anchor.

The first America's Cup challenger "Cambria" with the fastest NYYC boat, "Magic"

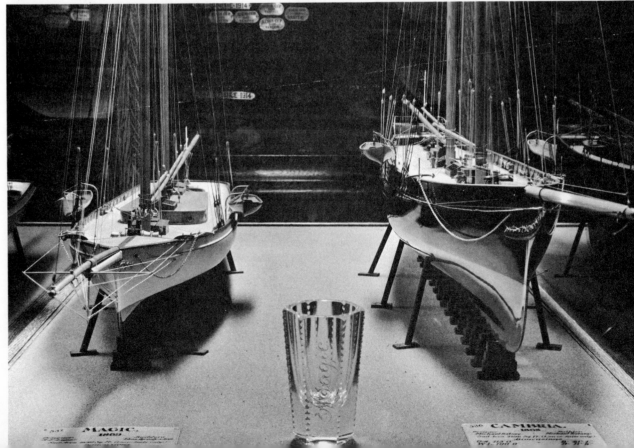

The race was just as predicted, a rout. The shoal draft, light schooner *Magic* won the race, beating the second place boat by three and one-half minutes and the challenger by about 27 minutes on elapsed time and by over 38 minutes on handicap time. Even *America,* despite her age and the heavy rigging, came in fourth place, beating *Cambria* by 13 minutes on elapsed time. The challenger finished eighth on elapsed time and tenth on handicap or "corrected" time. More than half the fleet had beaten the challenger.

Ashbury Tries Gamesmanship

Ashbury's second challenge letter pointedly asked that the NYYC put up one boat to defend the Cup against his new vessel, *Livonia.* He also asked that centerboarders be barred from the competition. Then came one of the most fantastic requests ever made of the NYYC. Ashbury said that he was a member of 12 yacht clubs in England and therefore under the terms of the Deed of Gift, he should be allowed to challenge 12 different times for the Cup, each time representing a different club. One writer of the day said in describing the negotiations, that Ashbury asked for a good deal, but got a good deal less.

In the spring of 1871 the sole surviving member of the *America's* syndicate, George L. Schuyler, admonished the club's officers by saying, "It seems to me that the present ruling of the club renders the *America's* trophy useless as a 'Challenge Cup,' and that for all sporting purposes it might as well be laid aside as family plate . . . When the word match is used in horseracing or kindred sports without any qualification, it means a contest between two parties—and only two . . . The same rule applies to yachts . . ."

Because a surviving signer of the Deed of Gift made it clear what was intended, the club capitulated and agreed to put only one boat up against Ashbury's new *Livonia*—but the officers reserved the right to pick a different defender each morning. Obviously if the weather was foul the club would send a heavy, keel boat to the line; if the air was light, a light-displacement centerboarder would be dispatched. The club also stood its ground on the course. They would not take Ashbury's suggestion of holding the race outside New York Harbor and away from the currents and headlands that give the advantage to whomever has local knowledge. Also, the challenger's request that he be allowed to represent 12 different clubs was denied, but the NYYC did agree to a best four-out-of-seven series, something that had been dismissed out of hand the year before.

The Second Match Begins

The second challenge for the America's Cup was to prove that the defense needed all the help that the New York Yacht Club could give it. The breeze was light on the morning of the first race on October 16, 1871, so the club predictably chose the shoal-draft centerboarder *Columbia*. She won by over 27 minutes. *Columbia* started the second race, but in the middle of it the wind velocity increased and parted the Americans' topmast staysail sheet. *Livonia* was leading at the outside turning mark by two minutes and jibed around the mark. *Columbia* came to the mark and tacked around it the opposite way, thus saving much time and distance. As a result she drew even with the English and went on to win.

Ashbury immediately protested *Columbia* for turning the mark the wrong way only to discover that the skipper of *Columbia* had asked that very morning which way the buoy should be passed. The race committee had responded that it could be passed on either hand, a bit of information that was not passed on to the challenger. Had the *Livonia* crew known this they would have also tacked around the mark thereby maintaining their lead.

The wind was blowing fresh the morning of the third race, so the club trotted out J. G. Bennett's *Dauntless,* a vessel that had gone transatlantic and was presumed to be good in heavy weather. However, as the American vessel was being towed to the starting area her topmast was carried away by the wind. The committee hastily scurried around to find the back-up boat *Sappho,* but she was nowhere to be seen. It seems that the only boat that was even near the yacht club's pier on Staten Island was *Columbia.* When asked to race, the *Columbia* crew vigorously objected because they had been up late the night before celebrating and were exhausted from the previous two races. Finally, the yacht club insisted that *Columbia* make a third race and the boat was towed to the starting line.

Columbia bungled the start, but was beginning to catch up with *Livonia* when the American jibstay parted, letting the sail stream out to leeward. After rounding the outer mark *Columbia's* steering gear failed and she made it home by steering with sails alone. Ashbury won the first race by 15 minutes over the disabled *Columbia.*

The committee calculated that the next race would be sailed to windward in a breeze so they picked the heavy displacement *Sappho* to meet *Livonia.* The club officers were right about the weather and *Sappho* romped home to victory in that race and the following one. *Livonia* had lost the Cup challenge series against two other boats, four to one.

The decision of the race committee against Ashbury in the second race protest upset the Englishman, and so after the series he claimed that the score was only three to two and that he would appear at the starting line the next day for the sixth race. The yacht club was incredulous and didn't bother responding to the millionaire's notification. In the meantime, Ashbury had talked Bennett into allowing his *Dauntless* to make a race; but again *Livonia* lost. The next couple of days it blew a gale and the only boat that left the anchorage was *Livonia.*

Because of that, Ashbury later claimed that he had won the America's Cup.

On October 18 of that year, the "New York World" editorialized: "The American public ought to be thoroughly proud of its yachtsmen, who have exhibited all of the proverbial national shrewdness in managing the contest with Mr. Ashbury . . . by their astuteness that may be fairly said to have organized victory in the majority, if not in all races, as a matter of certainty . . ." The English had had enough of the American sense of sportsmanship and vowed never to return, a proposition that was agreeable to the club officers.

A New Challenger and a New Motive

Not every man who has challenged for the America's Cup has wanted to win it. Some have challenged for other reasons, such as merely to reap the publicity involved in going after what was becoming a famous international prize. It is not clear exactly when the Canadian Alexander Cuthbert realized what a challenge for the America's Cup might do for his career as a naval architect and boat builder, but there is no doubt that this was his reason for his second challenge for the America's Cup, if not the reason for his first attempt as well.

In early 1876 Cuthbert formed a syndicate with Major Charles Gifford, the vice commodore of the Royal Canadian Yacht Club in Toronto and a few other minor syndicate contributors. Major Gifford asked in the challenge letter that the Americans choose only one boat to race the Canadians and that the selection not be changed the morning of the race due to weather conditions. The NYYC officers allowed the match to consist of the best two out of three races and offered to hold the contest in the open water off Newport after the annual NYYC summer cruise. These were two gracious gestures on the part of the club, yet on the crucial matter of the number of defenders the NYYC first responded, ". . . a yacht will be at the starting point on the morning of each race to sail the match." At some point club officials voted on the matter of how many boats should be used to defend. The result was eleven to five being in favor of using only one boat for all three races no matter what the conditions.

The Canadians built the *Countess of Dufferin,* a shoal draft centerboard schooner that was knocked together as fast as possible. She was launched and sent packing for the American East Coast before the yard even had a chance to fair the bottom, and before an adequate suit of sails had been fitted to the vessel's spars. In short, she was a sorry challenger that was under-financed and lacked proper time for adequate building or preparation. On her way down the East Coast to New York she raced some American schooners off Newport and was so badly beaten that the crews of the other boats reportedly forgot the

Countess was even on the course. Once in New York the Canadians had the Wilson sail loft in Port Washington, N.Y., cut some new sails for their boat but they were of little help and the Cup defender, *Madeleine*, easily won the match.

After the race, financial problems befell the *Countess of Dufferin* and she was laid up at New York. Cuthbert—who was not only the boat's designer, builder and skipper, but also the syndicate's major financial contributor—attached the boat in an effort to force Major Clifford to sell his share of the vessel. Captain Cuthbert contended that he still had faith in her and wanted to gain control of the boat, re-syndicate her to raise more money, and challenge again.

Cuthbert's legal action fell through and the Cup challenger was sold at a sheriff's auction to satisfy debts. Cuthbert sailed her back to Canada and she was eventually sold to a Chicago yachtsman. One can imagine the extent of Cuthbert's popularity in the halls of the Royal Canadian Yacht Club after trying to force its vice commodore to sell out his share. One newspaper account of the day reported that members of the syndicate were rumored to feel they had been used.

But if Cuthbert's reputation was tarnished at the RCYC, it did not hurt his boat building business. The many newspaper accounts of the match had spread his name and business flowed in. But since there was no question of the RCYC even entertaining the thought of sponsoring another Cuthbert-instigated challenge, the builder cultivated new ground elsewhere. Press reports of the day record that Cuthbert convinced the mayor of Bellville, Ontario, that a summer of America's Cup publicity would do much to promote the town's interests. The designer was quickly made a member of the nearby Bay of Quinte Yacht Club and a syndicate was formed.

The Second Canadian Challenge

During this period the Bay of Quinte Yacht Club was in its infancy and its members were enamoured with the idea that their club could gain the prestige of one of the major clubs in the world by challenging for the Cup. In the words of yachting promoters, Cuthbert had found a "pigeon." In May of 1881 the secretary of the Bay of Quinte Yacht Club sent off a letter of challenge on behalf of Alexander Cuthbert and his new racing sloop, *Atalanta*.

The New York Yacht Club cordially agreed to the challenge, suggesting a two-out-of-three match series off New York and promising to choose one boat to defend, after clarifying that they need not make such a concession under the Deed of Gift. One American newspaper writer bitterly criticized the NYYC fathers for not recalling that *America* had won the Cup against the "fleet par excellence of the world" and that by not requiring the new challengers to also run the same gauntlet, the club was diminishing the reputation of the Cup. The article said, "It is an axiom in sport that 'a good match is won when made,' and really our yachting friends, guardians of the America's Cup, do not shine as matchmakers."

As it turned out, a match made with Cuthbert was a match well made. The *Atalanta* was finished long after her scheduled launching and as with her predecessor, her construction left much to be desired. Cuthbert came in for much abuse in the U.S. press because his design looked very similar to many Cary Smith designs (the foremost New York naval architect) and he was even accused of stealing a Smith half-model. The charge seems to have been baseless. The 70-foot *Atalanta* underwent some brief trials and then was sent south through the New York Canal system. The sloop was a beamy centerboarder much like the American boats and thus was more similar to the defender than any previous challenger. Cuthbert was quite clever in bringing the boat through the canal, because that not only saved him time but also meant that the boat could be more lightly constructed since she did not have to sail in the North Atlantic around Nova Scotia. The club fathers had overlooked this possibility and agreed among themselves to never allow it to happen again.

For the first time in Cup history, the NYYC decided to commission a new design specifically for the defense. Trials were then held in the summer to determine the fastest American vessel. The 67-foot *Mischief* was selected.

Mischief beat the Canadian challenger by over 25 minutes in the first race on November 9, 1881, and by more than 40 minutes in the second race. That was the last time in history the Canadians sent a challenger for the America's Cup. The Bay Quinte Yacht Club disbanded shortly thereafter and was not started up again until years later. The Deed of Gift for the America's Cup was altered by the club the following year to bar any yacht club from challenging that was not located on salt water and stipulated that challengers must proceed to the port of the contest on their own bottoms. This effectively shut the door on lightweight racing machines from coming through the canal from Canada and challenging the club's own lightweight racing machines. The match was still "well made."

The Third British Challenge

In December, 1884, the club received a letter from the English designer J. Beaver Webb stating that the NYYC would soon get challenges from two of his British clients. In 1885 Sir Richard Sutton brought over his challenger, *Genesta*. She was a 90-foot cutter built to the racing rules prevalent in England at the time which encouraged narrow boats with deep draft. The yacht club was concerned by the challenge but since they had spent $20,000 on an unsuccessful candidate for the defense in 1881, the officers encouraged a syndicate to be formed to build a new boat rather than dip once again into the club kitty. The club's syndicate went to Cary Smith who proceeded to design the sloop *Priscilla*. In the meantime a syndicate was formed in Boston to build a boat for defense of the Cup. The head of the syndicate was Gen. Charles J. Paine who asked a young and unknown naval architect, Edward Burgess, to design a defender. Paine's syndicate members were: J. Malcome Forbes, Henry S. Hovey, John L. Gardner, J. Montgomery Sears and others. The result was the 94-foot *Puritan*.

In trials held by the club, the Boston boat was decisively faster than the Cary Smith design owned by the New York syndicate. Although *Priscilla* was unquestionably the hometown favorite and the NYYC favorite as well due to membership in the syndicate, the club's selection committee chose *Puritan*. The Burgess design went on to defeat Sir Richard's challenger in two straight races—the first race by over 16 minutes (on the inside course) and the second race by a scant one minute 38 seconds.

A surprising incident occurred just prior to the start of the first race in the 1885 challenge. Near the starting line both boats were approaching each other, *Genesta* on starboard tack and *Puritan* on port. The American skipper misjudged the distance between the boats, and their speed, and *Puritan's* bowsprit stabbed through the English mainsail, ripping part of it away. *Puritan* was in the wrong by virtue of the fact that boats on starboard tack always have right-of-way over port tack boats. When *Genesta* sailed by the committee boat, the chairman yelled over that the American boat had been disqualified and that the *Genesta* need only sail over the course to win the race. In a display of sportsmanship rarely seen on an America's Cup course, Sir Richard Sutton said, "We are very much obliged, but we don't want it that way. We came over for a race, not a sailover."

The 1885 series had been close for the Americans. *Genesta* had led all around the course in the second race until the final leg and was then overtaken because she had carried a topsail in winds far too fresh. Had Sir Richard or his professional captain ordered the sail furled and accepted the *Puritan's* disqualification before what was to have been the first race, the 100 guineas cup would have gone right back to the Royal Yacht Squadron upon the occasion of its very first challenge.

A Challenger With Dash

One of the most colorful challengers ever to step foot on American shores was Lt. William Henn, R.N., who sallied forth in 1886 to pit his 102-foot *Galatea* against the NYYC's finest yacht. Henn was the son of a wealthy landed proprietor and served in the Royal Navy from

"Puritan" launched the career of Edward Burgess in 1885

1860 to 1875. His service embraced the Abyssinian campaign and the war against the slavers of Zanzibar and Madagascar. In 1872 Henn was the second in command of the pith helmet expedition sent to Africa to find the explorer Dr. David Livingstone and was in charge of the land party which met Henry M. Stanley on his return from his successful quest for the explorer. Stanley had been sent forth by "New York Herald" owner and NYYC commodore, James Gordon Bennett. After retiring from the Royal Navy, Henn and his wife lived for seven years on an 80-ton cutter and sailed extensively around Europe.

The unfortunate part of Henn's plan was that he didn't stand a ghost of a chance. His beautiful *Galatea,* like most of the other boats built in Britain that year, was long, deep and narrow—so narrow, in fact, that yachtsmen of the day called her a sailing "planks on edge." *Galatea,* for example, was 102 feet long overall, nearly 87-feet long on the waterline, had a draft of 13-feet, yet was only 15-feet wide. English boats were narrow because they were built to take advantage of a handicap racing rule used in British waters. To have built the yachts wider would have only taxed the vessels severely under the English measuring system and caused them to "give" handicap time to opponents. However, the NYYC used a different handicap system and one that penalized narrow, deep-draft boats.

"Mayflower" defended the Cup in 1886

Gen. Charles J. Paine commissioned Burgess to design an improvement over *Puritan*—the result was Boston's *Mayflower*. After losing the initial races against *Puritan* in the American trials, *Mayflower* finally got tuned up and was the consistent winner. For the second time in a row, a Boston boat defended the America's Cup. *Mayflower* defeated the challenger by over 12 minutes in the first race and by over 28 minutes in the second. Just before the second race, Lt. Henn took sick and had to pass command of his yacht to his professional skipper. Henn was so ill that he retired below and sent a message to the race committee asking that the course be shortened to 30 miles so that he could sooner "secure the services of a physician." His request was denied by the race committee, the officers saying they were powerless to change the conditions of the match.

The Scottish Challenge

The Royal Clyde Yacht Club sent a letter to the club in 1887 on behalf of the wealthy Scotsman James Bell, announcing his intentions to challenge in the summer. The NYYC responded curtly that challengers were supposed to give six months' notice and that it would consider the challenge when it came in "proper form."

The successful English naval architect George L. Watson was commissioned by Bell to execute the challenger's design and building was carried out under great secrecy. The challenger was named *Thistle;* she was 108-feet overall and was designed to be 85-feet long on the water with a 20-foot beam and a 13-foot draft. This was by far the most advanced underbody design the British had yet sent forth. Instead of being blunt, with full sections from bow to stern, *Thistle's* entry forward was sleek with the forefoot slightly cut away. The challengers had good reason to think that they had a winner and the boat was launched while covered with large sheets of canvas so that no one could see the shape of the underbody.

Because of his past success, Gen. Paine was asked by the yacht club if he would come forward with another defender. He met with his wealthy friends at the Eastern Yacht Club and they were more than happy to assist the NYYC. By this time the Cup had received so much publicity that the country in general considered it a national prize, not merely a private cup held by the NYYC. The Bostonians at the Eastern Yacht Club felt this way as well and in the process enjoyed beating the New Yorkers in their own backyard.

Paine again went to Edward Burgess and his new design, *Volunteer*, was 106 feet overall, 85 feet ten inches on the water, with a 23-foot beam and a ten-foot draft, exclusive of the centerboard.

1887 Match Nearly Cancelled

Both boats spread an enormous cloud of canvas with *Volunteer* able to hoist 9,271 square feet of sail and *Thistle* able to hang 8,968 square feet. A bit of a row was created by the NYYC when *Thistle* was measured in the water in New York. She was found to be 86.46 feet on the waterline rather than 85 feet which had been promised as a condition of the challenge. Designer Watson maintained that the boat came out longer than designed due to an error in either his calculations or in building but that it had not been intended to come out that way.

Nevertheless, officials of the New York Yacht Club were up in arms and threatened to call off the match because of this breach of promise on the part of the Clyde group. The club made no mention of the fact that once they learned that the challenger would be 85 feet that they commissioned a boat that would be 85 feet ten inches long l.w.l. Speculation was also rampant in New York that the Americans had finally

"Volunteer" defended against "Thistle" in 1887

met their match. The Royal Clyde Yacht Club requested a best-of-five series and was turned down flatly, the NYYC stating that three races were sufficient.

Finally, because of the gravity of the situation—the fact that the challenger was seven inches longer than the defender and nearly a foot and one-half longer than had been counted upon—the NYYC referred the matter of accepting the challenge to George L. Schuyler who was still living. Were it not for the longevity of this original syndicate member and his sense of fair play, there would have been no match in 1887. Schuyler, allowing that the Americans were at a "disadvantage," recommended that the match go on. And so it did.

The popular professional skipper Captain Hank Haff, who had sailed the previous Boston defenders, was at the helm of *Volunteer* and quickly worked his boat ahead of the challenger in the beat out of New York Harbor. It wasn't long until the Americans pushed out ahead, partially because *Thistle* did not cover. Before long the huge spectator fleet fell in behind the leader thereby creating great turbulence for the challenger behind. Twice, the crew aboard *Thistle* hung from her quarters a large canvas sign which said "KEEP ASTERN." It did little good and *Thistle* fell farther behind, losing the race by over 18 minutes. Afterward, James Bell criticized the inside course saying that it was the worst he had ever sailed over. The course was full of strong tides, eddies, areas of slack water known only to the local yachtsmen. The headlands diverted the true wind making the breeze all the more difficult to play for the challengers. Perhaps the remarks of Bell had some effect on the race committee, as this was the last America's Cup race held inside New York harbor.

Thistle lost the second race by 12 minutes over the outside course because she could not sail as close to the wind as the defender; nor did the English put up a proper cover.

The Deed of Gift is Changed

A new Deed of Gift was drawn up in 1887, while Schuyler was still alive, which changed the rules of the game somewhat. Included were the following requirements: that the challenging club would inform the defending club of the length, beam, and draft of the challenger; that the boats could not be shorter than 65 feet l.w.l. or longer than 90 feet; that the vessels must proceed on their own bottoms to the match; that centerboards or sliding keels would always be allowed and never be figured in as part of the boat for measurement purposes; all races would be made on ocean courses, free from headlands; the challenging club could only use one boat throughout the series; and, the ocean course would always be deep enough to accommodate vessels of 22-foot draft. The club fathers were once again operating under the "a-match-won-is-a-match-well-made" theory of sportsmanship, and the new Deed was very well made indeed. It stayed in effect until 1956.

Lord Dunraven's First Assault

Despite the advantages handed to the defender in the new Deed, in 1889 the Royal Yacht Squadron sent a challenge for the Cup on behalf of the Earl of Dunraven, Windham-Thomas Wyndham-Quin.

The fabulously wealthy English Lord was a small man with a frail build, a little red face, gray hair and a straw colored moustache. When he challenged for the America's Cup he was in his early 50's and already a bit stooped shouldered. At one time the Earl had been Parliamentary Under Secretary of State for the colonies. He was known around the House of Lords as an eccentric, which is an interesting comment coming from the English ruling class. As one contemporary observer put it when speaking of the Earl, "His sport undertakings, numerous estates and commercial enterprises leave him little time for the affairs of government." The Earl of Dunraven had taken up yachting rather late in life, its social trappings being a consideration, and it was only natural that conversation in the great sitting room in the Earl's country manor should get around to the America's Cup. With the Cup so firmly established as the most prestigious international yachting prize, it appealed to a man like Dunraven. It also appealed to his sense of lordly one-upsmanship, there being quite a contest among the landed aristocrats of England at the time to outdo each other in extravagant undertakings.

Letters were exchanged from 1889 to 1893 between the Earl of Dunraven and the New York Yacht Club over the conditions for the match. Because of Dunraven's numerous objections to the 1887 Deed of Gift, the challenge was even dropped in 1890 because of lack of enthusiasm on the NYYC's part. In early 1893 Dunraven pushed for the match giving up some of his requests and the NYYC gave in on others. Dunraven told the club the waterline length of the challenger but would not divulge any further information and the club did not require it, despite the new Deed of Gift. George L. Watson was the designer of the 85-foot l.w.l. English *Valkyrie II*.

Four Contenders for the Defense

Because of the outstanding success of the 46-foot waterline sloop *Gloriana,* and because of the phenomenal success of *Wasp* in 1892, their designer, Nathanael Herreshoff, became the man of the hour. (Burgess had died the year before.) A New York Yacht Club syndicate was formed, including such men as J. P. Morgan, F. W. Vanderbilt, W. K. Vanderbilt, and Archibald Rogers, and it commissioned Herreshoff to design and build an America's Cup defender with a waterline length of 85 feet. The result was the *Colonia*.

Gen. Paine commissioned his son to design a new defender called *Jubilee*. Yet a second Boston syndicate asked the successors to Burgess' company, Stewart & Binney, to design a third contender for the Cup defense, *Pilgrim*. As if three boats were not enough, another New York syndicate sprang up headed by C. Oliver Iselin. He, too, went to Herreshoff and asked for a design.

The boat that Captain Nat created for Iselin was called *Vigilant*. She was a radical design because of her moderately deep, long run fin keel which was fitted with a slot forward for a centerboard. She was the first large boat built of Tobin bronze and consequently she had a silky smooth, strong hull. Another noteworthy development was her cut-away forefoot. The boat was 124 feet overall, 85 feet load waterline, 26 feet wide, with a 14-foot draft with the centerboard up, and 24-foot draft with it down. *Vigilant* won two of three trial races and was selected to defend the Cup.

Nathanael Herreshoff, designer of six defenders

The 1893 Match

The first leg of the first completed race saw Nat Herreshoff aboard his *Vigilant* steering much of the way as first *Valkyrie II* then *Vigilant* took the lead. Finally, the Americans got the upper hand and stayed there to win the race by nearly six minutes on corrected time. The second completed race was sailed in a fresh 25-knot breeze with lee rails awash. *Vigilant* came romping home three and one-half minutes ahead of *Valkyrie II.*

The third race turned out to be the most exciting in a rather dull history of Cup defenses. Neither boat was ready at the starting time (*Valkyrie* was over three miles away) so the race committee postponed the gun. When the boats did finally get away in a very fresh breeze, *Valkyrie's* Captain Cranfield swung his boat from astern and to leeward of *Vigilant* into position to weather off the defender's quarter.

Cranfield's weather berth was a controlling position. He was to windward of *Vigilant* and therefore could point higher if he wished (he did and went just as fast), and he also kept the Americans from tacking until he peeled off first. *Valkyrie II* worked to weather and rounded the windward mark nearly two minutes ahead. When *Valkyrie* hoisted her spinnaker the material fouled and tore, and as the sail was sheeted in, the rip became worse in the 30-knot wind. Finally, the spinnaker split apart and had to be replaced by a lighter sail, which, by virtue of its light weight, quickly shredded to tatters in the strong wind. As a last resort, Cranfield set what amounted to a balloon jib-topsail. This disadvantage was enough to allow *Vigilant* to win by 40 seconds; the Cup had been saved once again.

After the series, Dunraven complained that the first races were not truly to windward and therefore did not fairly test the boats' relative speeds. He was quite right in that contention, but the yacht club responded that there was nothing they could do about windshifts. The Earl also complained about the spectator fleet getting in the way and creating a terrible wash. Again Dunraven was correct and again the yacht club was truly helpless to solve the inequity.

The Infamous Dunraven Affair

Dunraven brought Lord Lonsdale, the Marquis of Ormonde, and Lord Wolverton into his second challenge effort, *Valkyrie III,* which was brought to the United States in 1895. She was also a Watson design and a magnificent sloop that showed that her English designer had borrowed heavily from the American boats he had observed in 1893. Her forefoot was completely cut away making her forward sections flat like the American skimming dishes, as they were called, and her beam was pushed out for added stability as *Vigilant's* had been.

Iselin organized a new defending syndicate that year including E. D. Morgan and W. K. Vanderbilt. They commissioned Nat Herreshoff to design another defender of about 89 l.w.l. Nat showed his respect for Watson's work by designing a boat that, in many ways, looked more like *Valkyrie* than *Vigilant.* But the biggest trick of all that crafty Nat Herreshoff had up his sleeve was the boat's construction materials—manganese bronze, a very expensive and strong metal by standards of the 1890's, was used for bottom plating. The hull frames were steel and the deck was of aluminum. The end result was an extremely light hull.

The boat was called *Defender* and she certainly lived up to the charges that the English had been making for years that the defenders were light shells and not capable of going to sea. She was used four years later as a trial horse for the American defender but because corrosive electrolysis had set up between the diverse metals in the boat, *Defender* was literally falling apart by the end of the decade and had to be scrapped on City Island.

The first race between *Valkyrie III* and *Defender* saw the former start under the American's lee then work out from under by footing faster. In the 15-mile beat to windward, Capt. Hank Haff finally split tacks and sailed away from the faster challenger. *Valkyrie* made the mistake of not covering. When they crossed tacks again *Defender* just barely made it across Dunraven's bow and stayed ahead to win the race by nearly nine minutes.

Immediately after the race Lord Dunraven charged that ballast had been added to *Defender* the night before—after she had been measured—and he demanded a re-measurement. Everyone was shocked by the English Earl's accusation. He also complained bitterly to the committee about the crowding of the excursion steamers, claiming that his boat had been bothered by the chop. The next afternoon both boats were examined and found to be essentially the same as when first measured. Dunraven appeared to be satisfied.

As the boats approached the starting line for the second race, it was obvious that *Valkyrie III* was going to go over the line before the starting gun and thereby lose valuable minutes in re-starting. To avoid going over early, *Valkyrie,* which was to windward of *Defender,* bore down on the American boat in hopes that she would drive off and allow the

English to run the line. But Capt. Haff was too smart to let the challengers out of a box that they had sailed into. *Valkyrie* luffed up quickly head to wind in order to kill her way and as she did her long boom swept across the deck of *Defender* hitting the starboard shrouds and snapping the topmast stay. The topmast sagged off to leeward but did not fall down. Capt. Haff immediately sent men aloft to string up a jury-rig. *Valkyrie* started the race as if nothing had happened and the partially disabled American boat set out in pursuit. Haff was never able to catch the challenger because of his disabled rig and Dunraven finished first.

Iselin protested the challenger and was upheld by the New York Yacht Club race committee, which handed the victory from *Valkyrie III* to *Defender*. After the committee's decision had been made, Iselin suggested to Dunraven that the race be re-sailed but Dunraven turned down the sporting recommendation on the grounds that, although he did not agree with the committee's decision, the matter had been ruled upon and was closed. He had lost and would not consent to resailing the match.

After the start of the third race *Defender* crossed the line and began the beat to windward. *Valkyrie III* crossed close behind and then withdrew from the race and sailed back to her anchorage. *Defender* sailed over the course, her time was taken and that concluded the 1895 defense of the America's Cup—the club had kept the Cup by virtue of a win, a protest and a sailover.

Dunraven Creates an Incident

It has always been unclear exactly why Dunraven withdrew from the third race. The day before he had sent a note to the race committee saying that unless the spectator fleet stayed clear he would not race. The excursion steamers were under no more control for the last race than they had ever been, so possibly this was the reason for his quitting. More likely it was a combination of events that, to Dunraven, added up to an intolerable, unsportsmanlike match in which he had scant chance of victory. The night before the first race his crew had seen men putting ballast aboard *Defender* and that is why he had asked for the remeasurement. Also, he was firmly convinced that the committee had wrongly disqualified his boat for the starting line violation before the second race, even though *Valkyrie* had broken an elementary rule of yacht racing. Thirdly, the spectator fleet was making life miserable for the challenger. Dunraven is usually characterized as the most villainous of all of the America's Cup challengers because of his unsportsmanlike behavior, particularly after the second match. However, the NYYC and the *Defender* syndicate did little to smooth over the bones of contention that were sticking in Dunraven's throat. His crew had

"Defender" was a controversial Herreshoff design that defended in 1895

seen with their own eyes men loading lead pigs aboard *Defender* the night before the race, yet no responsible American ever offered an explanation.

When Dunraven arrived in England he publicly charged that ballast had been put aboard *Defender* before the first race. This is the first time the English Lord ever made his thoughts public on the ballast matter and it received front page treatment in papers both in England and the United States. The American national honor soon became the issue.

Iselin, upon hearing the news from England, denied any wrong-doing and asked the NYYC for a full investigation. The club immediately called a special meeting and appointed a select committee to get to the bottom of the matter. The committee was composed of J. Pierpont Morgan, William C. Whitney and George L. Rives from the club, in addition to Captain A. T. Mahan of the U.S. Navy and The Hon. E. J. Phelps, the U.S. Minister to England.

A five-day hearing commenced on December 27 and Dunraven sailed to New York to take part. The hearing was as thorough as one could expect and the testimony taken fills a thick book. Anyone who had anything to do with *Defender* was closely questioned by both the yacht club's attorney and by the Earl's barrister. During the hearing it was proved that although *Valkyrie's* crew had seen ballast put aboard *Defender* late the night before the race, it was ballast that had been aboard, lying on the cabin sole, when the boat was measured. The lead pigs had been taken off the boat in order to cut them in half so that they could be properly stowed in the bilge. Dunraven did not have a leg to stand on.

The Earl of Dunraven

Traditionally, builders of America's Cup yachts have discouraged the prying eyes of journalists

The club expected an apology from the Earl and not receiving one by the end of February, asked for and received his resignation as an honorary member of the NYYC.

4

Two Knights Challenge

It was left to Sir Thomas Lipton to wash away the bad feelings about the Cup in a gush of publicity that spread the fame of the international prize into every literate home in the Western World. Ironically, it was a member of the English House of Lords who had done harm to the Cup's reputation and the successful son of a poor Irish farmer who would raise the America's Cup to the pinnacle of its popularity. The Royal Ulster Yacht Club in Ireland challenged on behalf of Lipton in the late summer of 1898. The challenge was accepted and the details worked out within 24 hours between a delegation representing Lipton and NYYC officials. The club was interested in being as accommodating as possible and for the most part terms of the previous match were adopted.

Sir Thomas Lipton was the first of the self-made-men challengers. Others, men like T. O. M. Sopwith, Frank Packer, and Marcel Bich, would follow in Lipton's foot steps—in more ways than one. Born in 1850 to poor Irish parents who moved from Ireland to Glasgow, Scotland, during the potato famine, Thomas, at the age of 15, came to the United States by himself to work. For four years he toiled on the East Coast at low paying jobs. It was during this period that Lipton first grasped the importance of advertising. He returned to Glasgow in 1869 and went to work in the modest provisioning store which his poor parents had managed to keep open. Through inexpensive advertising techniques that relied heavily on gaining free publicity in newspapers, Lipton was able in the span of twenty years to expand his parents' business from one shabby store into a chain of grocery stores extending throughout the United Kingdom. By the late 1880's Lipton had become a millionaire.

In 1890, while on a trip to the Far East, he purchased a number of bankrupt tea plantations in Ceylon. Overnight he got into the tea business, from grower to retailer. Lipton could not have chosen a better commodity than tea to sell in Britain. In short order his campaign of national advertising brought his product into nearly every home in England. Tea made Lipton a multi-millionaire within a few years and the benevolent Irishman passed on hundreds of thousands of dollars of his good fortune to charitable causes. These donations resulted in Thomas Lipton's knighthood in 1898, the same year he first challenged for the Cup. In 1902 he was made a Baronet and his instant rise in English society is legend.

Lipton arrived in London society very much as though he was a complete foreigner. In 1897 virtually no one had heard of him, but by the fall of 1898 everyone had. There were no ties to hold Lipton back from social success; he had no wife, no friends, no relatives, he had only his business. Overnight he entered British society and his self-assured manner and urbane wit, to say nothing of his bank account, insured his success among the world's most demanding social set.

Sir Thomas Lipton's America's Cup challenge was the master stroke of his marketing career. In the fall of 1899 after his first unsuccessful challenge, Lipton returned to London to find that he was as popular as any Englishman on the scene and that during the summer he had become a national hero. In the fall and winter of 1899, for the first time in his life, he was mixing with men and women in the top strata of world society and became a fast friend of Prince Albert. Entry into the fun-loving Prince's court was relatively simple if a few basic qualifications were met: Women had to be beautiful and amusing, and the men rich and amusing. Albert had assembled the liveliest elements

"Columbia" (background) racing against "Shamrock" in the last 1899 race

of international society in terms of vivacity and charm, and there is no doubt that Lipton very much enjoyed his new associations.

An Advertisement for Himself

Will Rogers wrote of Lipton, "I defy anyone to name a more universally loved character than Sir Thomas Lipton." Although he may have been loved, many of his contemporaries were cynical about his yachting motivations. A friend and good acquaintance of Lipton's, Anthony Heckstall-Smith, said of Lipton that, "He did not go yachting for sport. He went because it was all part of that great advertising campaign to sell Lipton's Tea . . . Win or lose, what an advertising that was for Lipton's Tea . . . No, there can be no doubts that Tommy's repeated attempts to win the America's Cup were virtually the finest advertising stunts the world has ever known . . . He fooled the entire U.S. and most of the world into believing that he was a good sportsman. In the end, I think he even fooled himself."

There seems to be no doubt that in the beginning Lipton sincerely wanted to win the Cup. In fact, he spoke to his aids about challenging in 1897 with an all Irish boat—designed by an Irishman, crewed by Irishmen, and built in Ireland. No one took him seriously then and even after a number of America's Cup challenges many English yachtsmen still considered him a newcomer to the sport. When Prince Albert notified the Royal Yacht Squadron that he was going to put Lipton up for membership, the Prince was told to reconsider in order to save embarrassment. Club officials said that Sir Thomas would surely be blackballed as being unacceptable to the conservative members of the RYC because of his "mercantile past." More likely they were concerned with Lipton's humble beginnings, his use of the America's Cup for commercial reasons and his utter ignorance of anything nautical. It was said that Lipton wouldn't have been able to find his own boat had it not been painted green.

Lipton's own motto was, "He who on his trade relies, must either bust or advertise." The Irish grocer, as he was called by his detractors, liked to tell an old advertising analogy: "When a chicken lays an egg, she cackles and tells the whole farmyard. But when a duck lays an egg, she makes no sound at all. And how many people eat duck's eggs?" he would ask.

The America's Cup was still the biggest news in international sports throughout most of Lipton's five challenges. The front page press coverage he received was enormous. The $200,000 that a Cup challenge cost him was nothing compared to the free publicity he reaped across the country all summer long during his challenges, and he was a master at dribbling out news bit by bit over a long period of time so that each new nugget of information would be worth yet another newspaper

Sir Thomas Lipton was a master of publicity

article. Present-day yachtsmen would be astounded at the prominence of yacht racing in the American East Coast press around the turn of the century and Lipton used that publicity to make his greatest strides in penetrating the American market with tea.

One of the most cynical portraits of Lipton appeared in the inflamatory "Town Topics" published in New York City in the early 1900's. It said, "Since the days of the late lamented Barnum no such past master in the art of humbugging the gullable public of all nations has risen and shone with such elegant luminosity. He beats Barnum and goes him one better at least in one respect. The great showman, for the life of him, could not help chuckling and giving himself away whenever he successfully played the populace for suckers. Lipton on the contrary either candidly believes that he is a sportsman and philanthropist or he is the finest actor that ever lived." Possibly Lipton's theory was that there was a potential customer born every minute.

Lipton's First Challenge

The New York Yacht Club has never questioned the motivations of the America's Cup challengers and it is always assumed that the foreigner's intentions are sport. In the case of Lipton, the club was pleased to have another English challenge so soon after the unpleasantness of Dunraven. Lipton picked William Fife Jr. as his designer. The new challenger was built by Thorneycroft & Co., a famous English torpedo boat builder experienced in ligł. weight hull construction. The first of five *Shamrock* challengers was built, then tied together with stingers and braces to make her temporarily strong enough to make the transatlantic crossing.

The New York Yacht Club defender in 1899 was *Columbia*, a Herreshoff design that was owned by an Iselin-run syndicate with J. Pierpont Morgan as an important financial participant. *Columbia* was 131 feet overall and drew 19 feet 3 inches, nearly the maximum that could be launched at Herreshoff's Bristol yard.

Although the Deed of Gift expressly stated that the challenger should sail over on her own bottom, the club granted Lipton special permission to tow *Shamrock* behind his steam yacht *Erin* whenever it seemed advisable, which, as it turned out was much of the way.

The 1899 NYYC Lipton Match

Because of the great Lipton publicity there were more boats than ever out to watch the greatest of international sporting events. The New York Yacht Club had taken the criticism offered by Dunraven to heart and had enlisted the aid of the Federal Government to control the fleet. Washington, trying to curry favor with some of the club's Wall Street members at the time, was only too glad to help. A large fleet of revenue cutters and torpedo boats under the command of Capt. Robley ("Fighting Bob") Evans of Spanish-American War fame made sure that spectators stayed well clear of the course. The Navy and the Coast Guard have cooperated in every Cup year since to control the ever-growing horde of spectators.

In the first completed race, Capt. Barr swung *Columbia* on *Shamrock's* weather quarter in the controlling position and was thus able to keep the challenger from splitting tacks while at the same time being free to work to windward. *Columbia* rounded the windward mark over nine minutes before *Shamrock* and won the race by more than 10 minutes. In the second race *Columbia* got to windward of *Shamrock* and stayed there as the challenging crew repeatedly tacked to get free. Each time *Shamrock* tacked, Barr covered. After half an hour of good racing *Shamrock's* topmast snapped in two, fell off to leeward in 12-knots of wind, and the challenger retired. The defender sailed over the course and won the race.

Columbia won the third race by about six minutes, primarily due to a very smart rounding of the leeward mark. Both boats were relatively even in speed with *Columbia* having a bit of an edge and a decided advantage in crew handling. Lipton was good natured about the defeat and soon after was proposed and accepted for membership in the NYYC.

Sir Thomas' Second Challenge

Following his return to London, Lipton immediately challenged for 1901. He commissioned George Watson and ordered that no expense be spared. Watson developed a 137-foot boat even more radical than his previous designs.

A new NYYC syndicate was formed consisting of August Belmont, Oliver H. Payne, F. G. Bourne, James Stillman, and Henry Walters. They commissioned Herreshoff to out-design his earlier *Columbia*. His new design was christened *Constitution* and displayed much of the design thinking used in *Columbia* and *Defender,* yet was even lighter in construction. Uriah Rhodes was chosen as captain, which was a surprise considering the fine job that Charles Barr had done in 1899. But the crusty Scot had rubbed some people the wrong way—including his all-American crew—and there was still some lingering doubt about a "foreigner" driving an American defender.

Seeing an opportunity for a strong contender for the defense, E. D. Morgan bought Iselin's share of *Columbia* and signed up Barr as skipper. Barr picked a crew of Scandinavians and drilled them into a smooth functioning team.

More Bad Publicity for the Club

A third contender for the defense was announced from Boston. Thomas W. Lawson would "defend for the American people," not as a member of the NYYC. This came as a shock to the America's Cup fraternity in New York. Thomas Lawson was a wealthy Boston stock broker and speculator. He was not a NYYC member and he did not want to become one. News of the progress on his boat was received at the club with all of the enthusiasm normally accorded word of a disaster at sea. Privately, NYYC officers wrote Lawson that the boat could not compete unless it was owned by a member of the club. However, the NYYC Commodore wrote that it would be permissible to sign the boat over to a member and that the officers very much wanted the boat to contend for the defense.

Lawson was the son of an uneducated Nova Scotia carpenter. The family had migrated to New England to get out of the cold and at age 12 Thomas started out as an office boy in a Boston brokerage house. By 1901 he was worth $50 million dollars. He had gotten the idea for a Cup defender a decade earlier when Gen. Paine of Boston built a Cup defender. Unfortunately, Lawson had grossly misjudged the New York Yacht Club. The inner circle was not particularly pleased to discover that Lawson was trying to make a cause out of his participation in the sport with his newly-constructed *Independence*. Lawson refused to sign the boat over to a member of the club and the NYYC maintained that it could not allow a boat to participate unless it was owned by a member. After weeks of bitter newspaper articles, and after numerous cordial letters between Lawson and the club, the NYYC publicly announced that *Independence* would not be allowed to compete in the trials for the selection of a defender because she was not owned by a member of the NYYC.

For weeks, newspapers from New York to Boston and across the country picked up the conflict between Lawson and the club and sensationalized it in banner headlines and front page stories. In article after article the newspapermen of the day asked how NYYC members could call themselves sportsmen when they were not allowing a boat

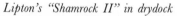

Lipton's "Shamrock II" in drydock

"Resolute" and "Shamrock IV" in 1920

specifically built for the defense to even have a trial. Club officers responded that the NYYC had to administer the match, under the Deed of Gift, or else chaos would result.

Public opinion and the press gave the club its share of lumps but people like Morgan and Iselin were inured to criticism and held their ground. Although Lawson had become the popular hero for standing up to the club, and the $500,000 *Independence* was the people's choice to win the trials, she was never allowed to compete. The experience was personally devastating for Lawson. Although he conducted himself as a gentleman at all times and is never recorded to have made even a sharp remark against the club, his public rejection was a terrible psychological and social blow from which he would never recover. Later, Lawson's fortune dwindled and he died a relatively poor man.

Although *Independence* did not take part in the official trials, she was involved in a number of informal races against *Columbia* and *Constitution* which established her speed in relation to the two yacht club favorites. *Independence* was the largest boat built up to that time to defend the Cup, being 140 feet overall and 89 feet on the load waterline. She was designed by B. B. Crowninshield, a well-known Boston naval architect, and had the appearance of a gigantic scow with 51 feet of overhang. *Independence,* with Hank Haff at the helm, sailed six races in all, four against both *Columbia* and *Constitution* and two against *Columbia* alone, and the Lawson boat lost every contest. Thanks to these "unofficial" races the NYYC was off the hook as far as *Independence* was concerned. She was broken up later that year.

The 1901 America's Cup Summer

In the trials between *Columbia* and the new Herreshoff-designed *Constitution,* skipper Charley Barr showed that aggressive steering tactics combined with quick, efficient crew work could give an old boat dominance over a new one. Barr bullied and bluffed *Constitution's* Rhodes at nearly every start until Barr got into the controlling position. Occasionally, Barr would threaten to ram *Constitution* and called for right-of-way when he actually had no rights and each time Rhodes allowed the Scot to get his way. *Columbia,* the old Herreshoff design, was finally selected defender.

On September 28, 1901, *Columbia* won the first race against *Shamrock II* by one-minute twenty-seconds, corrected time, after being behind at the weather mark by 41-seconds. The second race was as exciting as the first with *Shamrock II* leading the whole race until the wind breezed up to 15-knots toward the end and *Columbia* shot by. The third race was the closest in America's Cup history up to that time, with first *Shamrock II* and then *Columbia* being slightly ahead. Ultimately, *Shamrock II* finished the 30-mile course two-seconds ahead of the defender with both boats overlapped. Unfortunately for Lipton, *Shamrock* had a time handicap requiring her to finish 43-seconds ahead of the *Columbia* before she could win. Once again the Cup had been kept on American soil.

Lipton's Third Challenge

Lipton challenged again for a match in 1903 and went back to William Fife Jr. to design his third *Shamrock.* A NYYC syndicate was formed, among whose members were Cornelius Vanderbilt, William Rockefeller, James J. Hill, W. B. Leeds, Henry Walters, and practically unlimited backing was offered for a new Nat Herreshoff design. The hull alone is reported to have cost $175,000. Ironically, Herreshoff drew heavily on some of the design characteristics of *Independence.* The scow-like overhangs of Lawson's boat had been successful on certain points of sail and Herreshoff remembered that when he drew the 1903 Cup defender, *Reliance*—the most radical boat ever to defend the America's Cup.

Reliance was extremely flat with a shallow, skimming-dish underbody and a thin, deep keel. She was 143-feet overall, 89 feet 8 inches on the water, with a beam of almost 26 feet and a draft of 20 feet. Most outstanding of all, was the 16,160 square feet of canvas the boat carried. This was 2,000 square feet more than the defender would carry, and was the most yardage ever supported in a cutter configuration. The steel mast was one of Nat Herreshoff's engineering masterpieces and to his credit it held up throughout the summer.

The Americans appointed C. Oliver Iselin as the *Reliance* manager and Barr was chosen helmsman. Other syndicates were formed to campaign *Columbia* and *Constitution,* but *Reliance* was selected after only one trial race, her performance being so outstanding. It would be up to the defender's enormous sail plan—which reached 175 feet into the air—to overcome the nearly two minutes of time penalty.

In the first race, the boats were about even at the first mark with *Reliance* slightly behind, but then a severe windshift and poor crew work on the part of *Shamrock III* put her behind and the defender won by over 7 minutes. In the second race, *Reliance* led all around the track to win by one minute 19 seconds.

In the third and final event of the series, Barr got a good start and steered *Reliance* into a commanding lead. On the way home a fog bank rolled over both boats and the spectator fleet. *Shamrock* lost her way, missing the finishing line completely, then she dropped out of the race. *Reliance* found the finish line, winning the race and the match.

Lipton Refuses to Give Up

In 1907, Lipton challenged, conditionally, for the America's Cup for the fourth time. He suggested that the club adopt the Universal Rule for rating Cup yachts as that would discourage the fantastically large sail plans that were being designed. The club officers turned down the suggestion—and therefore the challenge—probably more because they had grown tired of Lipton rather than because of any commitment to the Deed of Gift. In 1912, Lipton sent another challenge to the club, saying that his boat would be 75 feet l.w.l. and stipulating that the NYYC defender be the same length. The club declined the challenge on the grounds that the Deed of Gift allowed any length boat to be built up to 90 feet. But Lipton was determined to have his fourth Cup match, no matter what the conditions. In April, 1913, Sir Thomas sent an unconditional challenge for the following year through the Royal Ulster Yacht Club and the NYYC accepted. Later, while drawing up the terms of the match there was mutual agreement that both boats would be 75 feet l.w.l. Lipton commissioned C. E. Nicholson of Camper and Nicholson to design *Shamrock IV.*

In New York, Henry Walters formed a syndicate of Commodore J. P. Morgan, Cornelius Vanderbilt and others. They commissioned the master, Nat Herreshoff to design *Resolute.* A second syndicate went to William Gardner who had designed, among many successful boats, *Atlantic,* the yacht that won the 1905 Transatlantic Race, setting a record from Sandy Hook, New Jersey, to Land's End, England, that still stands today. Gardner's America's Cup design was called *Vanitie.* Yet a third syndicate commissioned Boston designer George Owen to build *Defiance.*

More than a ton of Egyptian cotton went into this 5,000-square foot mainsail made in 1930 for "Enterprise"

While *Shamrock IV* was on her way across the Atlantic, under tow by Lipton's luxurious power yacht, World War I broke out, and Lipton put in at Bermuda for instructions. He proceeded to New York and the challenger was hauled out and stored for the duration of World War I. In 1920, the third Lipton challenge was resumed.

Amateur Charles Francis Adams Defends

Charles Francis Adams II was one of *the* Adams'—a direct descendant of John Adams, second President of the United States, and John Quincy Adams, sixth American President. Charles had been sailing since he was ten, first in catboats and later in 36- to 46-foot cruising-type sailboats. He and his brothers had cut a wide and fancy swath through the New England racing fleets, and he was considered to be the best amateur helmsman in the country.

The first race for the America's Cup was held on July 15, 1920 in light 5- to 8-knot zephyrs and *Resolute* worked to windward of *Shamrock IV*, generally making better tactical decisions than the challenger. At one point the English went into the New Jersey beach in hopes of more wind, only to find less. Toward the end of the race, when it looked as if the defender had won, the wire throat halyard for the mainsail gaff parted at the winch below deck. The gaff jaws jumped the mast and the great mainsail came tumbling down in one uncontrollable mass of canvas. Adams ordered the main furled, the staysail struck, and dropped out of the race. Lipton won his very first America's Cup race! The only other race ever won by a challenger was in 1871 between *Livonia* and *Columbia*.

Because Adams dropped out of the race he came in for some criticism. It had been the first time an American boat ever failed to finish a Cup match. Armchair yachtsmen contended that Adams should have set a spinnaker and finished the match with that old Yankee try.

Adams Loses His Second Race

In the second race, *Resolute* took the lead at first, in spite of the fact that she was supposed to be a slower boat according to the rating rule. (She received 7 minutes 39 seconds in time allowance from *Shamrock IV.*) Since the challenger could not foot as fast as the defender she pointed higher on the beat and Adams chose not to cover. A slight windshift favorable to the English allowed them to merely grind in sheets a bit and fetch the mark but Adams could not point with the English on the new slant. The wind shifted a second time and *Shamrock* got ahead, never to lose her lead, thus beating the defender for the second race in a row.

This was the first race in 69 years of America's Cup history that a defender had been beaten when she was not disabled. Defenders had been defeated only four times and Adams owned half of those defeats. Further, Lipton needed only to win one more match out of the three that remained to win the America's Cup. Never before had a Cup come so close to being taken. Charles Francis Adams and his *Resolute* would have to win the next three races or suffer humiliation. The third race was the closest race in all of America's Cup history. The two boats finished in a dead heat, both covering the course in exactly the same elapsed time. But because the challenger had to give the defender over seven minutes of handicap time, *Resolute* was the winner. In the following two races Adams simply covered *Shamrock*, never allowing her to break away. The Cup was saved.

Era of the "J" Boats

The NYYC suggested a new set of conditions for the 1930 match which brought the America's Cup into its "J" boat era of racing. First, the boats used would be built to a rating formula under the Universal Rule and would fall into what was called the NYYC "J" class. Second, because all the boats rated the same—76 feet—there would be no handicaps, and the match would be run on a boat-for-boat basis for the first time. (This is exactly what Lipton had requested in 1913.) Third, the time for the races would be taken at the gun, not when the boats crossed the starting line. Fourth, the match would be held at Newport.

Sir Tom's Last Try

In May, 1929, Sir Thomas Lipton challenged for the fifth time. A year later the real contest was as much among the American contenders for the defense as it was between the challenger and defender.

Chandler Hovey's Boston *Yankee* was superior in heavy weather because of her increased displacement and a waterline length greater than either Vanderbilt's *Enterprise* or Morgan's *Weetamoe*. The L. Francis Herreshoff-designed *Whirlwind* was eliminated from everyone's thinking in the early trials. (Capt. Nat had retired a few years before and had passed on his business to L. Francis.)

NYYC Picks the Slower Boat

By the beginning of the August and final trials, Clinton Crane's design, *Weetamoe*, had beaten all of the other contenders except *Yankee*. But the Boston boat only excelled in heavy air racing and was pretty much eliminated from the selection committee's thinking. As the August trials began, the contest was between *Enterprise*, designed by Burgess and sailed by Vanderbilt, and *Weetamoe*, which was sailed by George Nichols. Harold ("Mike") Vanderbilt was not easily defeated and kept tinkering with *Enterprise*, trying new approaches throughout the summer to get her moving faster. Her 4,000-pound duraluminum mast and her extremely wide "Park Avenue" boom were two examples of some of the ideas that Burgess and Vanderbilt explored to increase speed.

In the final trials, *Enterprise* defeated *Weetamoe* in a 12-knot breeze, then beat her in the following race in even fresher breezes. Surprisingly—given the prolonged early success of *Weetamoe*, particularly in light airs—the selection committee called off the trials and selected *Enterprise*. They had seen enough. *Weetamoe*'s skipper had made tactical errors in the last two races which gave victory to a slower boat. *Weetamoe*'s designer Clinton Crane was bitter about this NYYC decision and later harshly criticized the officers for their selection methods.

The Cup match itself was a rout, the worst defeat suffered by any of Sir Thomas Lipton's five challengers. Aboard his power yacht *Erin*, the 82-year-old Lipton watched what he knew was his last chance dissolve before his tired eyes. It is said that Sir Thomas in his shriveled and weakened condition did not always know where he was that summer. But at the conclusion of the last match, he said, "I canna' win . . . I willna' try again."

When Lipton returned to England he was voted into the Royal Yacht Squadron, the same club that had told Prince Albert years before not to put up Lipton's name because of his "mercantile past." When invited ashore to enter the RYS for the first time, Lipton sent his regrets, saying that he had broken a "wee bone" in his foot and could not walk. All of his life, Lipton never went where he was not wanted, and when he was wanted, he was careful where he went. He died the following year.

English Flying Hero Challenges

Early in the fall of 1933, the Royal Yacht Squadron sent a challenge for the Cup on behalf of T. O. M. Sopwith, and the gauntlet was taken up by the NYYC for 1934. Although no one could possibly realize it in advance, this challenge would come painfully close to taking the America's Cup.

Thomas Octave Murdoch Sopwith at age 21 took up the sport of flying in 1909. Like many young men of this era, he was fascinated by airplanes and flying. In 1910 he made headlines around the United Kingdom by flying alone from England, across the English Channel and deep into France. By 1911 he had organized a flying exhibition that went barnstorming across the United States putting on stunt shows. This daring young man in his flying machine won the heart of the Honorable Beatrice Mary Leslie Hore-Ruthven. With her help the young flyer built Sopwith Aviation Co., which he had founded a few years earlier, into what would be one of England's major aircraft producers during the First World War. The aircraft company was the foundation of his fortune, and during the war he turned out the Pup, the Dolphin and the famous Sopwith Camel.

After the war Sopwith raced powerboats and won the famous Harmsworth Trophy, the closest prize that sport has to the America's Cup. He actively took up sailing in the 1920's, and won the English 12-Meter championships four times in a row from 1927 to 1930. After Lipton's death, he bought *Shamrock V,* so by the time he challenged in 1933 he was well acquainted with "J" boats. Sopwith, who was later

T.O.M. Sopwith and his wife Phyllis Brodie Gordon

knighted, was the first challenger to steer his own boat, and he was just the kind of romantic gentleman-sportsman that the America's Cup needed to freshen its image.

Hometown Justice?

Vanderbilt went to Burgess for a new "J" boat design—*Rainbow.* The summer of 1934 was almost a repeat of the trials of 1930 as far as Vanderbilt was concerned. This time, instead of *Weetamoe,* his new boat was soundly beaten in race after race by the old *Yankee.* The Boston boat *Yankee* was sailed by Charles Francis Adams, then Secretary of the Navy.

Yankee beat *Rainbow* regularly through summer. Then, toward the end of the trials, *Rainbow* beat *Yankee* by three minutes in light air. In the following race, while *Yankee* was out in front, her jumper strut broke, and she had to drop out. Later, the club officials allowed as how they were ready to pick *Yankee* if she had won that race. *Rainbow* took the next race by two minutes, and in the following trial, the Boston boat ripped her spinnaker, recovered, then came from behind to gain an overlap, finishing one second after *Rainbow.* In another 50 yards, *Yankee* would have been ahead. The six-man selection committee announced that they had seen enough and chose the Vanderbilt boat.

This probably came as close to a hometown decision as the club ever had. Over the summer *Yankee* proved herself to be faster in a greater variety of wind strengths. Even in the last four races, the Boston boat was faster than *Rainbow.* Working in *Rainbow's* favor were the facts that she was a new boat, a Burgess design, and was sailed by Mike Vanderbilt. There were NYYC members who would contend for decades after the event that the biggest thing against *Yankee* was that she was from Boston and therefore not part of the club's New York inner circle.

"Endeavour" leading Vanderbilt's "Rainbow" in 1934

Rainbow's syndicate read like a "Who's Who" of American industry and high finance: George F. Baker, Walter P. Chrysler, Joseph P. Day, Marshall Field, Edward S. Harkness, Charles Hayden, Gerard B. Lambert, W. G. McCullough, Ogden L. Mills, J. P. Morgan, Henry H. Rodgers, George E. Roosevelt, Alfred P. Sloan, Alfred G. Vanderbilt, Frederick W. Vanderbilt and William K. Vanderbilt. The syndicate spent half a million dollars on the boat and the campaign. *Rainbow* was rushed to completion in 100-days at the Herreshoff yard and launched on May 15.

"Endeavour" is Faster Than "Rainbow"

It was obvious almost from the first moment the Americans saw the Nicholson-designed *Endeavour* that she was faster, and even Mike Vanderbilt was saying he was worried about the future of the Cup. But, as yachtsmen of the day pointed out, Vanderbilt had already beaten one faster boat, *Yankee,* maybe he could do it again. The big blue challenger was an impressive sight as she slipped out to the starting line for the first time with a crew of 14 amateurs and 14 professionals aboard. Sopwith was at the wheel and had in his afterguard his second wife (his first wife died in 1930) Phyllis Brodie Gordon, Nicholson and Frank Murdoch, the aviation engineer who had designed *Endeavour's* rig, possibly the most aerodynamic in the world.

Ten thousand people traveled to Newport to see the 1934 match and were not disappointed by the ensuing struggle. At the start of the first completed race, Sopwith was tardy in hoisting his mainsail.

The halyard fouled on a spreader and a man was sent aloft to clear it. In the choppy seas, the crewman was slammed against the mast and injured. The race committee, seeing what had happened and realizing the challenger would not be able to start in time, postponed the match 15 minutes, allowing Sopwith to get reorganized. Vanderbilt's afterguard discussed the advisability of protesting the race committee for the postponement but finally decided against it. The race was bow-to-bow all the way up the first windward leg with *Rainbow* rounding slightly ahead, but once the boats got their spinnakers drawing *Endeavour* drove by to windward and left *Rainbow* in her wash and won the race by over two minutes. Challenger: 1–0.

In the second race in moderate breezes, *Endeavour* slowly worked to windward of *Rainbow* and was ahead by over a minute at the windward mark and maintained her lead the rest of the course for Sopwith's second victory. Challenger: 2–0. Vanderbilt's fears were confirmed.

Sherman Hoyt to the Rescue

In the third race *Endeavour* was leading at the leeward mark by over six minutes in light air. It looked as if the Cup was finally lost. After rounding the lee mark on the last leg of the race, Vanderbilt unaccountably turned the helm over to Hoyt instead of Parkinson and then went below to eat a sandwich and reflect on losing the Cup. Hoyt described what happened next in his autobiography: "Although we couldn't see the finish line, I knew that we were both fetching it. All the same I luffed *Rainbow* well out to weather of Tommy in *Endeavour*, on the off chance that he might tack to keep between me and the (finish) line. The bluff came off. Tommy tacked right into a calm patch. Immediately I bore away and sailed right through *Endeavour's* lee, crossing the line three minutes ahead."

Incredibly, Hoyt had banked on Sopwith following a cardinal rule of match racing—always cover the opponent—rather than holding course to the finish. Sopwith tacked four disastrous times in light air to cover, and in the process killed his boat speed to almost nothing and fell into a hole in the wind that *Rainbow* had avoided. Challenger: 2–1. Sherman Hoyt, because of his clever downwind tactics in this and in a later race, is probably more responsible than any other single individual for the America's Cup not being lost to T. O. M. Sopwith in 1934.

The Controversial Protest

After the third race Vanderbilt knew he was still in deep trouble and asked John Parkinson to enlist Frank C. Paine's assistance in the *Rainbow* defense, asking that he bring with him *Yankee's* parachute spinnakers. Despite Paine's disappointment of having *Yankee* short-changed by the selection committee, he agreed to help the defense.

The fourth race has lived on through the years as an example of what the club's critics—and even some well-versed members—consider an example of the NYYC's most high-handed race committee decisions. The fourth race was over a triangle course with the first leg to wind-

Harold S. Vanderbilt and C. Sherman Hoyt

ward. The two boats approached the windward mark on port tack with *Endeavour* on *Rainbow's* weather quarter and in controlling position—Vanderbilt could not tack for the mark until Sopwith peeled off for it first. Predictably, the challenger drove the defender beyond the lay line then tacked for the mark, rounding 23 seconds ahead of the NYYC yacht.

At the start of the reaching leg, Sopwith's crew was slow in hoisting the boat's gigantic genoa. The Americans hoisted their genoa and smartly sheeted it home, thereby accelerating past *Endeavour* to weather. Immediately, Sopwith spun his wheel to windward to luff Vanderbilt. Under the rules in existence at the time, Vanderbilt was legally forced to alter course to keep from hitting Sopwith, which meant that he, too, would have to point his boat head to wind and kill way. The challenger hoped by this maneuver to stop the overtaking *Rainbow* and then re-start *Endeavour* ahead of the defender. But, Vanderbilt didn't bat an eyelash as *Endeavour* shot in front of him, and he kept all 127 feet of *Rainbow* barreling down upon the challenger. Rather than risk a collision between the two leviathans and thereby threaten the lives of those aboard with a dismasting, Sopwith quickly bore off. No one will ever be sure if Sopwith would have hit *Rainbow* forward of her mast or not—the criteria for a legal luff. Afterward the Vanderbilt crew said that *Endeavour* would have struck *Rainbow* abaft her mast and would have been disqualified. The English contended that Sopwith would have hit *Rainbow's* bow, thus disqualifying the defenders. Many American observers on the scene contended later that the British could have proved their point had they wished to risk their topsides. *Rainbow* swept past *Endeavour*—which had killed much of its speed in the luffing maneuver—and went on to win the race. Sopwith finished with a red protest flag flying in *Endeavour's* rigging.

Racing rules to this day state that the protest flag must be flown as soon after the alleged infraction as possible, yet there has never been a uniform method of applying this technicality. Some race committee's

"Rainbow," the 1934 defender

"Ranger," the 1937 defender and the fastest "J" boat in the world

are apt to accept a protest flag raised hours after an incident and others are just as likely to declare that a flag raised minutes after an incident "too late." In the case of *Endeavour*, the NYYC race committee said that the protest flag was not displayed immediately after the alleged infraction but at the end of the third leg and therefore refused to hear the protest. *Rainbow* won. The match was even 2–2.

Mike Wins—With Help From His Friends

The fifth race was a windward/leeward course of 30-miles in total, and *Rainbow* took an early lead because of poor crew work aboard the challenger. Calamities befell the defender on the leeward leg with first the spinnaker ripping and having to be replaced and then a crewman being knocked overboard. As the man went over the side he grabbed the loose end of the running backstay, held on for dear life, and was dragged along, mostly underwater, for nearly 30 seconds before he was pulled out. Had the crewman let go of the wire stay, *Rainbow* would have had to go back and pick him up, and the race would have been lost. As it was the defender stayed ahead and won. Defender: 3–2.

Before the start of the sixth race, the two mammoth boats circled each other like gladiators locked in a death struggle. During the pre-start maneuvers, *Rainbow* had to luff to keep from hitting *Endeavour* and lost all speed. When the gun fired, *Endeavour* got away with an incredible 48-second lead. It was a reach to the first mark of the triangular course, and when *Rainbow* caught up with *Endeavour* Sopwith threw his bow into the wind using the same luffing tactic that he had tried before.

This time the challenger was no doubt determined to hold his course and let the Americans come crashing into him. However, *Rainbow* promptly responded, luffing head to wind. Sopwith then let his beautiful blue machine fall off and pick up steam and beat *Rainbow* to the mark by over a minute.

On the second leg, which was supposed to be a beat to windward, *Endeavour* set a genoa while *Rainbow* set her quadrilateral jib. This sail selection was critical. The quad could be easily and quickly tacked while the genoa, because of its greater area, was by far more difficult to tack smartly and sheet home. Further, the amateur English crewmen's hands were by this race a mass of bandages and sores. Their winches were also underpowered, handicapping them with yet another disadvantage. The Americans split with the English and Sopwith tacked to cover, but in the freshening breeze trimming his genoa home became even more difficult and the next time Vanderbilt tacked, Sopwith did not cover. *Rainbow* headed out to sea, and her afterguard prayed for a windshift that would give them a better slant to the next mark. In the meantime, Sopwith's gang was having difficulty changing from the genoa down to their quad.

Vanderbilt's prayers were promptly answered as he got a header, tacked on it, and was abeam and to windward of Sopwith and able to fetch the mark with only one short hitch; *Rainbow* rounded two minutes ahead of *Endeavour*. On the final leg, downwind, the *Rainbow* foredeck gang set the wrong spinnaker, a notoriously "miserable" one loaned from *Weetamoe*. *Endeavour* set a beautiful chute and drew alongside; it was obvious that the challenger was on a sleigh ride to the finish line and her third victory.

It was reported by those aboard *Rainbow* that as *Endeavour* came galloping down on the Americans, Vanderbilt became extremely nervous. Never before in the history of the America's Cup had the defense been so difficult, and never before had the challenger been so markedly faster than the defender. Vanderbilt suddenly asked Hoyt to take the helm from Parkinson and he went below, despondent, just as he had been during the third race. Once again, lacking boat speed, Hoyt had to fox Sopwith out of victory. Counting on the challenger's tendency to cover—which had just been reinforced during the last leg when Sopwith lost the lead by not covering—Hoyt steered for a point one mile to leeward of the finish line. Instead of heading directly for the finish line, Sopwith bore off to cover *Rainbow* as she fell away from the rhumb line. In order to cover, Sopwith began sailing by the lee which slowed him up a trifle and *Rainbow* began to pull away. One mile from the line, *Rainbow* sharpened up, got a slight wind shift that gave the defenders a slightly faster sailing angle, and thereby beat *Endeavour* to the finish line by 55 seconds. The defender had managed to win the match: 4-2. The 1934 match was the closest a challenger had ever come to winning the America's Cup.

"Endeavour II" became the second fastest "J" boat

Tom Sopwith Tries Again

In 1936 T. O. M. Sopwith challenged a second time for the Cup. Charles E. Nicholson designed a new "J" boat, *Endeavour II,* and there was every indication that she was even faster to windward than the old Nicholson design. There was no doubt on 44th Street that a new boat would have to be built for the 1937 challenge. This time, club members were not scrambling over each other to become part of the new syndicate; the Depression had made itself felt even in the cozy parlors of the New York Yacht Club. The club was bound by the Deed of Gift to accept properly tendered challenges, yet if the America's Cup was defended by one of the existing American "J" boats, the Cup would be lost. The club's America's Cup committee turned to Mike Vanderbilt for help.

Vanderbilt formed a syndicate, but as time went by it became clear that substantial money would not be forthcoming, and in October, 1936, Vanderbilt made the decision to shoulder the $500,000 expense single-handedly. His financial generosity would save the Cup the following year.

Vanderbilt, who was a master at organization and at sizing up the right person for the right job, set up a curious arrangement for the designing of his new boat, *Ranger.* He asked Starling Burgess, who had designed *Enterprise* and *Rainbow* to work on his new boat in collaboration with the 28-year-old Olin J. Stephens II, a young naval architect who had been having considerable success with ocean racers. Both designers made small models and tested them in the new Stevens Institute of Technology towing tank. Models were also made of *Enterprise* and *Rainbow* for purposes of comparison. Incredibly, C. E. Nicholson had given Burgess the lines of *Endeavour I* and a model was also made of what was known to be the fastest "J" boat in the world. Nicholson might have considered the gesture sporting or maybe he was so confident in his ability that he figured that he could easily out-design her. In any case, it was a mistake.

Burgess Designed Ranger

For a long time after 1937, the designer of *Ranger* had been kept secret. Burgess and Stephens had collaborated on all aspects, and an agreement between the two parties stipulated that it would not be made public which man had designed the various aspects of the boat. However, as time went along, more and more yachtsmen were given to the feeling that Stephens had been the guiding light behind the fastest "J" boat that was ever built. Stephens uncovered the secret in the late 1950's writing, "Models for tank testing were drawn up by Burgess and myself, individually, and by draftsmen under close supervision, and the model selected to become *Ranger,* as the result of tank tests, was a Burgess model."

"*Ranger's* success naturally induced speculation as to the individual reponsibility and credit for her lines. Because of some minor detail of rudder configuration, Harold Vanderbilt, her owner, believed the model chosen was my design, but no publicity occurred until 1956, when he was quoted in an article in "Sports Illustrated," stating flatly that the *Ranger* lines had been drawn by Olin Stephens."

The result of the tank testing contest and the efforts of Stephens and Burgess was *Ranger,* a boat that was designed and built "on the cheap" by the parties involved in deference to Vanderbilt's undertaking of the entire financial burden. Rod and Olin sailed aboard the boat in the afterguard, and she quickly demonstrated her talents in races against *Rainbow* and *Yankee.* She then met the challenger in the sixteenth defense of the America's Cup and dusted off *Endeavour II* by fantastic margins of from three to 18 minutes in a display of superior boat speed that had never before been seen on an America's Cup course and which would never again be attained. *Ranger* whipped the challenger in four straight races. It would be over 20 years before anyone would ever again challenge for the America's Cup.

5

The 12-Meter Era

The seventeenth match for the America's Cup was held in 1958 and a new generation of yachtsmen had grown up since the 1937 contest. Many of the old guard had faded away. The officers of the New York Yacht Club were a new breed. Yachting itself had changed radically since the days of the "J" boats and somehow the continuity of the old America's Cup mentality had been broken. It was now a new game with different players.

In the mid-1950's serious talk about the America's Cup began at the New York Yacht Club. It was well known that the English wanted to continue the business they had begun in 1870 and the question before the club was in which direction the America's Cup competition should go. What kind of boats should be used? The "J" boats were long dead, fossils of an extravagant age long past. Everything from dinghies to 73-foot ocean racers were being recommended to take their place.

Any consideration of dinghies, small one-design boats, or medium-sized ocean racers was quickly tabled because such types would make the Cup easy prey and would break the tradition of the trophy being a prize for big boat competition. Debate among the club's influential inner circle centered on two types of boats: 73-foot ocean racers, largest allowed in the race held by the Cruising Club of America from Newport to Bermuda every other year, and the International 12-Meter Class. The 12-Meter Class was not unlike the "J" boats in that the yachts' measurements, when cranked through a formula, had to all equal the same number. In the case of 12-Meter boats, that figure was "12 meters." That meant sail area, length, draft and most of the other aspects of the design could vary within certain parameters. As it turned out, the biggest guns in the yacht club favored 12-Meter yachts, and the matter was settled.

Commodore Henry Sears went to the Supreme Court of New York State for permission to make two changes in the 1887 Deed of Gift from George Schuyler. In December, 1956, the court granted those changes: 1) the reduction of the minimum load waterline length from 65 feet to 44 feet; and, 2) the elimination of the clause requiring that boats proceed under sail on their own bottoms to the port where the contest was to take place. As before, the particulars of the match would be agreed upon between the challenger and the club. In June 1957, the Royal Yacht Squadron challenged for the America's Cup for an English syndicate made up of Group Captain Joel Guinness, Major Harold W. Hall, Sir Peter W. Hoare, Major R. N. MacDonald-Buchanan, Viscount Runciman, and four others. The syndicate asked four leading British designers to work up designs from which models were made and tank tested. David Boyd, a Scot, designed the fastest model and won the contract.

The selection of 12-Meter yachts as racing vehicles, if not the first break the NYYC ever gave to the challengers, was certainly the biggest. In choosing the 12-Meter, the club was opting for a class which had been developed in England, with rules made in England, and with most of the racing in the class done in England.

The Club Forms Its Defense

Commodore Henry Sears and Briggs Cunningham, a flamboyant member of the NYYC who had been a sports car racing driver at one point in his varied career and a successful 12-Meter skipper during the 1930's, formed a syndicate with Gerard B. Lambert, James A. Farrell, A. Howard Fuller, Vincent Astor and a few others and commissioned Olin Stephens to design a new Twelve. This was the primary syndicate and certainly the most "clubby" of the four groups that formed to defend the America's Cup in 1958.

A second group formed around the family of Captain John Matthews, who owned the old 12-Meter *Vim* at the time. Matthews spared little cost in putting the boat into fighting trim. She would provide a reliable measure of design progress if nothing else in the summer trials. As it turned out, *Vim* nearly won the trials. Matthews had assembled an all-star crew, including Emil "Bus" Mosbacher, Ted Hood, Dick Bertram, Buddy Bombard, Jakob Isbrandtsen, and others, who not only got the maximum out of the old design but gained valuable experience that would be utilized in later challenges. Matthews' selection of Bus Mosbacher to be part of the afterguard launched Bus' 12-Meter career.

The New York Yacht Club's selection committee was a combination of some old faces who had participated in America's Cup action during the Thirties and who knew its subtleties, and some new faces to Cup competition. It would be up to this group to make sure that the club had the strongest possible defender. The committee was made up of Mike Vanderbilt, Charles F. Havemeyer, Henry S. Morgan,

W. A. W. Steward, Luke Lockwood, and George Hinman. With only one new boat, *Columbia,* and one old one, *Vim,* gunning for the defense, the selection committee was not at all certain that the Cup would be safe and encouraged the formation of other syndicates. Harry Morgan called 78-year-old Chandler Hovey, who had owned *Yankee* when she lost the final race of the 1934 trials by one second, and asked if he would consider forming a 12-Meter syndicate, since there was always the chance that the New York group would fall apart. As if on cue, a half hour after Morgan's call, designer Ray Hunt walked into Hovey's office and showed him some preliminary plans for a 12-Meter design. The dean of American yachtsmen told Hunt to go ahead. He would swing another contender for the defense, *Easterner.*

At about the same time, Henry Mercer learned that the New York syndicate was having trouble raising money (about $500,000 was needed to build and campaign a Twelve in those days) and commissioned Phil Rhodes to design *Weatherly.* Both Hovey and Mercer committed themselves to those large outlays of money in almost a casual way, although they had both, no doubt, been thinking about a defender for some time. Mercer had lunch with designer Phil Rhodes and the meeting concluded with Mercer saying, "We'll shake and you go ahead. I want you to handle the whole thing. Get the best builder and select the finest crew. And, if we don't win, don't worry—there will be no gripe." Mercer was a designer's ideal client.

Columbia's syndicate was made up of a small group of industrialists and financiers; however, the other three boats were underwritten by three individuals. Chandler Hovey was a partner of Kidder, Peabody Inc., investment bankers in Boston. Hovey was also the patriarch of the Eastern Yacht Club, located in Marblehead. Eastern had been the only group that stood between the English challengers and the Cup during a decade in the late 1800's and for a time rivaled the New York Yacht Club as the nation's most prestigious yacht club. The Hovey family had been rooted in the tradition of the sea since one of Chandler's great-grandfathers, August de Peyster, had been a clipper-ship captain for John Jacob Astor in the early 1880's, sailing from the Orient to England in the great China tea trade.

In light of the Hoveys' lack of success with *Yankee,* his new interest was surprising to some. Hovey said, "I chose Charles Francis Adams as skipper in 1934. I thought the New York Yacht Club would look with more favor on *Yankee* if he were the skipper. I was wrong. In the last trial race in 1934 we didn't know which boat had won. The committee told us *Rainbow's* mast had crossed the line a second earlier. I should have demanded a rematch, but we were dumb—we knew we had a better boat. That brings me up to why I'm still in it. I was irked. So in 1957 when I heard the NYYC syndicate was getting a little wobbly, and they called me, I decided to build a Twelve."

Mercer's entry into the 12-Meter arena came as somewhat of a

surprise to the club. Although he had been a member for years, no one had approached him to become a member of the Sears-Cunningham syndicate. Evidently, Mercer's interest in the America's Cup had been sparked in the 1930's on a transatlantic steamship trip when he met Sir Thomas Lipton. He had nurtured a quiet desire to get involved in America's Cup action ever since. Mercer was, in every sense, a self-made-man, starting out as a stenographer for the Erie Railroad at age 17 in 1910 and working his way up to owner of States Marine Lines shipping company, which at the time of the challenge had a fleet of 143 freighters. The other members of his syndicate were officers in his company.

The trials during the summer of 1958 were probably the most exciting ever held in 12-Meters. Three of the skippers—Briggs Cunningham in *Columbia*, Arthur Knapp, Jr., in *Weatherly* and Bus Mosbacher in *Vim*—were all top-ranking International One-Design sailors and had raced against each other on Long Island Sound for years during the 1950's. Because the IOD fleet was considered the hottest on the East Coast at the time, it was from that group that the syndicates drew their helmsmen. On *Columbia, Vim*, and *Weatherly*, the afterguards and the crews (all amateurs) were stocked with some of the finest sailors in the United States. For example, aboard *Columbia* in addition to the helmsman, was Harry Sears, Olin and Rod Stephens, Colin Ratsey, Wallace Tobin, Vic Romagna and Halsey Herreshoff, a descendent of Capt. Nat. *Weatherly* counted Frank MacLear, Carleton Mitchell, Ed Raymond, Warwick Tompkins Jr. and Phil Rhodes in the crew. *Vim* had Ted Hood, Dick Bertram and Buddy Bombard aboard. *Easterner's* crew was made up of three Hoveys in the afterguard, which sports writers picked up on with the "coveys of Hoveys" phrase. *Easterner's* effort was the most low-pressure of the four.

"Vim" and "Columbia" Battle

Easterner and *Weatherly* were the first to be eliminated from the trials, with the two Olin Stephens designs left to slug it out for the honor of defending. Amazingly, the 19-year-old *Vim* was able not only to hold her own, but to consistently beat the new *Columbia* throughout the early trials. The final contest between these two boats was among the best 12-Meter racing ever seen, with *Columbia* taking the first race and *Vim*, the second. *Columbia* led all the way in the third race and the public expected the new boat to be picked—which was almost a forgone conclusion, anyway. But the committee, largely at the urging of Mike Vanderbilt, asked for one more race. *Vim* won the fourth race as a result of the starting line tactics of Bus Mosbacher who by this time had proved that superior steering and strategy could make a slower boat a winner. The fifth race was held in a breeze which seemed to

Crewmen hang on the windward rail for added boat stability

favor *Columbia,* and Cunningham won the start. There were scores of tacks in the eight-mile windward/leeward course and the crews on both boats were ready to drop dead by the time the boats reached the weather mark. *Columbia* lost her lead on the run by hoisting a large spinnaker but later regained the lead to win in a seesaw battle. In the end, *Columbia* had won and was selected to defend the Cup against the RYS's *Sceptre.*

The First 12-Meter Cup Match

The British challenger was steered by Lieutenant Commander Graham Mann, R.N., who at 34 had proved himself as one of the best small boat skippers in England. But the blue stadium off Newport was the big time, and the series was literally over 15 minutes after it began. Cunningham easily won the start and pulled away. Almost immediately, it was obvious that the challenger could not point as high as *Columbia,* nor could she foot as fast. In five minutes the defender had worked her way into a large lead. In 15 minutes it was obvious that *Sceptre* didn't have boat speed. Despite the relatively smooth waters, the English boat hobbyhorsed and with each pitch slowed herself down. At the windward mark, *Columbia* led by seven minutes 38 seconds. It was a rout. *Columbia* had advanced a small margin over the 1939 design of *Vim,* but English design had progressed not at all. *Columbia* won four races straight by margins of from seven to nearly 12 minutes.

Like many 12-Meters, "Columbia" was dismasted in practice

The 1962 Challenge

On April 20, 1960, the club received the eighteenth challenge for the America's Cup from the Royal Sydney Yacht Club on behalf of the Australian publishing magnate Sir Frank Packer. The challenge came just when rumors were flying that the English might try to set up a Commonwealth challenge for the Cup. Obviously, Sir Frank wanted to have no part of a group effort and fired off his challenge as soon as possible. Eight days later Commodore George Hinman announced that the NYYC had accepted the Australian bid—the first ever from that emerging country and the first challenge from a country other than the United Kingdom or Canada.

The way that Sir Frank was going about things indicated that he meant business. The previous October, Australian Olympic Finn sailor and one of the country's most avid yachting enthusiasts, Colin Ryrie, had secretly chartered *Vim* from Capt. Matthews, with an option to buy, on behalf of Sir Frank. In January, Australian designer Alan Payne had flown to New York and obtained an understanding from club officials that in the event of a challenge he would be allowed to use the Stevens Institute test tank since there was none available in Australia. With *Vim*, Payne would be able to take her lines, make a model, and determine how fast his own boat would have to be. Had the English gone about their 1958 challenge in this manner, it probably wouldn't have been as catastrophic. Later, Sir Frank got a concession from the yacht club allowing the Australians to use sail cloth from yarn made and woven in the United States. Through quiet, low-key negotiation, Sir Frank had significantly improved the changes of his challenge, and had gained concessions that would not be allowed later.

Sir Frank Packer—Man From Another Age

Frank Packer was born to a prosperous family, but that didn't keep him from scrambling just as hard as someone who hadn't when he entered the business world. He started sailing at three years of age when his father would tie him to the centerboard trunk of his 15-foot daysailer. Frank inherited his father's confidence and made his first big killing in the publishing industry in the 1930's by promising not to publish a newspaper in competition with an existing success. He collected $178,000 from his would-be rival and plowed it into the "Australian Women's Weekly," which by 1962 had a circulation of 820,000—eight percent of Australia's population. With the huge profits reaped from the women's paper he bought Sydney's "Daily Telegraph," which became the centerpiece of Packer's media empire, later encompassing T.V. and radio stations in addition to publications.

Sir Frank was a big man, strong and tough like the Australian

Sir Frank Packer, twice an America's Cup challenger

outbackers and he liked to hunt, shoot, fish and raise hell when things
got dull. He was a man born 200 years too late and probably would
have been more at home shooting game on an English moor and
swilling down ale at a roadside inn, surrounded by his hunting dogs.
Packer was known for being intensely loyal to his friends and even
picked up their debts on occasion. In describing him, a friend once
said that if he had told Sir Frank that he had just shot someone,
Packer's only question would be, "Where do we hide the body?" He
was just as rough in his business as he was in his sport and often fired
his editors out of hand. His employees called his company "Packerstan."

Packer's most classic remark was one he made to Queen Elizabeth
when she was visiting Australia in 1954. The two were sitting together
on a reviewing stand watching a parade go by in the Queen's honor
when he leaned over and said, "You are costing us a lot of money,
but we are very glad to see you here." Five years later he was knighted
by the Queen at Buckingham Palace.

Sir Frank's weakness had always been sports. He liked them and
he usually succeeded in making business ventures out of them; he
invested heavily in Australian squash courts and bowling alleys. It
should be noted that none of these sporting ventures hurt his publishing
business a bit and most provided even more news for his "Daily Tele-
graph." But, by far, Packer's biggest sporting venture of all was sealed

in his challenge for the America's Cup. Winning the America's Cup at age 55 would be a noble way of rounding out a rather dashing career, even if it did cost $700,000.

Alan Payne Designs the Fastest Twelve

Although Packer was paying the bills and reaping the publicity, it was Alan Payne who had to do the work. Payne, in his 30's, a bachelor and Australia's only full-time designer at the time, quietly went about designing, tank testing, lining up spar and winch manufacturers, and working with the sailmaker and the boat builder. It was his painstaking attention to every detail that would make the boat competitive off Newport. He, perhaps more than anyone else in Australia realized what a difficult task it would be to try to catch up to Olin Stephens in just a year and a half. As it turned out, Payne's hard work paid off. The Australian challenger, *Gretel*, had a faster hull than the ultimate American defender, both in the test tank and on the course.

Rally to the Defense

Paul V. Shields, senior partner of Shields & Co., a Wall Street brokerage house founded in the 1920's, picked up *Columbia* in 1960 for about $150,000 for the Shields family. When the Australians chal-

Alan Payne, designer of "Gretel" and "Gretel II"

lenged, he had in his hands the fastest 12-Meter in the world, so he handed the boat over to his brother and legendary Long Island Sound racing skipper, Cornelius Shields. Corny's 28-year-old son, Cornelius ("Glit") Shields, Jr., was named skipper and Corny, who was recovering from a heart attack, stayed on the sidelines.

Mercer's *Weatherly* had been doing better during the years between the challenges, and he was convinced that his boat had a good chance of being chosen to defend in 1962. In the spring of that year, the Luders yard in Stamford, Connecticut, sliced off two feet of her stern to save 160 pounds, put on a new keel with a slightly different shape and added about 1,000 pounds more ballast. Mercer asked Bus Mosbacher to be his skipper because of Bus' outstanding showing in *Vim* in 1958 and his obvious grasp of match racing tactics.

The New Twelve

As the fall of 1961 turned to winter, it became obvious that there was not going to be a new American 12-Meter built to defend the Cup. Quite possibly this could have lead to disaster. Had Australian Alan Payne succeeded in substantially improving on *Vim's* design, and thereby also improved slightly on *Columbia's*, the America's Cup would have been all but unguarded. Finally, 67-year-old Boston millionaire management consultant E. Ross Anderson, at the urging of Don McNamara, a hotshot Boston small boat sailor, jumped into the Cup fray. Later, Robert W. Purcell, who was chairman of the board of the Rockefeller I.B.E.C. in New York, joined up with Anderson in the financial underwriting of the project. Anderson commissioned Marble-head sailmaker and cruising-boat designer, Ted Hood, to create the new 12-Meter.

Because Anderson had made his decision so late to support a new boat, there was scant time left for her design. Hood wasn't given the greenlight to begin designing or tank testing until the end of October. A bright, young, would-be designer named Britton Chance went to work in Hood's design department and Hood utilized Chance's experi-ence in the Stevens Institute testing facility. Early in the project, both Hood and Chance spent many evenings running models in the Ho-boken tank, analyzing the results in a hotel room nearby, modifying the models with clay, and then testing them again the next morning. Hood was quite literally starting from scratch, since neither the lines for *Vim* nor any of the modern Twelves were available. He had to cram into two brief months all the work it had taken American designers six to eight months to accomplish in 1957. The lines were finalized in January and work was begun.

On May 19, at Graves Shipyard in Marblehead, after four months of work, the new American Twelve was launched at midnight to take

Bus Mosbacher, defending skipper in '62, '67

advantage of high tide. Over 5,000 people showed up to see the launching and to find out the name of the new boat—*Nefertiti*.

Although Hood's design looked just like any other 12-Meter to the layman, in actuality she was radically different. Her foretriangle was larger and she was beamier than the 12-Meters launched in 1958. The larger foretriangle would allow *Nefertiti* to carry more sail area, and thus have more power, than the more conventional Twelves, and her greater beam would give her increased stability.

The NYYC Eliminations

Midway through the American trials, it became evident that *Columbia* wasn't going to make it. Her early defeats brought on crew changes, but the boat never matched the finely-tuned machine she had been in 1958. Hovey's *Easterner* was still a family gathering although George O'Day was signed on as the boat's sharpshooter. The grand Boston yachtsman refused to turn his boat over to the young and hungry hotshot professionals in the industry who ached for a chance for front-line duty in the defense of the America's Cup. Chandler Hovey maintained all of his life that sailing was a sport, not a business. *Easterner* and *Columbia* were quickly eliminated in the American trials.

That left the new *Nefertiti* and the modified *Weatherly*. Just as *Columbia* had shown herself to be superior to *Vim* in a moderate breeze, so *Nefertiti* liked fresh winds and began holding her own with *Weatherly* in the 12-knot range, gaining superior performance as the wind increased. Three of the five trial matches were held in light air and *Weatherly* posted a 4-1 record, good enough in any selection committee's book. Mosbacher, who had by now spent a summer on *Vim,* one on *Easterner,* and a third on *Weatherly,* was the most experienced 12-Meter helmsman racing in Newport. His skill at starting was evident during the trials and it would pay off against *Gretel.*

Although Mosbacher didn't know it, *Weatherly* was slower than *Gretel* according to the tank tests carried on by both designers at the Stevens Institute. In addition to Pierre DeSaix, the director of the Stevens testing facility, a few members of the *Weatherly* crew had discovered the bad news and decided to keep it from their helmsman. Bus said later, "It's quite true that after the last race I was told that the Australian boat *Gretel* was faster in tank tests. No one wanted me to know before the races for fear of upsetting me . . . but, never underestimate the value of a good excuse."

The Politics of Defeat

Packer's first mistake was not selecting a skipper at the outset. Instead, he chose to switch off helmsmen and crews, trying first one then the other. A formal 11-man challenging crew was never organized and allowed to drill together to smooth out their performance. Instead of *Gretel* and her chartered trial horse *Gleam* simulating actual America's Cup course racing, Sir Frank put his crews through endless drills that only exhausted and demoralized the crewmen.

At the last minute, Packer made out the crew list and announced that Jock Sturrock would be helmsman. Even more incredibly he tossed one man out of the afterguard the morning of the first race and put in two new men. Indeed, Sir Frank behaved like a man transported from the feudal age. The Australian helmsman, Sturrock, had long since realized he would not be allowed to be the "skipper" of the boat, only its driver. Although Sir Frank would not be aboard for the races, he would call the shots—all of them. Sturrock was good natured about his impotent position and took the attitude that he was just another hired hand in Packerstan.

The Match Begins

Because of the 2,500 spectator boats crowding in on the match racers, the course could not be cleared in time and the start was postponed. Sept. 15, at 1:10, the race started; it would be twice around a 24-mile windward/leeward course. Mosbacher fell in behind Sturrock in the "round-de-round," a 12-Meter sparring pattern where one boat tries to get behind the other in order to be in a controlling situation. Mosbacher won the sparring duel and forced the challenger over the line just before the gun fired, compelling *Gretel* to come back below the line and restart. As *Gretel* dropped back, *Weatherly* shot ahead, eating up the much needed yardage she needed to beat the faster *Gretel*. Because of a wind shift, *Weatherly* was able to reach to the layline in two tacks and be ahead by 1:28 at the mark. In the second circuit of the course *Gretel* overstood the mark, had a running backstay fitting break, and was forced into an unnecessary tack. The reason for both of these errors was that the last-minute navigator simply had not been prepared to take the responsibility at such short notice. *Weatherly* won the race by three minutes 43 seconds.

The Australians Win

At the start of the second race, *Weatherly* was in what is known as a "safe leeward" position; that is to say, she was to leeward of *Gretel* but slightly ahead and had free air. When the boats tacked from starboard to port, as they must, *Weatherly* would be in the controlling position. This is exactly what happened, and as the boats made their way up the course on port tack, *Weatherly* began climbing out to windward and away from *Gretel*. Midway up the course the Aussies initiated a classic America's Cup tacking duel—the only time in the sport of yachting when such large boats became locked bow-to-bow in such grueling action. *Gretel* tacked to starboard, forcing *Weatherly* to do the same to maintain cover. As soon as *Gretel's* speed was up, Sturrock threw his wheel hard over, tacking the Twelve to port and forcing Mosbacher to follow. Thirty seconds later Sturrock slammed his wheel hard over again. Although the graceful boats looked as if they were tacking effortlessly, on the deck amidships the crew madly cranked in the genoa, turning the handles of the "coffee grinder" winches in a blur of movement.

Because the *Gretel* men were bigger and stronger, and because designer Alan Payne had been clever enough to design winches that were linked together, the challenger was managing to tack faster than the Americans. With each heart-busting tack, *Gretel* was gaining yardage on the defender. Finally, noting that *Gretel* was tacking faster and gaining, Mosbacher broke off the action and let *Gretel* tack away from him. Thereafter *Weatherly* only maintained a loose cover. Mosbacher would say later, "The Aussies had a better boat with much better winches and bigger men, while our gang was called Mosbacher's midgets. If they had made us tack and tack and tack, they would have beaten us. That's the art of match racing: finding your opponent's Achilles heel and sinking your teeth into it."

Mosbacher led at the windward mark of the triangular course by 12 seconds. The next leg was a reach and the two boats stayed locked together, still 12 seconds apart at the jibe mark. Later, *Weatherly* was slow in breaking out her spinnaker. *Gretel* set her Hood chute quickly

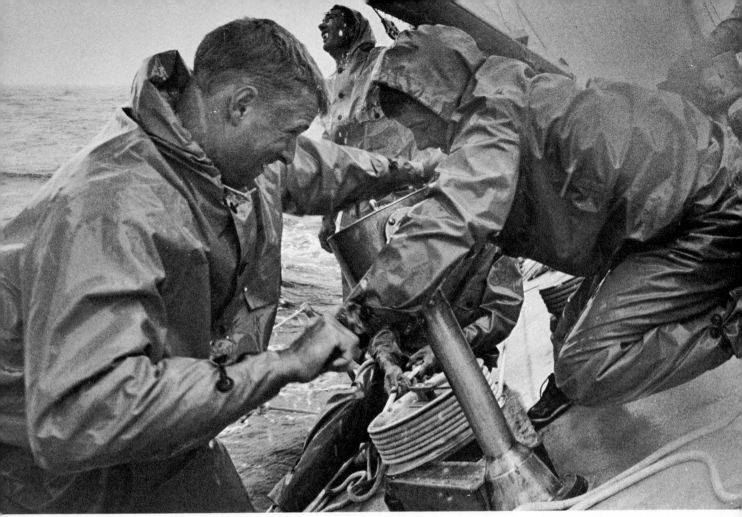

Grinding the genoa home in a tacking duel

and just as she did, something happened which had never occurred before (or since) in 12-Meter America's Cup racing. As *Gretel's* spinnaker was drawing, a big roller swept in underneath the challenger and picked her up on its crest, shooting *Gretel* down course on a plane. Just as *Gretel* sliced ahead, *Weatherly's* afterguy parted and her spinnaker pole slammed into the headstay, thus ruining any chance the defender had of coming back. The challenger stayed in front to win the race, the first match ever taken by a challenger in a 12-Meter.

That night the Aussies threw one of the biggest celebrations ever seen in Newport. They took over the waterfront Cameo bar, turning it into the "Royal Cameo Yacht Squadron," as hundreds of well-wishers joined the exuberant Aussies in a night of drinking, singing, and back slapping that only hinted at what these fun-loving men would do if they won the America's Cup.

In the next race Sturrock won the round-de-round start, crossing the line on port tack at the leeward end of the line with Mosbacher late. Later, the Long Island Sound fox worked his way even with Sturrock, and after the breeze slackened, he slowly moved ahead of the Australians and won the race. In the following race Mosbacher got his desired safe leeward position and refused to be drawn into a tacking duel by Sturrock, maintaining instead a loose cover. Running down wind, *Gretel* was noticeably faster and Mosbacher's tactic of reaching off away from the rhumb line, then setting a chute and heading back for the line on a better point of sail than the challenger's was in some respects similar to the tactic that Sherman Hoyt had used in 1934 against the vastly superior *Endeavour*. Like Sopwith, Sturrock chose to cover the defender and in so doing lost his advantage. *Weatherly* crossed the finish line 26 seconds ahead, the closest margin ever in an America's Cup match to that time. (Closer boat-for-boat races had involved corrected time differences greater than 26 seconds.)

In the last race, Sturrock got the safe leeward position, but midway up the first leg, Mosbacher slipped *Weatherly* along, going for maximum boat speed and refusing to be sucked into a disastrous tacking duel. Again Mosbacher gambled on a loose cover to pay off at the windward mark. It did by two minutes. *Weatherly* went on to win and saved the America's Cup from Sir Frank Packer.

Bavier Beats the Bird

Two new syndicates were organized for the 1964 defense. One was formed by Walter Gubelmann and Eric Ridder, who rounded up over 30 syndicate members. Each bought $25,000 shares of the new 12-Meter *Constellation*. Some of the syndicate members were John Astor, Briggs S. Cunningham, John T. Dorrance, Jr., Roger S. Firestone, Avard E. Fuller, Francis L. Kellogg, Charles S. Payson, Rudolph J. Schaefer and Harold S. Vanderbilt. Olin Stephens was commissioned to do the design. The other syndicate was started and heavily financed by Pierre S. du Pont III. Du Pont's boat was designed by Bill Luders, the Stamford boat builder who had successfully "Luderized" *Weatherly* for the 1962 defense. The boat was named *American Eagle,* after the vessel in which the first du Pont immigrants had crossed the Atlantic to the United States.

Ross Anderson brought back *Nefertiti* with Hood at the helm and *Easterner* returned for her third try with "coveys of Hoveys." A California group headed by Pat Dougan compaigned *Columbia*. Hood redesigned *Nefertiti* but was hampered somewhat, due to a problem in the testing procedures at MIT. From the outset the contest seemed to be between *Constellation* and *American Eagle,* with *Eagle* sweeping the early trials. Bill Cox, one of the nation's most outstanding one-design skippers, was the helmsman on *Eagle*. The Bird was sailing high, wide, and handsome; by mid-summer she looked to be the obvious choice.

Constellation, with Eric Ridder at the helm, could not seem to beat *Eagle* and on one occasion was nearly beaten by *Easterner,* which hadn't seen a new sail in years. In a race with *Nefertiti,* Ridder brought *Connie* so close to the committee boat that she actually scraped it and was technically out of the race. The *Constellation* afterguard decided to sail the race anyway just to show the selection committee what they could do in light air. *Connie* ended up beating *Neffie,* with Ted Hood at the helm, by 2 seconds—a disastrous margin considering that *Constellation* was a new boat and *Nefertiti* was obviously a heavy weather design. *Eagle* had won 14 straight races and was the obvious choice unless something startling happened on *Constellation.*

After the race with *Nefertiti* Eric Ridder told his co-helmsman, Bob Bavier, that he could steer at the start of the next race. But Ridder's generally poor showing through the trials and his slow grasp of 12-Meter match racing tactics was now admitted by the syndicate and the crew. Soon after the collision with the committee boat, the inevitable decision was made by the syndicate manager Gubelmann; Bavier would be given more time on the helm.

In the next race against *Eagle,* Bavier steered *Constellation* into a safe leeward at the start and led *Eagle* by four minutes at the weather mark. Later, fog rolled in and the race was cancelled. Bavier started most of the races in the New York Yacht Club Cruise and was over the line early in two out of three starts. As the cruise continued, *Connie* began doing better and better, beating *Eagle* in the last three races. Morale aboard *Connie* was on the rise; Bavier had reversed a disastrous trend. After the cruise, the syndicate decided that Bavier would start and steer in the final trials in August. Ridder would stay aboard as the skipper. At the same time it was decided that Rod Stephens, who had sailed the entire NYYC cruise aboard *Connie,* should be a permanent member of the *Constellation* afterguard. Rod had been the tactician

"Constellation" with Bob Bavier at the helm came from behind

on *Columbia* and had sailed on *Ranger* and *Weetamoe,* and probably had more America's Cup match racing experience than the whole crew combined.

Around Newport the watch word was "Beat the Bird"—a slogan spread by the *Connie* crew and one that was picked up by the many America's Cup aficionados rooting for a come-from-behind victory. Later, yacht club officials passed the word to the syndicates not to encourage the slogan as it was considered inappropriate.

In their second duel off Newport, Bavier got a slightly favored start, then sailed out of the wind. Cox took the lead and kept it until the last windward leg. The only way Bavier could get ahead was to force *Eagle* into a gut-wrenching tacking duel, and that's just what he did. This was the ultimate showdown of the 1964 summer and it still stands as one of the most monumental tacking ordeals in America's Cup history. The battle lasted for 42 tacks and with each one *Connie* ground down her opponent. Finally she smashed through *Eagle's* cover and surged into the lead to win and "break the heart of the Bird," as Bavier wrote later. *Connie* won the next three races and *Eagle* won the following match due to a wind shift. Bavier then beat the thoroughly demoralized Bill Cox in the next race by over four minutes. The selection committee made its decision: the Bird had been beaten.

The Odd Couple

In 1964, the British involved themselves in a curious challenge effort. The same designer who drew the disastrous *Sceptre,* David Boyd, was given the new commission by Tony Boyden. It was felt that Boyd could profit by his past mistakes. He was also the only designer in England with current 12-Meter experience and had worked extensively at the Stevens test tank while it was still available to foreigners. A number of syndicates were rumored to be sprouting up in England, but by early fall of 1963, it was obvious that no one else would come forward to sponsor a second British challenger. The English had come to the conclusion that it was absolutely essential for a successful challenger to have another new 12-Meter to tune up and race against. In September, two rather eccentric Australian brothers living in England stepped forward and offered to pay for a new boat if someone else would rig it and manage the campaign. The millionaire pair were Frank and John Livingston, who had made their fortune during their younger years as Outback sheep ranchers. Owen Aisher took the two elderly bachelors at their word and the second British challenger was born.

However, since there was only one 12-Meter design in England that anyone had any confidence in—the new Boyd design—it, too, was picked for the Livingston boat. Boyden graciously went along with the scheme and so the Robertson yard in Scotland turned out two

Action on the foredeck of a Twelve

12-Meters that winter—*Sovereign* and *Kurrewa V*. The latter had a keel and rig design that was a bit different than *Sovereign's* in hopes of doing a little design testing during the trials. The boats sparred in England and then were both sent to Newport for their final selection. *Sovereign*, with internationally famous Peter Scott steering, convincingly won the British series.

The showdown for the America's Cup between *Sovereign* and *Constellation* was a letdown. In the first race, as the two boats passed before the start, Bavier pretended that his men were not yet prepared. Once Scott was past, Bavier spun the wheel down and the seemingly disorganized crew sprang, cat-like, to action. Almost immediately the defender was on the challenger's stern and in the controlling position. Two minutes before the gun, Bavier broke away and sailed from the line, then jibed around and told his crew to "trim for speed." Quickly, *Constellation* accelerated until she was thrashing through the water at nine knots, heading for the windward end of the line near the committee boat. Scott had the same idea, yet he had not gotten a "running" start at the line as had Bavier. When *Constellation* approached the committee boat and *Sovereign*, Bavier headed up and shot to windward of the challenger, driving right over her, up and away. It was a fantastic start for the Americans as they powered into the lead, leaving the challenger in *Connie's* wash. The series ended up 4-0, with *Sovereign* losing by nearly twice the time of *Sceptre's* 1958 defeat.

The British weren't the only foreigners in Newport during the 1964 match. Sir Frank Packer, Alan Payne and his assistant, Warwick Hood, were also there. When the match was over, Sir Frank handed another challenge to the yacht club. The match would be held in 1967.

The Club Changes Some Ground Rules

After the *Sovereign* challenge, the club decreed that sails, sailcloth, rigging, gear, designers, and their design tools (the test tank) would all have to be from the country of the challenge, unless specifically exempted. Throughout America's Cup history challengers had freely used American lofts to re-cut sails and, on occasion, even had whole new suits made stateside. One of *Vim's* new spinnakers was used on *Gretel* against *Weatherly* in 1962. Now the club ruled that even the weaving would have to be accomplished in the nation making the challenge. It was said that the America's Cup should also represent the technology of each country as well as its design and sailing prowess. Needless to say, neither Australia nor England could approach the technical sophistication of American industry.

"Dame Pattie," the 1967 challenger

Australia Tries Again

There was a "grandfather" clause in the yacht club's new pronouncement as well, allowing any existing 12-Meters to race with the equipment already installed or purchased. Sir Frank Packer, who probably had a better understanding of America's Cup gamesmanship than any previous challenger, decided that he would keep *Gretel's* deck and rig the same—thereby falling under the grandfather clause—but make some "modifications" to the old boat's underbody. In fact, the underbody was completely changed and in actuality Payne designed a new boat.

A retired Australian ice cream millionaire named Emil Christiansen formed a second Aussie syndicate which was funded by contributions of 15 commercial firms. Christiansen commissioned Warwick Hood, Payne's former assistant, and immediately named Jock Sturrock as skipper, the latter having had his fill of Packer. The sailmaker for the challengers was Jan Pearce, the Ted Hood representative in Australia and a man who had learned his trade at the Hood loft in Marblehead, cutting American defender sails. The Christiansen syndicate boat was named *Dame Pattie* after the wife of the Australian prime minister, Dame Pattie Menzies. This was a *coup de maître* of public relations and insured the new Australian 12-Meter plenty of publicity, even in Sir Frank's press.

Jock Sturrock picked his crew and trained them just as one would expect from a strong and intelligent skipper. This was in marked contrast to the scene in the Packer camp. Sir Frank was carrying on his usual show. However, unlike 1962, this time the Aussies knew what to expect of Packer and were quick to step off the modified *Gretel* at the first sign of Sir Frank's erratic behavior. In the final trials in Australia, *Dame Pattie* defeated *Gretel* in match after match until it was obvious to all that there was nothing like the *Dame*. She alone was shipped to Newport for the showdown.

The "Intrepid" Syndicate Defends

William Strawbridge had worked in 1964 with the *American Eagle* camp running its tenders and had learned enough about the defense to have some definite ideas about how a campaign should be run. Strawbridge went to Olin Stephens for a design commitment. Before agreeing to a boat, Stephens recommended that Strawbridge first line-up a top skipper. Mosbacher's name was mentioned and Strawbridge tried to sign on the 1962 defender.

Because Mosbacher's father was ill, Bus did not want to commit himself, but did promise not to sign on with another group. Soon, J. Burr Bartram and Jack Dorrance promised to put up substantial amounts of cash and Bill Strawbridge found himself with a syndicate. With the entry of Harold S. Vanderbilt, the syndicate was able to put out contracts. Next, at Stephens' suggestion, Pat Haggerty was contacted and he agreed to join. That made four syndicate members, in for $150,000 each. Later, Bartram brought in Eleanor Radley and Gilbert Verney at $50,000 each for a total of $700,000

By the spring of 1967, Sparkman & Stephens had designed, and Minneford's Yacht Yard on City Island had built, *Intrepid*. She would prove to be as big an advancement in 12-Meter design as *Ranger* had been in "J" boat design. Some ideas that had been successful in ocean racers were applied to *Intrepid* with excellent results in terms of increased boat speed. The biggest improvement below the waterline was the design of two rudders, one at the stern of the boat and the other hung behind the keel. The rudder on the keel was called a trim tab and was not used for steering the boat except in tight turning situations or when the helmsman wanted instant response; otherwise, the small rudder aft was used. Twelves of this period had two or three wheels— the large one for the rudder aft, the medium-sized for the trim tab, and the smallest one to lock the tab. Normally the tab was used most effectively when going to windward when it was cocked from three to five degrees to windward. Also, about 40 square feet of surface area had been cut away from the after part of the keel; this was translated into less friction, less drag and therefore greater speed. *Intrepid* also had a little bustle on the afterbody called a "kicker."

Topside, the biggest changes were the winches. The big coffee grinders were no longer on deck. The Barient manufacturing company designed a system of cross-linked, below-deck grinders driving two drums on deck. The advantage of the system was that the four crewmen assigned to grind in the genoa could be kept below deck. The lowering of their weight, and the weight of the grinding machinery, would add to the stability of the boat and reduce windage somewhat. There were also two hatches forward, one to port and one to starboard to facilitate spinnaker handling. Much of the deck design came from Mosbacher and Vic Romagna. Romagna was a man who had crewed on three Cup defenders as well as having crewed on a 12-Meter every America's Cup summer since 1958.

From *Intrepid's* first brush with another 12-Meter, it was obvious that she was fast. She met *Constellation*, sailed by Bob Bavier, in a skirmish off City Island and it was quickly evident that *Intrepid* was closer winded and faster footing. There were no other new Twelves built for the 1967 defense, and *Intrepid* smashed the old 12-Meters from the beginning of the summer to the end. There was never any doubt about the fastest American defender.

The drubbing that the fleet of well-sailed and well-crewed American 12-Meters had gotten at the hands of Mosbacher and his men on *Intrepid* had a serious psychological impact on the challenging *Dame*

Pattie crew. Sturrock started *Dame Pattie* in a safe leeward position in the first three races, but *Intrepid's* superior pointing ability and speed meant that she simply walked away to windward. Sturrock seemed unable to deviate from the strategy that had worked so well for Bavier against Cox in 1964. When it didn't work for him, Sturrock was unable to try something different. The Australian challengers threw the defenders into a tacking duel, but this time the Americans had superior equipment and their tacks were quick and only helped *Intrepid* to eat farther to windward. Sturrock tried false tacking a couple of times, but Mosbacher and Romagna had been around the 12-Meter course more than any two men alive and they were hard men to take by surprise. The afterguard, the crew, and the beautiful *Intrepid* were simply an unbeatable combination. The America's Cup was successfully defended in four straight races with *Intrepid* winning by margins of from three and one-half to nearly six minutes.

In 12-Meter match races off Newport between challengers and NYYC defenders, only once had the defending boat been beaten. The legend of the America's Cup and the invincibility of the New York Yacht Club grew older and more entrenched by the end of 1967 because of the commanding performance of *Intrepid*.

"Dame Pattie," the 1967 challenger

6

Close Call for the Club

The 1970 match nearly brought the house down. Never, since the time of Sir Thomas Lipton, had so many people in the world been interested in the showdown at Newport, and never, since the time of Lord Dunraven, had there been such acrimony. World opinion turned viciously against the New York Yacht Club for what appeared to many to be highly unfair and prejudicial treatment of the challenger. The reputation of the NYYC race committee was at its lowest ebb since T. O. M. Sopwith's 1934 protest was thrown out. Cries of "hometown justice" could be heard from all over the sporting world. Newspapers and T.V. stations across the United States cried foul, as the club weathered its most vitriolic storm since the *Independence* affair at the turn of the century. Most important, the New York Yacht Club came very close to losing the America's Cup—far closer than the 4–1 final score indicated.

Not all of the criticism of the club during that stormy September was rooted in the controversial decisions of the club's race committee against the Australian challenger. There were other motivations. Indeed, few people even knew the actual facts of the protest. Rather, the bulk of the world's America's Cup watchers were reacting against the NYYC itself. Decisions of the NYYC race committee were not criticized on their own merits: the American Establishment itself was under fire. In the minds of many people around the world the NYYC is the actual rendezvous of the reactionary elite of the nation. World opinion had been convinced long before 1970 that America's industrial moguls would go to any lengths to impose their will, so when the NYYC race committee disqualified the challenger *Gretel II* in the second race, it was interpreted by "world opinion" as just another example of ruthless American behavior.

Moment of impact as "Gretel's" bow hits "Intrepid"

The Defenders

At the outset the leading contender for the 1970 defense was Robert McCullough's new S&S-designed *Valiant*. This boat seemed to have everything going in her favor. McCullough was vice commodore of the NYYC and had originally organized the *Valiant* syndicate, putting up much of the money for the boat himself. The boat was designed by Olin Stephens, the undisputed master of 12-Meters. And her crew was composed mostly of veteran 12-Meter sailors who had been through the America's Cup ordeal before. At the beginning of the summer, *Valiant* looked like she would be the ultimate defender.

But there were other strong-willed men around with ideas of their own. From the South, the popular Charles Morgan was organizing the first new-boat contender to ever come from a section of the country other than the Northeast. Morgan, a self-made man who had tried to put a syndicate together for 1967, was by far the most colorful person to hit the America's Cup scene in many years. The youthful Morgan was a savvy sailor who had grown up on Tampa Bay, first sailing anything he could nail together and later in sleek ocean racers that he designed and built at his Morgan Yacht Corp. Charley had won his reputation struggling up through one-design classes and later in ocean racers. In the early 1960's he was considered to be one of America's hot young designers. In just a few years he had parlayed his small boatbuilding concern into a multi-million dollar operation. When he sold out in 1966, he became rich overnight.

Morgan designed, built and sailed his own 12-Meter, *Heritage*. He also made the original suit of sails for the boat (he owned his own sail loft) and ultimately completely financed the cost of the *Heritage* campaign himself. Because Morgan was involved in most of the details of his boat, sportswriters were quick to call *Heritage* a one-man show. Charley, of course, saw it differently. He had draftsmen doing the lines, engineers helping with rigging details, and foremen overseeing the building; yet, every major decision was made by Morgan. No man in the history of the America's Cup had been so deeply involved with every aspect of the campaign as was the personable Charley Morgan.

The third contender for the defense was *Intrepid*. Syndicate manager Bill Strawbridge pulled together many of the original backers of *Intrepid* for a second time. The 1967 helmsman, Bus Mosbacher, was away in Washington serving as the Chief of Protocol during the summer of 1970, so Strawbridge picked Californian William Ficker to be skipper. Strawbridge had watched Ficker steer *Columbia* in the 1967 trials and had liked the former World Star Champion's style. Because the *Valiant* syndicate had a boat designed by S&S that would be in all likelihood faster than *Intrepid* had been in 1967, Strawbridge commissioned Brit Chance Jr., to modify the boat to make her competitive with the new designs. *Intrepid's* crew, like that of *Heritage*, was composed mostly of young men new to 12-Meters who would have many lessons to learn during the course of the summer. Both boats, however, had experienced men in the cockpit.

Rounding out the American armada was a fourth boat, *Weatherly,* built in 1958 and "Luderized" in 1962 for the defense. *Weatherly* started out the 12-Meter summer as a trial horse for *Valiant,* but as the season progressed the Cup selection committee asked that she officially enter the trials. Skippering the old Twelve was former NYYC commodore George Hinman, the syndicate manager for *Valiant.* Hinman had been involved in every 12-Meter America's Cup summer since 1958 and knew what he was about. For crew, *Weatherly* was manned by a band of young Long Island Sound sailors with some time on their hands who knew they had no chance of being selected to serve the American defender, but they scrapped as hard as possible nonetheless.

The Challengers

The French challenge came from the ball point pen tycoon, Baron Marcel Bich. Bich had been thinking about sailing for the America's Cup for a long time. He purchased *Sovereign* in 1965 and later bought

"France" races with her trial horse "Constellation"

Louis Noverraz at the helm of "France" in 1970

Constellation and *Kurrewa V.* In 1968 he commissioned Brit Chance to design a new 12-Meter, so that French designer André Mauric would have the most up-to-date product of American design thinking to use as a jumping off point for the new French challenger. Herman Egger built Brit's design, and she was launched in August, 1969.

Unfortunately for Bich's timetable, *Chancegger* was really launched too late for the French to adequately tune her and then race her against *Constellation*—the fastest 12-Meter in the Baron's flotilla. However, *Chancegger* did have a few brushes with the Baron's other Twelves before work was begun on building *France* in October. The most valuable aspect of *Chancegger* was probably the tank testing model that Mauric had made from Brit's lines. There were not many differences between *Chancegger* and *France*. In fact, it is said that *France's* lines differed only slightly from the American-designed boat. *France* was a bit fuller in the bow sections, she had the noticeable chine aft, her rudder was slightly smaller and her center of hydrodynamic pressure was said to be further aft. In effect, Mauric and the Bich challenge reaped the benefit not only of Brit Chance's knowledge but also, through Chance, the French obtained access to the Stevens Institute test tank, something which had been forbidden by the club to foreign designers. According to one member of the French effort, *Chancegger* proved to be the fastest boat in light air while *Constellation* was superior in a narrow wind band from 9 to 12 knots, and *France* the faster boat in anything over 12 knots.

The French knew that the Australians were ahead of them in sail technology—in both weave and cutting. The French knew also that their mast was inferior to the Australian mast and was a poor relative of the expensive, tapered titanium masts of the Americans. But French technology simply did not permit Bich to order such a sophisticated

mast. Nor could he get the titanium ribbon rigging which had far less weight and more strength than stainless steel.

Bich and his numerous sons who served the French effort were quite open about their expectations of being beaten by the Americans should they get by the Australians—and they were quick to point out the strengths of *Gretel II.*

Sir Frank's First Tactic

Sir Frank Packer had recovered from his 1962 defeat and was back, prepared for the fray. Considering that *Gretel II* ultimately turned out to be not only faster than the modified *Intrepid* but possibly the fastest 12-Meter ever built up to that time, the early reports from Australia of her poor showing against *Gretel* now seem to have been a smoke screen. Had Sir Frank carefully ordained that his *Gretel II* sandbag when racing against *Gretel* off Sydney?

The fact that *Gretel II* made no quarter wave should have been a tip-off that designer Payne had been as hard at work as ever. The quiet, pensive man undoubtedly knew that he had a fast design. *Gretel II* also had a couple of clever Payne innovations. Dual wheels, one to port and one to starboard, allowed the helmsman to be near the sheer of the boat to better see the sails. *Gretel II* also had collapsible spreaders that would allow the genoa to be sheeted in, closer to the centerline. The spreaders had a flexible joint in the middle, and by pulling a light string a crewman could open and close them when the boat tacked. The tapered mast, the finest ever produced in Australia, was fitted with a double row of vortex generators, (shaped like small rivet heads) which

"Gretel II" during her 1970 challenge

ran all the way up its forward side to improve the flow of air over the sails.

Sir Frank seemed to have learned a few lessons since 1962. First, he chose a skipper and made the announcement before the Aussies left their homeland. The man was 37-year-old Jim Hardy, heir to an Australian wine-making concern. Also, Sir Frank was not putting the crew through ridiculous drills as in 1962; instead they warmed up *Gretel II* against Ted Turner's *American Eagle*. Ted was itching for the chance to get involved in the America's Cup and had even tried to put together a syndicate for 1970 with himself as skipper. In chartering *American Eagle*, the young Atlanta television station owner was able to get involved in the 12-Meter drama. During the summer, Turner got the feeling that *Eagle* could be competitive and asked race chairman Dev Barker if *Eagle* could enter the trials. He was told that it was too late.

Even though Packer had definitely picked Hardy as helmsman, he was not fully confident in his competence at the start. Hardy was aware of Packer's doubts and refused to match starting tactics with Turner for fear that Ted would win and that Packer would replace him at the helm. Later, Hardy's ominous expectations would be justified. Packerstan still lived.

Bich Follows in Packer's Footsteps

Bich handled his crew much the same way that Packer had drilled his men in 1962; he also kept his options open on helmsmen. The excellent Swiss helmsman Louis Noverraz was the oldest and possibly the most skilled of a number of skippers in the French camp. Also in the wings was Pierre ("Poppie") Delfour, a young 505 champion. A third possible skipper, Jean-Marie Le Guillou, had left in a huff before the foreign trials even got started. The French helmsman was not named until the morning of the race, a tactic which surely could not have helped the French. After the first race, Bich announced that Poppie Delfour would sail the second race, an obvious mistake in light of the excellent job Noverraz had done. But, at 67, Noverraz was getting old and had himself requested that Marcel Bich have another man on hand in case he became ill or weakened. Throughout the series, it was obvious that Noverraz relished the helm of *France* and a chance at the America's Cup was for him the crowning of a very successful sailing career. Perhaps this tall, white haired 5.5 Olympic silver medalist knew it would be his last chance at the Cup. He died two years later.

The Challengers Duel

Viewed from the air, the first race between the would-be foreign challengers was as graceful as it was slow. Just prior to the start, the two boats began turning in a tight circle like two afghans at play one chasing the tail of the other. Suddenly, Hardy broke away from the circle and headed for the line. Noverraz was right behind him, and both got a good start. The day's light air did not suit *France's* windward capabilities; she needed 12 to 15 knots of wind to perform at peak, and from the beginning the Swiss skipper knew he was in trouble. Noverraz knew his own boat's strength and pointed *France* high. Hardy took *Gretel II* quite a bit lower, footing faster.

Hardy tacked but could not cross *France's* bow, and forced *France* into a tacking duel. The old man on the French helm covered smartly every time, keeping up his boat speed in the fluky airs, and rounded the windward mark first. Noverraz led the Aussies on the two reaching legs of the triangular course, and by the time they got to the weather mark again, *France* was one minute and 30 seconds ahead. Then, for the first time in the race, *Gretel II* showed the speed she was capable of and closed the time gap between the two boats to 13 seconds by the end of the downwind run. Noverraz rounded the leeward mark with victory in sight, but *France* sailed into a patch of water with no wind—a hole. Hardy, seeing what had happened ahead, sailed around the calm spot and into the lead to win the race.

Bich, unaccountably, announced that afternoon that Poppie Delfour would sail the next race. All that the old Swiss gentleman had learned of Hardy's sailing habits would be lost. The second race was as light as the first. The big summer high pressure systems which annually drift in over the Eastern Seaboard had long since arrived. The high extended from the Midwest to Bermuda and there was no relief in sight. The weather was just as it has been for the first race, but this time *Gretel II* led at the first mark by 200 yards—a fantastic lead. On the first reaching leg Delfour got *France* moving and astonished

"Gretel II" and "France" in close boat-for-boat action

the spectator fleet when the blue hull eased by the Aussies. Delfour stayed ahead at the next two marks. On the second windward leg, *Gretel II* got by *France* and Hardy again was out in front by 200 yards at the mark. Downwind *France* again closed the gap, there was a brief luffing match as the wind faded away into nothing, and *France* wafted by. Then both boats coasted to a stop. Two minutes later, Hardy called for the spinnaker to be dropped and her light genoa to be hoisted; it filled and *Gretel II* ghosted ahead staying there to win the race. It was a fantastic race which either boat could have won.

Louis Noverraz was back on France's helm for the third race, but by now the Aussies had the momentum of two victories and Jim Hardy knew his competition. *Gretel II* was again triumphant.

"France" in the Fog

What happened in the fourth and final race between the contenders for the challenge will be remembered for as long as men covet the America's Cup. With the wind light again, Bich felt that there was no chance for *France*. The man who had put up four million dollars for a crack at the challenge—more money than had ever before been spent by a challenger on one effort—made another change at the *French* helm. Now he, Baron Marcel Bich, would steer *France*.

This came as a surprise to everyone in Newport, except the French. They knew he had paid the price of admission, and now that his dreams for challenging the Americans had vanished, he would want the fun of sailing against the Australians in the last race. He didn't expect to win, but if his boat was going to lose, he might as well have the thrill of being at the helm. The result was tragic.

Fog horns bleated all over Block Island Sound as the blue stadium turned gray in a matter of a few minutes. *Gretel II* found her way around the course to win the race, but *France* got lost and ultimately dropped out because she couldn't find the marks. The press said that Bich had "abandoned" the race, which he had, yet he took offense at their use of that specific word because of its pejorative impact when translated into French.

Abuse was heaped upon the Baron by the spectators in Newport and by the press because he had taken the helm and then couldn't even find his way around the course. The industrialist responded by accusing the International Race Committee (not a NYYC committee) of "dishonoring" both him and his boat by not stopping the race when the fog "did not allow the contenders to normally find the marks." The committee's only response was that the Coast Guard had not ordered the race stopped.

Clearly, Bich did not deserve the harsh criticism that was being heaped upon him. It was not he, after all, who had been responsible for navigating *France*. That was the job of Eric Tabarly, a man who comes close to being a French national hero for his ocean racing victories. It was Tabarly, not Bich, who had gotten lost.

For the next two weeks the French cooperated fully with the Australians to help them prepare for the ultimate showdown. *France*

Baron Marcel Bich pulls on his gloves before "France's" last race in 1970

"Valiant," designed in 1969 by Sparkman & Stephens

and *Gretel II* held four more informal races to sharpen Hardy and crew, and the Aussies won every race. Then, the French switched to *Chancegger,* because she was equipped with American sails, and helped tune the challengers even more. When *Gretel II* finally met the American defender on September 15 in the 21st challenge for the America's Cup, she was the best prepared challenger ever.

The Americans Slug It Out

When the American Twelves came out for the last time in August they all meant business. *Intrepid's* success in the July trials meant that she was the boat to beat. Stephens added a piece to *Valiant's* trim tab and changed her mast rake to compensate for the modification to her bottom. A couple of new sails were also put aboard. Morgan moved *Heritage's* mast forward thereby closing-up the boat's large foretriangle and making it commensurate with those of the other boats. Morgan, like Hood before him, had found that a large foretriangle base was no asset. The boat was slightly re-ballasted and had the new suit of Hood sails aboard. Chance slightly modified *Intrepid's* bottom and added large faring flaps over her rudder.

Ficker had established himself in the minds of everyone at Newport as being one of the coolest skippers to have ever sailed a Twelve. The tall, thin, Southern California architect, became well-known to the yachtsmen around Newport and his calm demeanor and friendly manner won him many friends. Ficker had been sailing most of his 41 years and racing for the last 30 years. In two months he had molded a green crew into America's Cup caliber and he and tactician Steve Van Dyck showed themselves to be a winning combination.

McCullough, like Ficker, was cool and confident in the cockpit of a 12-Meter. With veteran Vic Romagna on hand there was a relaxed feeling in *Valiant,* despite the fact that much of Newport was saying McCullough should have been replaced. The six-foot-four inch vice commodore had had two months to show what he and his boat could do and he failed to beat *Intrepid* more than a few times all summer. Many people were saying that, like Eric Ridder, a good ocean racing skipper does not necessarily have what it takes to steer a Twelve. On the other hand, this textile company president was a highly competent skipper and leader who had the respect of his crew. McCullough was caught in an unenviable dilemma—should he give the helm over at the last minute to someone unfamiliar with the boat and hope that he could instantly gain success (highly unlikely), or should he hang on in hopes that the latest S&S modifications would bring the boat alive? There was no pat answer. McCullough chose to keep the helm and take full responsibility, win or lose.

Weatherly and later *Heritage* were eliminated early in August and the selection committee let *Intrepid* and *Valiant* slug it out day after day

"Valiant" crosses "Intrepid's" bow during the 1970 trials

George Hinman, Bob McCullough and Gerry Driscoll try to tune up "Valiant"

until the ultimate superior speed and tactics of Ficker's *Intrepid* were obvious with a 6–1 record over *Valiant*. It was the first time since 1901 that a previous defender was selected to protect the America's Cup for a second time.

The 1970 Showdown

Basically, the 1970 America's Cup was run under the same ground rules of every challenge since the first one 100 years before in 1870—the New York Yacht Club was the judge, jury and issued the verdict on the matches. The NYYC race committee started the races, set the course, heard the protests and settled any questions. The racing rules that applied were those of the International Yacht Racing Union, the same rules used all over the world.

On September 15th, the two great America's Cup boats came at each other gliding gracefully along in the light airs of Block Island Sound as thousands of spectator boats milled around trying to get a better view of the pre-start scramble. About seven minutes before the start the two skippers steered their 65 foot yachts beam reaching toward each other, Hardy on starboard tack, Ficker on port. The fencing began. Ficker, who was burdened on port tack to avoid a collision, bore off, and then Hardy did the same, meaning that both yachts were still on a collision course. Then, Ficker altered his course to windward to avoid an accident and Hardy followed him for the second time, thus keeping the two boats on a crash course. Ficker headed higher and then Hardy headed higher forcing contact unless he or Ficker tacked immediately. Ficker, who had altered course twice to avoid a collision, held on as the two boats were in imminent peril and it was Hardy who at the last moment spun his wheel over and tacked out of the way. Immediately, the Australians threw up a red protest flag and Ficker did the same. The match had not even begun (although the boats were technically racing) and already it was under the cloud of protest.

A minute before the start Hardy was on Ficker's tail and driving him away from the line in controlling position. With 30 seconds to go before the start, Hardy left Ficker and went for the starting line. The Australian boat arrived too early and Hardy had to kill his speed. Ficker, on the other hand, had timed his start perfectly and as the gun boomed on the 70 foot committee boat, Bill crossed the line at full speed leaving *Gretel* behind in her spray.

At the weather mark of the triangular course, *Intrepid* was ahead by over one minute. When the Australians rounded the weather mark they snagged their spinnaker on the headstay and it was nearly five minutes before they got another chute up and drawing. On the next leg *Gretel's* foredeck boss Paul Salmon was washed overboard by a green wave. Hardy jibed around and picked him up on the second try. The

Skipper Bill Ficker and tactician Steve Van Dyck

Aussies lost another two minutes and were out of it, but Hardy and his gang of wild and wooly Australians grimly held on.

Then, on the second windward leg, anarchy broke out in the spectator fleet as the 3,000-boat gallery broke through the patrolling screen of Navy destroyers, mine sweepers and 300-foot Coast Guard cutters. The day turned nasty and gray, the wind freshed and the sea was whipped up into a maelstrom of turbulence. A chop of from two to four feet slapped into the hulls of both boats but *Gretel* got the worst of it. *Intrepid* won easily. That night everyone criticized the Coast Guard, which had accepted the responsibility of patrolling the course. The next morning the NYYC race committee chairman, B. Devereux Barker III, announced that his committee had had a spirited discussion with the Coast Guard and henceforth they would keep the course clear. Neither one of the Twelves was bothered again by the spectator fleet.

Barker also announced that the two protests of the day before had been disallowed because there was "no indication that either yacht had infringed any rule . . ." Later, Hardy would say, "We left the protest meeting like little boys who have just been lectured by their school-master." The Australians felt that there was a difference in interpreting IYRU rule 34 before and after the start, and they also felt that any protest made over the point would come to nothing unless there was actual contact between the two boats. Hardy was probably right in his deduction, but wrong about the outcome of the protest. Had it been heard the Aussies would have been disqualified. A starboard tack boat cannot continually alter course to force a port tack boat about. There

Jim Hardy, the 1970 challenging skipper

had not been a protest in an America's Cup match since 1934 when T. O. M. Sopwith protested Vanderbilt over the latter's failure to respond to a luff.

The Second Race

It seems that Sir Frank had not learned his lesson in 1962 after all. He ordered that Martin Visser steer *Gretel II* at the start of the second race. This was obviously done because Packer doubted Hardy's starting ability all along and hitting the line early in the first race must have only strengthened Sir Frank's resolve. Visser took the start in the second race by beating *Intrepid* across the line by three seconds. Immediately, Visser stepped aside and Hardy resumed command of the challenger. The wind was fresh, the air damp and cold, and the sky was gray. Both boats headed out on starboard tack and after 15 minutes, *Gretel II* tacked to port and crossed the defender's bow—the challenger was ahead and a cheer could be heard all across the spectator fleet. Two minutes later, Ficker initiated a tacking duel in order to close the gap. In the next few minutes both boats tacked 12 times and the sight was unforgettable as fog closed in. The big Twelves silently, seemingly effortlessly, tacked back and forth, back and forth again and again with Ficker trying to break past, and Hardy slamming his boat around and staying on top of the defender with each tack like a wrestler who will not give the man below a chance to slip up from the mat.

As the duel continued, the boats cut deeper and deeper into the growing mist until they had completely disappeared into the fog bank. It was almost as if what was going on was somehow sacred or personal and should be kept from the prying eyes of those who really had no part in the affair. Visibility dropped to a quarter of a mile as Ficker and Hardy struggled unseen. Because of the fog, the gallery did not see *Gretel II* turn the windward mark nearly two minutes ahead of the Americans. The Australians hoisted a large spinnaker they had borrowed from the French and it proved to be a poor selection. Ficker caught up, then he drove past on the second reaching leg and rounded the leeward mark first. A wind shift turned the second windward leg into a reach, *Intrepid's* best point of sail. The fog closed in tighter until visibility was impossible beyond 50 to 60 yards. The race committee then notified the contestants that it was abandoning the race due to unsafe conditions. It was a good call on the part of the race committee for safety reasons. Ficker remarked later that he was glad that the committee had waited until *Intrepid* was ahead before cancelling the race otherwise the Australians might have justifiably had another bone of contention. The decision also confirmed Baron Bich's earlier criticisms of the international race committee.

"Gretel II" and "Intrepid" at the America's Cup buoy

The Protest Heard Around the World

What happened at the start of the next race (the second race completed) has been chewed over in yachting circles ever since. At one point it threatened to blow up the whole match and Sir Frank Packer made noises about taking the matter to the New York Supreme Court. Basically, what happened is this: both *Gretel* and *Intrepid* were heading toward the committee boat end of the starting line on starboard tack. As they approached, *Gretel* was ahead but to leeward of *Intrepid* in such a way that if both boats had maintained their same compass bearings *Intrepid* would have just cleared the stern of the race committee boat *Incredible.*

The Australians claimed that they were sailing close hauled when *Intrepid* sailed between them and the committee boat and contact was made. They further contended that the wind had backed and that as she passed to windward *Intrepid's* sails blanketed *Gretel* causing her sails to luff. The challengers also maintained that *Intrepid* was not sailing close hauled, but was coming in at a barging angle, and therefore, not entitled to room at the committee boat.

The Americans contended that they were sailing close hauled, had room between *Gretel* and the committee boat, and that *Gretel* had luffed head to wind when she hit *Intrepid* after the starting gun was fired.

One thing was agreed to by all from the start, and that was that the collision had occurred after the gun was fired. Protest flags were hoisted on both boats and *Intrepid* sailed off with almost a full head

of steam. *Gretel II* was completely stopped and had to fall off and get her sails driving again. Ficker led at the windward mark by 42 seconds.

At the leeward mark *Intrepid* led by a full minute, Hardy chipped away 30 seconds on the next windward leg again proving the weather ability of the new Payne boat. On the dead downwind leg, Australian David Forbes took over the *Gretel* helm and initiated a jibing duel with Ficker. Without his tactician Van Dyck aboard (he had been stung by a bee before the race and taken off *Intrepid* by helicopter), *Intrepid* was vulnerable. Her afterguard was a specialized one with Ficker in command, but concentrating on steering and maintaining maximum boat speed at all times. Steve Van Dyck was the tactician and it was up to him to keep a close eye on *Gretel*, check and recheck sailing angles and distances to the next mark and lay lines. Without Van Dyck, Ficker was severely handicapped. Navigator Peter Wilson was filling in but that was not his speciality and the second race of the America's Cup was a poor place to start learning tactics. The Australians got by on the run and kept their lead on the last windward leg to finish first and win the race. But did they win? There was still the matter of the protest.

At the Hearing

A hearing was held the following morning. The Australians stated later that they felt that the proceedings had been most irregular with the normal procedure giving way to an informal hearing which Bill

Ficker dominated until Martin Visser objected and was sustained by chairman Barker. Jim Hardy disagreed with the drawings that Ficker had submitted as evidence. Visser contended that UPI photos taken from water level confirmed that Ficker was coming in at an angle or barging. The drawings themselves were as different in execution as they were in what they showed, Visser's being roughly drawn and Ficker's being carefully scribed as if the architect were making a business presentation. Aerial photographs seemed to substantiate Ficker's position that he was close-hauled and that at the moment of contact *Gretel II* was sailing above close-hauled.

All the possibilities of what happened that day could fill a whole chapter and would not resolve the issue to the satisfaction of Packer and Visser. The two facts that seem incontestable, and the ones that ultimately persuaded the committee were these: 1) the foul had been committed after the gun, and 2) *Gretel II* was either sailing above close-hauled or above the first mark when the contact occurred. The applicable IYRU rule is 42.1 (e) which reads: "When approaching the starting line to start a leeward yacht [*Gretel*] shall be under no obligation to give any windward yacht [*Intrepid*] room to pass to leeward of a starting mark [the committee boat] surrounded by navigable water. But, after the starting signal, a leeward yacht [*Gretel*] shall not deprive a windward yacht [*Intrepid*] of room at such a mark by sailing either above the first mark [the windward mark] or above close-hauled."

From the numerous photographs taken of the start, both from the surface and from planes flying overhead, it is obvious that *Gretel II* had begun to point head-to-wind before the gun and continued going up. Because *Gretel II* was sailing higher than close-hauled there is no doubt that it was she, not *Intrepid,* that was in violation of the rules.

By the next day news of the NYYC race committee's decision to disqualify *Gretel II,* thereby taking away her win and giving it to *Intrepid,* had spread around the world and the New York Yacht Club, its race committee, and chairman Devereux Barker came under heavy fire. Some of the criticism resulted in misinformation as people thought that the NYYC had also written the racing rules under which *Gretel II* had been disqualified. Over 500 telegrams from all over the world were received and practically all condemned Dev Barker's group. One letter said that the whole mess would not have happened if the committee boat had not been in the way.

The Third Race

The dueling before the third race was probably the best of the series as first Hardy leaped on Ficker's stern, then the American wrenched himself free. It was a free-for-all but there would be no more testing of the rules since the Australians were convinced that the cards

would be stacked against them in any protest hearing. Hardy went for the line and Ficker slipped into the controlling position behind and to leeward forcing *Gretel II* over the line five seconds early. In a masterful start for Ficker, he dipped *Intrepid* back below the line then re-crossed without losing speed and drove by the struggling Aussies who followed 10 seconds later. Hardy threw Ficker into a tacking duel in a desperate attempt to get by, but each time the Americans skillfully covered and Hardy had gained little yardage after 20 tacks.

"Gretel II" Wins

In the beginning of the fourth race Ficker and company led Hardy around the course administering a *coup de grace* that would make Yankee superiority something to be remembered. But, on the last windward leg, with *Intrepid* over one minute ahead at the leeward mark, Jim Hardy instigated another tacking duel and Ficker decided not to cover with an exhausting tack-for-tack. Instead, Ficker and Van Dyck provided only a loose cover. By breaking a cardinal rule of match racing Ficker gambled and lost. *Gretel II* had a light air genoa set so when the wind dropped she was favored. Then, when the breeze headed *Intrepid,* the challengers were favored again and crossed the finish line over a minute ahead. The Australians went wild. There was no doubt who had won the race and no one could take the victory away. The match was 3–1, the challengers still had a chance.

U.S. Navy and Coast Guard patrol the course

Packer tapped Hardy to steer at the start of the fifth race, a belated demonstration of confidence in his soft-spoken and gentlemanly helmsman. Hardy repaid Packer by winning the start, driving *Gretel* over *Intrepid.* Ten minutes later the Australians had widened their lead to ten lengths. Finally, Ficker ordered *Intrepid* about. Hardy's men followed. The tacking duel was on. With each tack Van Dyck noticed that *Intrepid* gained a few yards and so the Americans continued to press the challengers all the way up the first windward leg until the defenders broke past the Aussie cover. *Gretel* stayed on *Intrepid's* stern for the rest of the race but could not get by. In the final beat, the Ficker-Van Dyck team took Hardy out to the lay line and a wind shift made it an easy reach to the finish.

The America's Cup had again been successfully defended, but it was the closest call for the club since 1934. Had *Intrepid* not been campaigned in the trials, *Valiant* would have surely been chosen. It is noteworthy that *Intrepid's* total time margin over *Gretel II* for the five races was far less than her time over *Valiant* during their last seven-race showdown. All things being equal, *Gretel II* had definite boat speed on *Valiant* and had the two boats raced the Australians might well have won the Cup.

7

The Challengers

After the 1970 America's Cup match, no fewer than five yachting nations were considering challenging for the Cup—England, France, Italy, Australia, and Canada. Perhaps foreign yachtsmen sensed that the NYYC was losing its grip. But with defense efforts running about $1,250,000 and challenges costing on the order of three to four million dollars each, the first to succumb to the harsh realities of an America's Cup match were the would-be challengers themselves. First the Italians and then the Canadians dropped any notion of such a grand venture. Since several clubs around the world had challenged for the match scheduled for 1973, the NYYC accepted the challenge from the Royal Thames Yacht Club in England with the stipulation that the RTYC conduct the elimination trials among all of the contending foreign yacht clubs. The NYYC would defend against the strongest of the challengers. Late in 1971, the RTYC asked for a postponement until 1974 and it was granted.

During the intervening years a great deal transpired. First, the English challenge withered and died. For a while it looked as if there might be two challengers each from both France and Australia. As time passed it became apparent, though, that only Baron Marcel Bich had the capability to represent France. Then, Australia's Sir Frank Packer let it be known that he would not challenge again, leaving only Alan Bond to represent that country. By 1972 the cast of players was set. There would be two challenges: one from the Cercle de la Voile de Paris and the other from the Royal Perth Yacht Club. The RTYC scheduled the final foreign trials to be held off Newport on August 22, 1974, and picked an international jury to run the races, with Robert Symonette from the Bahamas as chairman and A. J. B. Forsyth of Canada and Professor Ole Westerberg of Sweden as members.

"Southern Cross," Australian contender for the 1974 challenge

Bich Picks Elvstrom

In 1972 came the startling announcement from the French challenger that he had picked Paul Elvstrom as his helmsman. The selection of Elvstrom was a master stroke, and Americans organizing the defense efforts realized that for the first time in the history of the America's Cup, the skipper of a challenger might be more skilled than anyone the NYYC could muster.

Elvstrom is a legend in the yachting world. He is the only man to have ever won four Olympic gold medals in yachting and the only man who has ever won gold medals in four different Olympic Games. Moreover, Elvstrom has twice won the Star World Championships, in addition to having taken the European or world championships in almost every class he has seriously entered. Since the mid-1950's he has won more sailing championships than any other man in history, and for years has been called "The Great Dane." In 1972 he sailed a boat to first place in the Half Ton World Championships held in Sweden and proved that he could do in larger boats what he had accomplished so successfully in dinghies for two decades.

Elvstrom Takes Command

The French challenge with Elvstrom would be awesome. Not only was the Dane going to be the skipper, but he was also the "project manager" for the French challenge. He would put his keen sailing ability to work on the race course and employ his fertile and inventive mind to solving the many problems involved in producing a race winner. Elvstrom, like all world champion helmsmen, knew that more than skill was needed to win races. One must exploit every competitive edge possible. Elvstrom, the sailmaker, boatbuilder, gear manufacturer, inventor, tinker, and even boat designer, was going to do more than just steer the boat—he was going to run the show. But Bich's choice of Elvstrom raised more than a few eyebrows in yacht clubs all over the world. Many questioned the propriety of letting a Dane contribute so heavily to the French challenge effort. Throughout the fall of 1972 and the spring of 1973 rumors drifted slowly from yacht club to yacht club as sailors moved about from France and Denmark following the wind: "Elvstrom would have an all-Scandinavian crew," they whispered. Around the world yachtsmen were asking, "How long will the honeymoon between Elvstrom and Bich last?"

It was clear by the time of the 1972 Olympics that those most upset over the Elvstrom *coup* were the young French sailors, particularly those who had a chance at being the helmsman of a French challenger. At Kiel, Elvstrom was sailing in the Soling Class against some of the hottest sailors in the world, in particular the French representative, Jean-Marie Le Guillou, a young sailor from a racing family who had made a good name racing in the 5.5-Meter Class. From the start of the first race it became obvious that Le Guillou was attempting to topple Elvstrom, the pre-race favorite. The Frenchman was turning the Olympics into a grudge match, sticking as close to Elvstrom as possible and covering his every tack in an effort to out-sail the Great Dane. In one of the early races the Danish and French boats had come perilously close to a collision, and in the sixth race it happened. Le Guillou forced Elvstrom in the tight maneuvering situation before the start, with 30 other boats sailing about, to hit both the French Soling and the mark—Elvstrom was out. Paul sailed his boat back to the Olympic basin, packed up, and drove home to Denmark. The young Frenchman who wanted the helm of the French challenger had won the first round with Elvstrom.

That winter Elvstrom modernized *Constellation* with the modifications that he would want in the new aluminum Twelve, fitting her with a tiller and hikingstick so he could sit up on the weather rail and steer her much the same as he would a Soling. In the spring of 1973, it was a strange sight to see Elvstrom sailing a 65-foot 12-Meter just as he would a dinghy. Since the coffee grinders had been moved below deck and all of the crew were stationed there as well, it appeared as if Elvstrom was sailing alone.

"France" Founders

Since *France* and *Chancegger* were not being used by Elvstrom, there was little sense in keeping them in Denmark, so the decision was made to tow them through the Kiel Canal and the North Sea to Le Havre, 600 miles away. The plan was risky because the North Sea is treacherous in the middle of winter. The first night out the wind built to Force 8 and the seas grew high. The masts that were strapped on *France's* deck came loose and fell overboard (representing some $50,000 lost), and the 1970 hopeful filled with water and foundered in five fathoms. *Chancegger* quickly made for the nearest port and was saved.

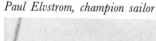

Paul Elvstrom, champion sailor

It was over a month before the weather and sea conditions cleared enough to allow crews to raise the half-million-dollar *France*. Considering what she had gone through, she was remarkably undamaged. Nevertheless, the incident did not speak well of the Scandinavian crew. Despite the fact that he had not been aboard at the time, Paul Elvstrom had lost round two.

In the spring, the French dinghy sailor Daniel Nottet tried to get a crew berth aboard *Constellation* but quickly gave up when faced with a solid wall of Scandinavians who spoke a sailing language all their own. Some of the crew were Danes, others were Norwegians and Swedes, and they used a combination of the most fitting words in all their languages when sailing the boat. Elvstrom explained later that he needed a crew with whom he could easily communicate and one that worked as a well-drilled team. To have some Frenchmen and some Danes, he said, would be too complicated and risk disastrous misunderstandings on the race course. Elvstrom would not budge. There would be no Frenchmen on *France*. It was this single point perhaps more than any other that aroused the patriotic ire of the French yachtsmen. Pressure began to mount on the French millionaire Marcel Bich to restore the French challenge to French yachtsmen. Elvstrom had lost round three.

In April, 1973, word got out through a Danish yachting magazine that Elvstrom's house designer, Jan Kjerulf, was using a Danish test tank to test a new 12-Meter design. The tank was the Hydro and Aerodynamiske Laboratory in Linby, just outside Copenhagen. Although Alan Payne and David Boyd had used the American test tank at the Stevens Institute of Technology in Hoboken, New Jersey, for their 1962 and 1964 challenges, since that time the America's Cup conditions have required that tank testing be done in the country of origin. That meant that not only did the designer have to be the same nationality as the challenger, but the test-tank facility also had to be in the country of origin. By testing a Danish design in a Danish tank, Elvstrom was in effect saying that he had little confidence in the French designer André Mauric. Moreover, if work done by the budding young Danish designer somehow got into the new French boat, all of the other teams involved might have strong grounds for protest. It was reported that when the Dane's designs were presented to Mauric, he would have nothing to do with them. Elvstrom had lost round four.

In August, 1973, Elvstrom entered a new version of his design *Bes,* done in conjunction with Jan Kjerulf, in the Half Ton World Championships. (The year before he and his Scandinavian designer had devastated the best Half Tonners in the world with his radical boat.) The Dane had not counted on the arrival of the French Michel Briand in a brand new Half Tonner designed by André Mauric. Elvstrom experienced bad luck throughout the series. He received a number of time penalties, fouled another boat at a windward mark and had to abandon the last race because of a crack in his hull. *Impensible* won the series. Briand had won in a Mauric-designed boat and Elvstrom had failed once again. Another round lost for the Great Dane.

French Pressure Mounts Against Elvstrom

Baron Bich actually looked in on Elvstrom's progress only once during the summer. Bich dropped in at the Elvstrom shop and the two, along with the all-Scandinavian crew, went through their paces. Reports have it that Bich insisted on jibing *Constellation,* without warning, to test the reaction time of the crew. This infuriated Elvstrom, as it is a maneuver that would never take place during an America's Cup match without advance notice. Elvstrom took the tiller and put the gold-colored 12-Meter through about 30 jibes to show Bich the efficiency and power of both his crew and his equipment. The two parted on friendly terms, but they would not see each other again.

In September, while Elvstrom was sailing *Constellation,* a fitting in the rigging gave way and her mast went over the side. Dismastings are not uncommon for 12-Meter America's Cup yachts, but this was the last straw for Bich. Unfortunately the spar had been made by an Elvstrom subsidiary in France at a cost of $125,000—three times the normal price of a 12-Meter mast.

The carping against Elvstrom was rising to a crescendo in France and Baron Bich was caught between his countrymen on one side and his commitment to Elvstrom on the other. There were also rumors circulating in Paris that the French government had threatened to take away the tax-exempt status that Bich's America's Cup challenge activities have enjoyed over the years, since the challenge was threatening to be French in name and money only. Of course, rumors such as these are hard to confirm since they involve such vast amounts of money— Bich spent around $4 million dollars on his 1970 sortie—and the matter was a private one between the multi-millionaire and his government.

To make matters worse, in the late summer of 1973, magazines in the United States and Europe ran several articles about Elvstrom that mentioned his history of mental breakdowns. Although the Dane's emotional problems were well known to his acquaintances and to yachtsmen in the highest levels of competition, they had rarely been mentioned in the yachting press, largely as a courtesy to such a respected member of the racing fraternity. Elvstrom's first emotional problem had manifested itself in 1959 when he "blanked out" for a few minutes during the Snipe World Championships in Porto Alegre, Brazil, and luffed the Duke of Arion (of Spain) without having the right-of-way. In the 1960 Olympic regatta in Naples, it is said that Elvstrom, had a nervous breakdown and was unable to sail the final race in the Finn Class. However, he had built up such an impressive point-score lead in the first races, he did not even need to sail the final race to win the gold medal. To many people he looked fit, yet his

doctors suggested that he retire from racing. Throughout the mid-1960's Elvstrom stayed away from the pressures of the race course.

Then in the late sixties he began racing again. One of the first major regattas he entered was the 1968 Olympics held in Acapulco where he sailed in the Star Class. He did not do particularly well, but nevertheless remained calm and relaxed throughout the tough series and took his defeats philosophically. It was not until the 1972 Olympics and his disqualification for hitting Le Guillou and the mark that he again lost control of himself.

Bich Drops Elvstrom

In October, 1973, a Frenchman arrived at Elvstrom's shop and handed him a plain white envelope. Inside was a note from Marcel Bich simply stating that his representative would take charge of *Constellation* and all of the 12-Meter equipment and would return it to France. Bich had made his decision and Elvstrom was out. What had had all the earmarks of a perfect challenge was now gone. Almost simultaneously Bich sent a letter to the Swiss builder Herman Egger, who was building the new aluminum French 12-Meter in Pontarlier, France, informing him that since the construction had been started late (it had been started over a month behind schedule), the boat could not be finished in time to properly challenge for the America's Cup. All work on the boat was to be stopped. Bich then announced to the yachting world that he would challenge with the old *France,* a boat that designer André Mauric considered still to be a viable candidate.

Bich must have anguished over his decision for weeks, maybe even months. The industrial titan knew Elvstrom had been working hard for the challenge for over a year and that it could well have been the culmination of the Dane's great sailing career. At 45, Elvstrom had a good chance to accomplish what no man had ever done before—the winning of the NYYC's treasured challenge Cup. Moreover, a man with the stature of Bich does not go back on his word at a whim.

Bruno Bich, son of Marcel and spokesman for the French challenge syndicate, stated, "If we had been sure of winning with the boat and Elvstrom and his Scandinavian crew, it might have helped with the criticism we have been receiving here in France. But we feel now it will be better to go with a French crew and skipper. We have appointed Jean-Marie Le Guillou as skipper. He is only 28, but he was with us during the preparations for the 1970 challenge and he is very good."

The Marcel Bich Success Story

What sort of man is Baron Marcel Bich? Born to a relatively modest family in the Italian part of France, Bich started his career selling housewares from door to door. After World War II, he got into

"France," the French contender for the challenge

the ball-point pen business on the ground floor and quickly succeeded in the French market with a well-engineered, low-cost product. When he first thought of trying to break into the gigantic American market, French economic advisors told him that the American public would never accept his 19-cent throw-away pen. Bich nevertheless went ahead, and his product's success in the United States made marketing history. His "Bic" pen was universally accepted and the French millionaire became a multi-millionaire. With his new-found riches he purchased his title of baron, and took up the sport of yachting. It was only a matter of time before he became interested in the America's Cup.

Like so many self-made men, Bich has always been a hard-driving industrialist who strongly relies on his own judgment. He demands long hours and complete loyalty from his employees and associates. Some have described Bich as a ruthless capitalist suffering from a severe case of megalomania, a trait not uncharacteristic of a number of challengers for the America's Cup. Other acquaintances of Bich paint quite a different picture. To them, he is more the classic gentleman-sportsman, in the best sense of the term. He is both a yachtsman and an avid hunter, and he follows many other sports in Europe. His company sponsors numerous sporting events in France, including bicycle racing.

Unlike many challengers for the America's Cup, Bich is an intensely private man who shunned all personal publicity until a story broke about him in the American press in 1969. Bich first considered legal action against the U.S. magazine and then dropped the matter, realizing, it seems for the first time, the public's interest in the adventure he had undertaken. Some of the Baron's detractors maintain that his 1970 America's Cup challenge had been a publicity stunt designed to promote Bic pens. This charge had no basis in fact. Bich's motivations were sporting rather than commercial or social. Indeed, there was never an advertising push in the United States connecting Bic pens to the America's Cup. The commercial ties involve only the tax arrangement Bich has established with the French government *vis-à-vis* his America's Cup challenge.

The Bich Fiefdom

One Frenchman who has worked closely with Bich over the years says that on yachting matters Bich is a "cake ready to be eaten." His love of yachting and his desire to win the America's Cup is consummate. Oddly enough, the biggest weakness in the 1974 French camp may well be that Bich wants the America's Cup too much. In 1970 he was so eager to win that he spared no expense in getting the best personnel, design, and equipment working in his favor. Many feel that much of the $4 million spent on the 1970 challenge was wasted. The entire French syndicate with the exception of the millionaire sailcloth manufacturer, Ferrari, was directly in his employ. Bich reigned supreme as the syndicate manager and master of the 12-Meter effort. His word was law. There was no one in Newport who could overrule a Bich decision and this ultimately led to problems.

Le Guillou, 24 years old at the time, was asked to be one of three possible helmsmen, but he turned the offer down after some negotiations. Bich had refused to name him unconditionally the skipper of the challenger, preferring instead to keep his options open among Le Guillou, the veteran Swiss sailor Louis Noverraz, and Poppy Delfour. Although Bich probably leaned toward the 67-year-old Swiss 5.5-Meter champion, Noverraz had asked that because of his age an alternate helmsman be available. Because of this, Bich refused to name any one person as the ultimate skipper, and there was less than the optimum relationship between skipper and crew. After dismissing Elvstrom for the 1974 challenge, Bich named Le Guillou official helmsman. Noverraz had passed away between the challenges.

With some of the innovations that Elvstrom introduced aboard *Constellation*, better sails, a unified crew under the direction of one skipper, and the independent force of Le Guillou—a man with his own mind and definitely not beholding to Bich—the new French challenge will undoubtedly prove stronger than it was in 1970. Unfortunately, the two drawbacks to the French challenge—the reversal on Elvstrom at the eleventh hour and the decision not to build a new aluminum boat—place the French at a disadvantage. A four-year-old design would be severely handicapped even if her competition were also built of wood. But to have to sail against new designs in lightweight aluminum makes *France's* chances of beating the Australians slim, indeed.

Designer André Mauric

The man who has been Bich's personal designer for ten years is André Mauric. Mauric had got his start in yacht design well before

Baron Marcel Bich

Jean-Marie Le Guillou, the French helmsman

World War II and was on his way to becoming one of the major yacht designers in Europe with his 5.5-Meter designs and large planing powerboats popular with the rich French along the Riviera. But the war was disastrous for Mauric's career. While it raged, there was, of course, no interest in racing-boat designs, and afterward the French nation spent long years struggling to its feet. It was not until the 1950s that Mauric got any sort of design work on a regular basis again, then sustaining himself for a time on commissions for military and commercial powerboats. Later, he designed the popular Draglia ocean racing class boat, built of molded ply, and found success with his *Challenger* and *Superchallenger,* which won the Half Ton and Quarter Ton cups. But it was not until Baron Marcel Bich came along in the early 1960s that Mauric found the patron he needed.

By 1965 the idea of challenging for the America's Cup was already evolving in Bich's mind. He bought *Sovereign* and *Kurrewa V* and before 1966 he also owned *Sceptre* and *Constellation.* Mauric was the logical choice for Bich since he was still reputed to be the most outstanding French designer, despite the setbacks the war had inflicted on his career. Bich also had owned a Mauric-designed boat built before the war. Mauric embarked on the design of an America's Cup challenging 12-Meter in the mid-1960s.

With each new Twelve that Bich bought, Mauric could learn more about what made these boats move. Like everyone else getting into 12-Meter design, Mauric had to gather all of his information from scratch. Models were made of all the Twelves that Bich purchased and slowly Mauric evolved a design. To help his efforts, Baron Bich attempted to buy the successful *Intrepid* in the fall of 1967, but was rebuffed by the NYYC syndicate. The New York group's refusal to sell may well have been the most important decision in saving the Cup since Harold Vanderbilt had asked Sherman Hoyt to take the helm of *Rainbow* in 1934.

Since Mauric could not get *Intrepid*, he did the next best thing and assembled hundreds of photographs of her, clipped from magazines from all around the world. Slowly, he pieced together *Intrepid's* lines. A model was then made and tested in the National Engineering School of Mechanics test tank in Nantes, France. Despite the fact that Mauric had spent a large part of every year since the early sixties working on the Bich 12-Meter project—and in the process had become one of the highest paid designers in the world—still many Frenchmen seemed not to have full confidence in the boat Mauric was producing. At the urging of the Swiss builder, Herman Egger, and the hot young French helmsman, Jean-Marie Le Guillou (then in his early twenties), Baron Bich commissioned the American designer Britton Chance, Jr., to design a 12-Meter to be used as a French trial horse.

The Australian Challenge

The fourth Australian challenge in just over a decade comes from the 36-year-old Western Australian land developer, Alan Bond. Never, in the 123-year history of the America's Cup, has there ever been a challenger that even remotely resembles the irrepressible Alan Bond. Bond is younger than any previous challenger and the most flamboyant since Lt. William Henn. He speaks his mind about the club as no challenger had ever dared before. Over a year before the match was to take place, Bond had already fired a number of salvos at the NYYC, accusing the club of not hesitating to change the rules to keep the Cup, among other things. Bond publicly stated that he would protest the club before the match even began if the American boats were allowed

André Mauric, designer of "France"

to use a mainsail made of the new DuPont Kevlar material. (Since then, Kevlar has been ruled legal for sails, but not for rigging.) Bond further expressed his regard for the America's Cup race committee and international jury by announcing that he would have his own video-tape camera crew in Newport to record any infractions of the rules. If all that weren't enough, the five-foot-six-inch challenger said that he was bringing his own lawyer to Newport.

Alan Bond—From Paint Rags to Riches

Bond emigrated from England to Australia with his parents when he was 13 years old, in the days when the Australian government was offering passage, a job, and a small nest egg to anyone who settled Down Under. Alan grew up in Perth and started his career as a sign painter and handyman at $6.00 a week. From the beginning, he displayed the qualities that make him an exceptional character. Bond was not just a sign painter but a man who would take on all the jobs that no one wanted because they were either too big or too far buried in the Australian Outback. He quickly became famous as the sign painter who would paint water towers and wheat silos in the middle of no-where. In his early twenties, Bond bought some cheap land in Western Australia and resold it for a quick and tidy profit. Soon he was buying and selling land, building a pile of capital with remarkable rapidity until within a few years he was a millionaire, then a multi-millionaire. By the late 1960's he owned all or part of 27 companies, and his vast land holdings in Western Australia contributed to his net worth of $80 million dollars.

Bond made no attempt to hide his new wealth and one of the first things he bought was the posh Australian glamour yacht, *Panamuna.* Often he could be seen sailing the boat from her mooring, down the river that runs through Perth to the sea. Bond was beginning to be recognized. Because of Bob Miller's success with his 41-foot design *Mercedes III,* which Australian Ted Kaufman had sailed to an individual highpoint victory in the 1967 Admiral's Cup in England, Bond struck up a relationship with Miller. It did not take the two men long to agree that what Alan Bond really needed was a 58-foot ocean racer—the boat was designed and built on a crash program and launched in time for the 1969 Sydney to Hobart Race. Nobody in Perth had anything that could even approach it.

No sooner, though, had Perth resident Alan Bond reached the sailing center of Sydney than he discovered that there was yet a greater yachting horizon. In 1970 he went to Newport, Rhode Island for the start of the Newport to Bermuda Race. It was there that he saw America's Cup yachts for the first time. The story goes that while Bond and Miller were closely inspecting *Valiant,* Vic Romagna, a member of the *Valiant* syndicate, chased them away. As they left, Miller shouted back that Bond would challenge and win the Cup and drive a bulldozer over the "damned thing right on 44th Street and be done with the

America's Cup foolishness." A few months later Bond challenged for the Cup, sponsored by the Royal Perth Yacht Club.

Bond is a short, barrel-chested man supported by spindly legs. His round, full face is connected to his body by a short, thick neck and it is because of these physical qualities that the challenger has a sort of a roly-poly appearance. His quick and easy smile and eager involvement in any discussion has won him friends all over the world. At a cocktail party it is … to see Bond darting from group to group aggressivel… circle of conversation.

…itured way with people (except in … nces call him "Bondy." When … icial venture or sailing gaff, his … id this" and "Bondy did that," … child pilfering penny candy in … Brown quality about Bond that … but no one can quite pin down. … d, the appearance of a friendly … r of a mischievous fraternity …

… e and moon face, there is noth- … knows exactly what he wants … gamble because that is how he … d has made since he put down … ated risk involving big invest- … as Bond launched the biggest … at his America's Cup challenge … also embarked on one of his … d be his economic Waterloo, … mining project in Western … the big time, wheeling and … with some of Japan's most

…overseas … excluding the U.S. and …services and specialist catering … U.S.

Meanwhile, ARA, a services group, would acquire the remaining part of the U.K. catering unit and the U.S. contract catering business, Forte said.

Bond Gets 2½-Year Term Stemming From 1987 Case

Special to THE WALL STREET JOURNAL

PERTH, Australia – Businessman Alan Bond was sentenced to 2½ years in jail after being convicted of dishonesty in a 1987 deal.

A jury found Bond guilty of dishonesty in inducing Brian Coppin to contribute eight million Australian dollars (US$6.1 million) to the rescue of Rothwells Ltd., an investment bank that failed in 1987.

Mr. Bond, 54 years old, was found to have concealed from Mr. Coppin that he had negotiated a fee of A$16 million for his company, Bond Corp., for its role in organizing the rescue.

Once ranked among Australia's richest men, Mr. Bond recently was declared bankrupt.

Judge Peter Blaxell said a custodial sentence was his only option. He said Mr. Bond's dishonesty could have cost Mr. Coppin as much as A$15 million.

… that his America's Cup challenge is d…gned to make his business pastures even greener. He claims defiantly, "Anyone who considers that racing for the Cup isn't a business proposition is a bloody fool. There can be no other justification for spending six-million dollars on the Australian challenge unless the return is going to involve more than just an ornate silver pitcher. Let's see what they say about commercialism and sportsmanship after we win."

The "commercialism" referred to is Yanchep Sun City, a $200-million land development project that the Bond Corporation is undertaking 35 miles north of Perth on Australia's Indian Ocean coast. Bond bought up 20,000 acres of sand and rock and is slowly turning this "moonscape" into a gold mine. Already Bond has sold off parcels of his future sea-side resort to Japanese investors to augment his cash flow. By the time the new Australian 12-Meter was delivered to the West Coast, Yanchep Sun City had a large, oyster-shaped breakwater protecting what will be the country's single biggest West Coast marine facility. It cost nearly $2 million. The giant marina will be the focal point of Bond's Sun City, which is scheduled to have tennis courts, golf courses, swimming pools, restaurants, and all of the other trimmings of a Miami resort. Now it is little more than a concept, but with development and promotion (that's where the America's Cup comes in) it will be worth every one of the millions of dollars Bond is investing.

For the last year Bond has reaped a harvest of free publicity in all of the world's boating magazines. In 1974, as the showdown at Newport approaches, Yanchep Sun City will receive more and more publicity in the daily newspapers and weekly news magazines. Should things get dull, Bond has already demonstrated that he will not hesitate to drum up a protest and blast the NYYC (and therefore guarantee newspaper space) for anything that he feels is harmful to his cause. In the fall of 1973, after designer Alan Payne had sold an article on the new boat's design to the American magazine "Sail" and the Australian "Modern Boating," Bond charged Payne with giving away secrets. Newspapers around the world ran articles of Bond threatening to sue the magazines involved and to protest any American boat which showed evidence of having appropriated features of the Aussie design. Bond said that if an American designer copied the Miller 12-Meter, it would contravene the clause in the conditions of the match that states the design has to be from the country of origin. Bond also fumed when told that the American syndicates had asked for a postponement because of the international oil crisis. He fired off word to the American and Australian press that the talk of postponement was just another NYYC ploy to keep the Cup.

"A great deal of nonsense is spoken and written about the America's Cup being purely a sporting contest," Bond asserts. "The Americans certainly aren't sporting about it. They have always defended the Cup with big company money. Of course it's a sporting challenge, but to suggest that it is nothing more than a sporting challenge is absolute rubbish. You can't expect to compete successfully against the Americans with their space technology, their 123 years' experience, and their preparedness to amend the rules, without the sort of money that will buy the very best of everything."

The Killer Instinct

Although Bond blatantly uses the challenge for publicity purposes and is writing off his campaign costs against taxes as an advertising expense, he nevertheless seems to be a bit sensitive on the subject when confronted. When reminded that Bich and the American syndicates are noncommercial, he has been piqued. "It's all very well for the 'old money' people in London and New York to look down their noses at my challenge," he responds. "They're the very people who wouldn't hesitate to change the rules if they thought it might help them. The good old days when gentlemen sailors could say 'jolly good show, sir . . . well done' are gone forever. America's Cup racing is far too competitive for that sort of sentimental nonsense today."

Clearly, Bond is sounding the horn for a challenge unlike any the NYYC has ever endured before. Although Packer bellowed and growled, it was mostly for the benefit of his own ears. The rest of the challengers of this century seem mild-mannered and docile compared to Bond, and one has to go all the way back to the Lord Dunraven affair in the 1890's to find any challenger as verbally aggressive as Alan Bond. To mentally prepare his team for the attack on the NYYC, Bond has said that "Australian yachtsmen generally lack the killer instinct that the American defenders have in plenty. We will cultivate the American approach for the 1974 challenge."

Bond's yachting career was not interrupted at all with the announcement of an America's Cup challenge. In 1972 when the Miller-designed *Ginkgo* ocean racer showed that she would be a hot contender for the Australian Admiral's Cup team, Bond immediately put in an order for an aluminum version of the same design. *Apollo II* would not only give the Halvorsen, Morson and Gowland yard good building experience in working with aluminum, it would also give Bond a shot at the Australian Admiral's Cup team—the most prestigious team racing offshore. With a little help from *Gretel II* skipper, Jim Hardy, champion small-boat helmsman David Forbes, and an all-star crew of young lads who had been sailing all of their lives, Bond won a place

Alan Bond

in the three-boat alliance for the 1973 summer regatta in Cowes, England. *Apollo II* did well in England and Bond actually steered the boat during part of the Admiral's Cup races, while experts Hardy and Forbes sat on the windward rail and watched him enjoy himself.

Cowes at Admiral's Cup time was just the sort of environment in which Bond thrives. With racing during the day and cocktail parties, balls and formal dinners at night, he was a center of attention for days on end. Bond rented a house for the crew of *Apollo II* and had a telex and other communication equipment set up there so that he could keep in close contact with his Australian land ventures. He would work in the early mornings and late afternoons with his secretary, dictating commands to his mini-empire. The rest of the time he was racing or socializing. At night, Bond liked to sport about in a navy blue evening jacket, complete with gold braid epaulets on his wide shoulders. It must have amused him to think that only a few years before he had been painting signs; now he could afford to paint whole towns red—indeed, even create the towns.

A Corporate Attack on the Cup

Alan Bond's challenge may well prove to be the best organized in NYYC history. The Australian contends that his effort has not been a gamble and that he has carefully analyzed every eventuality. Bond's entrepreneurial talents have shown themselves in top form and the effort has run without a hitch.

Southern Cross, the new 12-Meter, was delivered to Yanchep Sun City only a week late. The boat, shrouded throughout the move from the prying eyes of journalists, was ensconced in a specially-constructed, 200-foot concrete building at the Yanchep marina. Not only can the air conditioned, virtually windowless structure house up to three 12-Meters, it also accommodates a full-sized sail loft, spar shop, repair shop, office space and many other facilities. Bond spared no expense. Construction costs exceeded $200,000. A high chain-link fence was erected around the concrete building and inside attack dogs were unleashed at night to keep out any eager journalists or American spies. Whenever the boat was launched or hauled a protective curtain covered the bottom.

The Australian timetable had called for the challenger to train against the two *Gretels* from December until early summer when *Gretel II* and the aluminum challenger would be shipped to Newport. Inevitably, there were delays. The cross-linked coffee grinders mounted below deck on the centerline failed and key parts had to be re-made. By the middle of January, *Southern Cross* had only been sailed ten times and only the suit of sails from the Miller & Whitworth loft had been tried. Nevertheless, the Australian crew members had been installed in Yanchep since December and had four months of intensive crew training. Bond provided housing and covered minor expenses for the men and their families, and he found jobs for the entire army—over 30 men. Practice was carried out on the weekends and on two or three afternoons per week. The rest of the time the challengers ate, slept, and talked about sail shape, America's Cup, 12-Meter tactics, and . . . Bondy.

Bob Miller, a Free Spirit

The most important decision of all made by Alan Bond in 1970 was his selection of designer, Bob Miller. To many observers it seemed strange that Bond would not ask Alan Payne, the Australian who had twice before created 12-Meters that were faster than the American defenders. Miller had only two ocean racer designs and a few dinghies to his credit and was virtually unknown. Selecting Miller was an incredible move on Bond's part and a tremendous show of confidence in a young man who had not finished high school, was adverse to math and reading, and who designed by the seat of his pants. Alan Bond calls Miller a "genius."

Bob Miller came from a broken home in a small town north of Sydney and worked on the Australian railroad in his youth. Having spent his early years living near Lake Macquarie, it was only natural that an outdoorsman like Miller would find his way to the docks and try his hand at sailing. Because he had no money, he would find boats that were so old and beaten up that they would not float and then would patch them up. Many of his early boats lacked proper framing, but he used to tell his critics that the boats were nevertheless strong because it had all been worked out "scientifically." One of his early Star boats was indeed fast, despite the fact that pieces kept falling off her. He attracted the attention of some of the Star Class sailors up from Sydney for an Easter Regatta and one of them encouraged him to move to Sydney, himself. Miller took his advice.

The 16-year-old boy was dazzled by the Sydney boating scene and became a fixture in the Star Class, racing for Ted Kaufman. The Star-owner liked Miller's reckless enthusiasm and took Bob in. Miller lived with the Kaufman family for over two years while he worked for sailmaker Peter Cole. Later, Norm Wright, an 18-foot skiff champion, persuaded Miller to go to Brisbane and make sails there, and the good-natured Miller took him up on the offer only to end up in the hospital. While measuring a 45-foot mast for a new suit of sails, Bob fell from the masthead and severely hurt his back.

Wright encouraged Miller to design some 18-footers while laid up in bed for three months; *Taipan* was the result. Later Miller designed *Venom*, which won the 18-foot skiff world championships in 1961. Miller's design approach to these boats was characteristic of his later efforts. Since he wanted a fast 18-footer, Miller reckoned that a cut-down Flying Dutchman, one of the fastest planing dinghies in the world, would do just fine. It worked, although he was accused of building "rule beaters." On one occasion he was showered by a barrage of empty beer cans from the disgruntled partisans on a spectator boat.

While trying out for the 1960 Olympics in Brisbane, Miller met a young man named Craig Whitworth. Two years later the partnership of Miller & Whitworth, Sailmakers was formed. Miller provided the expertise, and Whitworth contributed the business head and arranged for the company's financing. In 1966 Miller designed *Mercedes III* for his old benefactor, Kaufman. Also in the mid-1960's, Miller designed a one-man, centerboard dinghy with a trapeze called the Contender. The boat was seriously considered for an Olympic class but was turned down in 1968, because it was relatively expensive and hard to sail.

It has never been stated whether Miller or Bond was the first to originate the idea of the challenge, but it was an extremely rash proposal coming from either one—Bond had only a few years of sailing under his belt and Miller had only a few designs to his credit. There couldn't be a more unlikely pair to assault the America's Cup. Since the challenge was issued in 1970, Miller has designed two more boats which have been highly successful—*Ginkgo* and his new *Ciel III*, a 40-foot One Tonner that won the 1973 Sydney to Hobart Race by over three hours on corrected time.

The 38-year-old Miller is tall, strongly built, and as agile as a cat. This hail and hearty fellow loves nothing more than to spend time with friends singing, joking and telling tall tales. He is immediately liked by all who meet him for his outgoing and ebullient personality.

In the office, Miller is a designer and a sailmaker who uses common sense rather than a computer. He eschews reading and any mathematics beyond multiplication and division. In the Sydney University test tank, one of the most modern in the world, Miller found himself in a trial-and-error situation as he tried desperately in 1972 to better Alan

Bob Miller, designer of "Southern Cross"

Payne's design of *Gretel II.* Day after day, Miller would ride along on the towing gantry in a seat just a few inches above his model, as she made her way down the tank. He would tie a string on a stick and hold it at key spots along her hull to see at what point the string would flutter. Then he would add putty to the area where he had noted the disturbance, in an effort to smooth the flow of water over the bottom of the model. After a year of work, it was reported that Miller was able to slightly improve the test-tank results of the Payne design.

Payne himself was called in for consultation early on, but worked with Miller for only a few weeks. Later, John Bertrand, an M.I.T. graduate and member of the *Gretel II* crew, joined Miller. Bertrand did the extensive wind-tunnel tests that eventually led to the special "D"-shape of the new Australian mast and handled much of the higher mathematics.

Southern Cross is the longest and, predictably, one of the most radical Twelves ever built. She is 70 feet overall, is extremely narrow forward with a 12'4" beam, and has long, low overhangs both on her bow and stern. Just below the waterline on the forward edge, there is a slight bulbous section. This is similar to some Brit Chance 5.5-Meter designs and is basically intended to give the effect of increased waterline. The leading edge of the keel sweeps back at a sharp angle to a very narrow base. The afterbody slopes up gradually into the rudder which is shaped like the bottom half of a tiger shark's tail. This is a design that Miller has been working on for years and it gives far better steering control than rudders on the 1970 American Twelves.

On deck the boat is much more conventional, although a number of Miller refinements are evident. As on *Intrepid '70,* her boom is as low to the deck as possible. She has a double vang track, one of which is in a semi-circle as seen on *Ginkgo.* Three large coffee grinder drums are mounted down the centerline and grinding stations are below. There is one unusual opening in the deck just abaft the mast, which will be used for spinnaker takedowns and other sail evolutions. Aft, the boat has two steering wheels. In her first trials against *Gretel II,* the new boat proved to be faster to windward but could not point quite as high. The Australians attributed this to their baggy mainsail and predicted improved windward performance. Off the wind, *Southern Cross* was definitely faster than *Gretel II.*

John Cuneo Will Skipper

The man who will be sailing the mustard-colored (Sun City yellow) Australian 12-Meter is the 44-year-old, balding Brisbane optometrist, John Cuneo. In 1972, after he had won the second race in the Dragon Class at the Olympics in Kiel, he received an odd telegram from a person he hardly even knew. The cable said, "Looking at results with great interest." It was signed Alan Bond.

Cuneo went on to win the gold medal in the Dragon Class and upon his return to Australia he was signed up for the helm of Bond's challenger. Like Bond, Cuneo is short; unlike Bond, he is quiet, soft-spoken, and shy. His speech is slow and measured as he searches for the most accurate word possible to articulate his thinking, and his approach to yacht racing is just as methodical. Cuneo was born to a sailing family, his grandfather having won the inter-colonial 18-footer championship in 1888. John has been racing nearly from the time he was eight. Over a period of 13 years, Cuneo won seven Australian Sharpie titles and excelled in a number of other classes as well. In 1966 he came in third in the World 505 Championships in Adelaide and in 1968 he finished fifth in the Dragon Class in Acapulco.

"No, I'm not confident of winning the America's Cup," Cuneo said in the fall of 1973. "I believe confidence leads to over-confidence and I reckon that anyone who is over-confident is a fool." Cuneo knows what odds he's up against, and indeed, even Bond was only giving his men one-to-five odds on success.

Cuneo moved to Yanchep in November 1973 to train with his America's Cup crew. First they sailed in *Gretel I* and *II,* with Cuneo sailing the slower boat so that he could sharpen his aggressive tactics. By the time *Southern Cross* was launched in December, Cuneo and his crew had sailed 83 match races over a short America's Cup course. Throughout the Australian summer (December, January, February) and into their fall (March, April), the Australians worked out in sail drills and match racing in a planned program of ever-increasing intensity, so that by the time the team was shipped off to Newport, everyone would be at their peak of efficiency.

"Australia has never started planning and training as early as we have this time," Cuneo says. "I believe that our crew will be fitter and trained to the minute. There won't be much difference between the boats, and the Americans might even have slightly better sails than ours. But our crew, because they have trained so much longer, should have the edge." Cuneo feels that this has been one of the problems in the past. "The Americans train in 12-Meter boats while our blokes sail in 12-footers. But management is what wins the Cup. The Americans are good managers, but so is Alan Bond."

The Australians have learned quite a bit from their unsuccessful attempts at the Cup in the past. It is generally agreed that Aussie crew work in 1970 was frightful for top levels of competition. That is why they have started so early this time and that is why there will be more than two full crews training at all times. Cuneo has laid down the dictum: "Every member of the back-up crew will be expected to replace the primary crew on a minute's notice in the event of sickness or accident. And he will be expected to be as good as the man he replaces." If the Australians get by the French to challenge the Americans, their crew will have had nearly three times the practice that the defenders have had. It could mean the difference between winning and losing.

The Australians also know that the syndicate manager cannot be picking and choosing the crew and changing the helmsman at the last minute. Bond understood that concept early in the effort, picked Cuneo, and then gave him the authority that a skipper should have. Cuneo is the boss on the boat, not Bond, and it is Cuneo that the individual crew members are responsible to. One crew member has remarked, "Cuneo drives himself hard and he expects the crew to do the same. He really lets you know when you make a mistake and he demands 100 percent effort from everyone."

Backing up Cuneo in the cockpit will be Miller's design back-up man, John Bertrand. His fourth place in the 1972 Finn Olympic regatta and his success in Solings, Sharpies and Sabots, not to mention his 1970 experience on *Gretel II,* will make him a valuable man in the cockpit.

Crew positions were announced in December and included Norman Hyett, Jack Baxter, and John Shaw among others. There were 13 men on the list, yet only 11 are permitted to sail in an America's Cup match. One of the names on the list was Alan Bond, and there is the possibility that Bond will be in the afterguard. He may even take the helm, as did Baron Bich in 1970, if the Australian cause seems lost.

There is no doubt that the flamboyant Bond loves every moment of the show and, like former Aussie challenger Sir Frank Packer, he enjoys being in the center of the hubbub. In December of 1973 the challenger commissioned an author to write a book on himself and his America's Cup challenge, scheduled to come out in time for Bond's victory celebration. In addition to the Bond video-tape crew that will follow the boats around the course, Bond has also budgeted $150,000 for a documentary film to be made. With an historian at his side to write down his every word and a film crew on hand to photograph his show, Bond will fête Newport with a challenge that should long be remembered.

John Cuneo, skipper of "Southern Cross"

8

The Defenders

After the 1970 match, new challenges poured in from all over the world and immediately the America's Cup committee of the NYYC had to begin thinking about new defense efforts. William J. Strawbridge, who had organized the two successful *Intrepid* defenses, made it known to the club almost immediately that he would be forming a new syndicate to champion the Cup in the twenty-second challenge. The syndicate would be called "Courageous" and would commission Sparkman & Stephens for the design. Later, George Hinman, the former NYYC commodore who had been instrumental in the *Valiant* syndicate, announced that there would be a second defense boat to be designed by Britton Chance, Jr. For awhile a group in Rhode Island talked about forming an all-Rhode Island syndicate as well, with Halsey Herreshoff as the designer, but it never survived the planning stage. Efforts were also initiated on the West Coast by the California International Sailing Association, which opportunely won a ruling from the Internal Revenue Service declaring contributions to the group tax deductable. This was the first time that a potential American syndicate had successfully lobbied for tax exempt status, and though the California group later dropped out of the defense picture, it did pass along the idea of seeking tax exemption to Hinman and, later, to the *Intrepid*/West syndicate.

Strawbridge's *Courageous* syndicate, consisting of primarily the same people who had been with him through the *Intrepid* campaigns (J. Burr Bartram, John Dorrance, Mrs. John Radley, with the addition of George Coumantaros and others). They opted to forego seeking tax exempt status as they felt it would be "inappropriate." On the other hand, Hinman, feeling it would be impossible for two syndicates to raise the necessary money without tax exempt status, contacted the Kings Point Merchant Marine Academy, (from which *Weatherly* had been chartered as a trial horse for *Valiant* in 1970) and asked if the Kings Point Fund might be interested in arranging a defense syndicate.

They were in favor of his proposal and made an arrangement whereby contributions for a new 12-Meter would be routed through the fund and the school would ultimately own the boat. Hinman then contacted Reynolds du Pont, Perry Bass, Robert Timkin, and Charles Payson, who all agreed to contribute significant sums of money and put the syndicate nearly halfway to their $1 million dollar goal. Hinman carried on an active fund-raising campaign from 1972 until well into 1974 and ultimately gained over thirty-five syndicate members.

Early in 1973 it was announced that the *Intrepid*/West syndicate, led by Gerry Driscoll, would be mounting a third defense effort which would campaign a redesigned version of *Intrepid*. Driscoll had been involved in the modifications to *Columbia* when she was a contender for the defense under the California management of Pat Dougan. An old and close friend of Olin Stephens, Driscoll felt that *Intrepid*, with modifications, could be made a viable candidate for the defense. The boat was sponsored by the Seattle Sailing Foundation, a non-profit organization formed in 1971 to help train Seattle-area youngsters in sailing and racing. As with the *Mariner* syndicate, the *Intrepid*/West group was also established on a tax exempt basis and the effort was basically funded by George S. Schuchart of Seattle, George F. Jewett of San Francisco, and Charles J. Hughes of San Diego. A special fund was set up within the foundation to accept contributions towards the America's Cup effort. Eustace "Sunny" Vynne, Jr., was made chairman of the special committee which would mount the *Intrepid* campaign. Although the plans for the syndicate were worked out in the first half of 1973, *Intrepid* was not trucked from her resting place on city Island, New York to Driscoll's San Diego yard until early fall. By November, 1973, the *Intrepid*/West group had raised $168,000 of the $750,000 they needed to mount the campaign.

Defense Efforts Setback

In light of the preparation of the Australians, and of even the French before they dropped Elvstrom, the supposedly "well organized and invincible" Americans seemed anything but that. The first set back came with the announcement that aluminum scantlings would be written into the 12-Meter rule and that lead compensators would not be required to equalize weight distribution in the new aluminum boats with that in the old wood ones. This automatically dashed the hopes that 1970 contenders Charley Morgan or Bob McCullough might have had of revitalizing *Heritage* and *Valiant*. Morgan, who designed, financed, built and skippered *Heritage*, had not been consulted on the decision to go to aluminum and was understandably infuriated. His boat would no longer have a chance to defend and, in fact, she sat at the St. Petersburg Yacht Club for the next two years. Another surprise came when the Royal Thames Yacht Club asked for a postponement of one year for the challenge, pushing it forward to 1974.

While the new Australian 12-Meter was being lofted in Sydney in the Spring of 1973, the American designers were just beginning to get into their design work. Chance had worked during the Fall of 1972 under a limited budget and likewise Sparkman & Stephens had laid some of the ground work for their new design. Yet, it was not until March, 1973 that Chance got the go-ahead on phase two of the *Mariner* design work, and it was not until about then that the tempo really picked up at the S&S Madison Avenue office. While the Australian boat was being plated and the *Gretels* were being moved to Yanchep to begin practice, the American boats were still in the test tank and the *Mariner* syndicate had not even announced who would skipper its boat. In fact, actual construction work did not even begin on the two defenders until after Bond's boat was sailing.

Oil Crisis Hits "Courageous"

In October the Mid-East erupted in war and the Arab oil potentates eventually curtailed all petroleum shipments to the United States. As the implications of the oil embargo began to be realized by the big investors on Wall Street, the New York Stock Market took its greatest tumble since the crash of 1929. Problems were brewing for the American defense.

In late November the America's Cup committee called a special meeting to discuss the club's position for the America's Cup summer in light of the fuel crisis. The Committee and the syndicate heads agreed that the match should go on as scheduled and that although the syndicates might have to limit the use of their powerboats as

Thousands of boats fill the blue stadium for the Cup matches

tenders, they could still get along. A week later word leaked out that *Courageous* syndicate manager Bill Strawbridge had asked the America's Cup committee for a one year postponement of the America's Cup match in light of the energy crisis. To him, it seemed "inappropriate" to hold such a match in a time of distress. The club officers denied the request. The showdown would go on. But the next day Alan Bond blasted the club through the papers, both in the United States and in Australia. He said talk of postponement was another NYYC trick. Of course, it had not been the club at all that had proposed the one-year delay, but one of the syndicates. As soon as possible, NYYC Commodore Kipp stated that the match would be held on schedule. Calls and letters poured into the club in early December and twice more the NYYC issued statements affirming the match.

A few days later further complications developed. Joe Bartram, the *Courageous* syndicate's co-manager, announced "We will definitely not proceed . . . because we were refused a year's postponement. Because of the economic situation, our people felt that it was not feasible to put up a lot of money for this sort of project at this time." The *Courageous* syndicate, the group which more than any other seemed to have so much going for it, the group that had old and established names like Strawbridge, Dorrance and Bartram, the group that had selected and had been accepted by the prestigious firm of Sparkman & Stephens, had succumbed to the uncertainties of a too-eventful year.

Work stopped at the Sparkman & Stephens design offices. The order was given to Chuck Sadler, Project Manager at Minneford's Yacht Yard, to stop all work on *Courageous*. But despite the fact that the syndicate had folded, Sadler had his men continue lofting the boat so that if the effort did start up again, time would not have been wasted. A couple of days later Olin Stephens also resumed work, gambling that *Courageous* would be revived.

For months it had been known that the *Courageous* syndicate had been shaky, but that was nothing new for an America's Cup syndicate. There had been many groups in the past that hadn't completely raised their required funds until the very summer of the challenge. No one had given the *Courageous* group's financial plight much thought. In addition to having landed S&S and the big names on the committee list, the syndicate had signed on William Ficker, the skipper of the 1970 defender and a man who was considered by many to be one of the hottest helmsmen available. But even before the oil crisis *Courageous* had commitments for only $600,000, while the *Mariner* group had $850,000 pledged. (Further, Hinman had received assurances from certain people that if he could not receive the remaining $150,000, he could count on help.)

Obviously, the reason that the *Courageous* effort crumbled in early December had very little to do with the "inappropriateness" of America's rich playing games in million-dollar toys while houses went unheated for lack of fuel and the unemployed stood in line on the dole. The cause of the syndicate's sudden twinge of social conscience was as evident as the plummeting stock market and the rise in fuel prices. In the space of a few months, the net worth of some of the New York Yacht Club's wealthiest members was undermined drastically, some by as much as half. In fact, two syndicate members involved in the trucking rental business dropped out because of the devastating effect of the oil crisis on their economic base.

The officers of the New York Yacht Club are not a particularly talkative group of gentlemen when it comes to the inter-workings of the club and its activities. Their discussions are private and although word might occasionally ooze out onto 44th Street as to the general thinking of the club and the America's Cup committee on a particular subject, there are relatively few public statements. It is safe to say that the club's officers were a bit surprised and chagrined at what seemed to be a rather hasty closing-up of shop on the part of *Courageous*. A conference was called between the club's officers and a few key men in the *Courageous* camp and the syndicate was "encouraged" to try to continue its effort and renew its search for funding. After the meeting in late December, Bill Strawbridge polled the syndicate members once again and found that they favored renewing their efforts and getting *Courageous* built; new financing would surely turn up by summer. After a 10-day dormant period, work was ordered renewed at Minneford's and Sparkman & Stephens. In fact, both had stopped working on the boat for only a few days and had resumed on their own, thus saving the syndicate valuable time. Their gamble paid off.

With one crisis barely mastered, the *Courageous* effort met still another stumbling block in its attempt to mount a viable defense for the 1974 challenge. During the two weeks that the project had been abandoned, skipper Bill Ficker had taken on business commitments for the coming summer. When *Courageous* was eventually back in the running, she suddenly found herself without a skipper.

Immediately the search began for a new skipper of a caliber equal to the challenge ahead. A few days later, the syndicate named Robert N. Bavier, Jr. as Ficker's successor, and it seemed that the defense effort was finally back in the race to stay. Bavier had skippered *Constellation* in 1964 with great aplomb, having both triumphed over *American Eagle* in the trials and trounced the challenger, *Sovereign,* in the actual Cup races. A ground-floor member of the Eastern yachting Establishment and popular with everyone at the club and in the syndicate, Bavier was an undeniable asset to the *Courageous* team. His hand at the helm was expected to interest new contributors to the cause, as well.

But the propitious selection of Bavier was followed by more unfortunate reversals. Two weeks later, Steve Van Dyck and Peter Wilson withdrew from their positions as tactician and navigator, because of disputes over design details. Almost simultaneously, a substantial syndicate backer also began to reconsider his support. Another round of syndicate meetings was called. This time the design and construction efforts didn't miss a beat and work went on as if the future of the new boat was not in doubt; but everyone knew that it most certainly was. In late January the syndicate's leadership was re-organized and Strawbridge assumed a lesser role.

"Mariner" Gets a Helmsman

If money posed the greatest problem for the *Courageous* group, quite a different dilemma beset the *Mariner* syndicate. It was the matter of who should skipper *Mariner.* The logical choice and one that sprung to almost everyone's mind was Ted Turner, the colorful, 34-year-old Atlanta hell-cat who had been cutting a handsome figure across the American yachting scene since 1965. Although Turner was always in the back of George Hinman's mind as a possible skipper, Bus Mosbacher and 1972 Soling Olympic gold medalist Buddy Melgis were both offered the *Mariner* helm first and both turned it down. Mosbacher had recently given up his grueling duties as Chief of Protocol for the United States Government and being unsure as to what his future plans might involve, he could not commit himself to a summer of racing. Melgis was deeply involved in his Wisconsin sailing business and evidently felt that he could not in good conscience spend so much time away from his work and family. That left Ted Turner.

Turner had won the World Ocean Racing Championship in 1972, capping a determined three-year campaign in his converted 12-Meter, *American Eagle,* that took him all over the world. Earlier in his career he had been extremely successful in world 5.5-Meter racing and in the Flying Dutchman Class. With a background of success in dinghies, meter boats, and ocean racers and by virtue of his having sailed more miles in a Twelve than anyone else alive, Turner was a natural for the helm of an America's Cup defense yacht. Yet, there were two big problems with Ted Turner. First, while he and his rag-tag gang of devoted young crewmen had criss-crossed the world, chewing up the best racing fleets in yachting, he had managed to offend a number of people. Second, some of those people were members of the NYYC.

In 1966, at the age of 26, Turner had accomplished what most ocean racing yachtsmen could only dream of—he had won the Southern Ocean Racing Conference, the toughest and most prestigious ocean racing series in the Western Hemisphere. It is even more impressive that he did it in the production Cal 40 *Vamp X,* against a fleet which included many expensive, custom-built boats. In 1970, Turner again won the Southern Circuit, becoming the only person in history to win the series twice. Along with his famed racing prowess, Turner had got the reputation (partially deserved) of being brash, outrageous and loud.

He always spoke his mind and sometimes his thoughts were not complimentary. Somewhere along the line, he managed to alienate enough important people to warrant his first bid for membership in the NYYC being turned down cold. When his name was brought up in the spring of 1973 as a possible candidate for the helm of *Mariner*, one of the big factors was his run-in with the NYYC membership committee years before.

Although there is no formal requirement that the skipper of a defending boat be a member of the NYYC (back in the days of professional helmsmen many were not members), it is the general consensus of most club members that if a man is good enough to defend the America's Cup, he's good enough to be a member of the NYYC. Obviously, it would be an embarrassment to everyone concerned if Turner were selected to defend a trophy for a club that excluded him from membership. If Turner could make it into the club, he would be the ideal choice to skipper *Mariner*. Turner had two important people working on his behalf at the club. One was the *Mariner* syndicate manager, George Hinman, the man who wanted him for the *Mariner* helm. Hinman had been involved in the America's Cup since the first 12-Meter challenge in 1958 and in every defense since, serving in one capacity or another. Widely respected throughout the yachting world as one of the great gentlemen of the sport, former commodore Hinman was no doubt important to Turner's eventual election to the club in December 1973, just six months before the trials. Ironically, Turner's other key support and the member who formally sponsored his name for nomination was Bob Bavier. It was soon after Bavier worked so strenuously to get Turner accepted into the club that he himself was selected to skipper *Courageous*.

The irrepressible Ted Turner after a dismasting at sea

Problems Out West

The *Intrepid*/West syndicate, also, was having its share of problems, mainly those involved in the complex process of yacht construction. Although *Intrepid*/West went "public" to finance its operation, soliciting thousands of West Coast yachtsmen for their tax-exempt financial support and even took magazine ads, the *Intrepid* campaign was guaranteed at the outset by the group's three principals. Finances were not one of the *Intrepid*/West syndicate's most pressing worries. The launching date for *Intrepid* was postponed from the middle of January to the first of February and as time passed it became obvious that the boat would be launched at even a later date. Built in 1967, she had undergone two rigorous 12-Meter summers and she was beginning to show her age. When she arrived at Driscoll's yard for her modifications, her second underbody designed by Chance for the 1970 defense, was torn away. At that time it was discovered that much more work was necessary than had originally been planned. In November the International Yacht Racing Union ruled that wood 12-Meters could replace old or weakened framing with aluminum if necessary, and this added even more work to that which had been scheduled at first. However, the use of aluminum facilitated a significant weight reduction and this was just the break that *Intrepid* needed to become more competitive. Gerry Driscoll was caught in a dilemma. The more time he spent rebuilding the boat, the better she would perform on the race course, but every day spent working on the hull meant one less practice day for the crew on the water.

While the French practiced in *France* on the Riviera and while the Australians sharpened their skills at Yanchep, the Americans were still struggling to get their boats built.

Ted Turner Rules the Waves

Robert E. ("Ted") Turner has led one of the most fantastic sailing careers of any American yachtsman alive. An aggressive competitor and colorful personality, Turner personifies the spirit of American sportsmanship at its most dynamic.

Turner's father introduced him to sailing at age nine on the family schooner in the waters of Savannah, Georgia. A year later young Ted became the willing charge of Jimmy Brown, the man hired to take care of the Turner schooner, and Brown tutored the youngster in the sport that was to play a major role in his life. They remained constant companions throughout years of racing, as Ted graduated from Penguins to various other classes and went on to ocean racing. He was hooked from his very first contest, despite the defeats and capsizings that checkered his less than illustrious early career. In the seven years that Turner raced at the Savannah Yacht Club, he never managed to place better than second in the club championship. Even throughout his high school career, he never exhibited the championship prowess that would later dazzle the yachting world. While at Brown University he made the sailing squad, but it was not until 1961, at the age of twenty-two, that he won his first major championship—the "Y" Flyer Nationals held in Savannah. In 1964 he placed seventh in the Flying Dutchman Olympic trials, and a year later he won the Nationals in the same class. The "late bloomer" had finally come into his own.

Turner chartered his first ocean racer in 1965, without even having crewed previously on an ocean-going boat. "I didn't know anybody who owned one," he off-handedly says. With Jimmy Brown and two other crew members, he ventured offshore for the first time to sail the stock design from Morehead City down to the 1965 Southern Ocean Racing Conference. Leaving the protection of the coast, they sailed straight into the teeth of a gale. Turner describes the trip as "a comedy of errors," but in truth they were lucky to make it alive to Charleston, two hundred miles south.

That year, Turner's SORC crew was made up of anyone he could find hanging around the dock and mostly of people who had never sailed in an ocean racer before. Sometimes the boat didn't even have a navigator and Turner just followed the fleet. As a racing venture, Turner's first SORC was a disaster, with two exceptions. He picked up trophies for third in class in the Miami to Lucaya Race and for second in class in the 30-mile Lipton Cup race off Miami. Turner confesses "that was all I needed, I decided then that I liked ocean racing."

For his second assault on the Southern Circuit, Turner ordered a Cal 40, which he believed to be the fastest production boat made at the time. By 1966, he had lined up a couple of crew who knew how to sail and had trained a couple of others. He met Buddy Friedrichs (who later won a gold medal at the '68 Olympics) in New Orleans and talked him into sailing the 404-mile St. Pete to Ft. Lauderdale

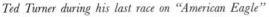

Ted Turner during his last race on "American Eagle"

Race in his new *Vamp X*. Amazingly, Turner won the race and he was just as surprised as anyone else.

Everyone thought that victory was a fluke, but when Ted got a fifth in fleet in the race to Lucaya, the veteran ocean racers began to inquire about the young lad from Atlanta. The next weekend he won the Lipton Cup, and with a high finish in the Miami to Nassau Race and a good show in the final Nassau Race, Turner won the whole SORC by over 100 points. It was as if David had beaten a whole army of Goliaths.

"We were young and exuberant," Turner says. "I didn't know anyone and no one knew me. We were just a bunch of kids that were cutting up—I'd only sailed five other ocean races in my life. That was probably when some people got turned off. I was the youngest guy down there and probably the youngest guy who had ever campaigned an ocean racer. Nobody likes to get beaten, particularly by a 26-year-old kid who didn't know anything about ocean racing. We didn't know anything about seamanship because no one had ever shown us. We learned by doing and we did the only thing we knew how to—sail the boat like a dinghy just the way I did in the club regattas on the inland lakes."

Besides having a Cal 40 that rated well, the key to Turner's first SORC success was that he knew nothing about how ocean races customarily were sailed. He had never crewed on the goldplaters and didn't know that at night most of the boats stopped strenuously competing and that at meal time, more attention was given to dessert than to sail trim. Turner and his men simply worked their little boat as consistently hard as they would have in a "Y" Flyer regatta. Though Turner would not realize it for years, he was changing the very nature of the sport of offshore racing, by bringing dinghy tactics and small-boat racing-sense to the ocean.

After the Southern Circuit, Ted took *Vamp X* to Long Island Sound to race against Bus Mosbacher in his Cal 40. He then went on to Newport for the Bermuda Race. Two weeks later, he was off on the Transatlantic Race, in which he won his class. Ted Turner's 15th ocean race was across the Atlantic, 3,600 miles from Bermuda to Copenhagen. "We learned a lot of seamanship in that race, I'll tell you. We had a lot of problems, but we went fast. The big thing was that we didn't just sheet the sails in and then cleat them off like the rest. We constantly trimmed our sails. I learned on Flying Dutchmen that little nuances in trim made a big difference. People who have only sailed big boats don't know that . . . they don't have a delicate feel for boat speed."

Turner met Bob Derecktor, the boat builder from Mamaroneck, New York, for the first time in 1966 at a party held for the Transatlantic Race competitors. The two happened to sit together during a slide presentation of all the boats in the race. "The 70 or 80 people in the room clapped for all of the boats that were shown except for Bob's

Ted Turner, first World Ocean Racing Champion

and mine," Turner related later. "They booed our boats and I asked Derecktor why. We've been friends ever since." Derecktor a leading American custom-boat builder, was chosen to build Turner's 12-Meter for 1974.

The 5.5-Meter world championships were being held in Copen-hagen at the conclusion of the Transatlantic Race, and Turner bought a Chance-designed 5.5 which he had shipped to Denmark. At the conclusion of the Transatlantic Race, Turner picked up a couple of crew and hopped aboard the 5.5, taking off to sail against some of the best skippers in the world, including Paul Elvstrom. But the series was another one of Turner's disasters. The next year Turner collaborated with Derecktor on the building of *Vamoose,* a custom boat much like the Cal 40, and the two men sailed together in the 1967 Southern Circuit.

After only three years of big boat experience, Turner was already beginning to think about the America's Cup. "I was thinking about everything," he admits. "I've always had the capacity to quickly lift my sights. When I reach one plateau, I start looking at the next higher one. I actually entered the Transatlantic Race before I even got *Vamp X.* . . I had only sailed five ocean races."

In December 1968 Turner paid $70,000 for the converted 12-Meter *American Eagle*—the 1964 America's Cup defense contender—to race in the 1969 SORC. For a third time Turner struck out into the Atlantic in the dead of winter, leaving New Bedford, Massachusetts on January 10th with Jimmy Brown, Warwick Tompkins, Jr., and a couple of other good sailors. This time there were no problems going South. In the back of his mind, Turner knew that his experience with *American Eagle* might help his American's Cup plans along.

In 1969 *American Eagle* showed for the first time what she could do in an ocean race by winning the long race to Ft. Lauderdale. That victory, combined with a good Lipton Cup finish, put *Eagle* in the fleet lead and it looked as if Turner might have his second SORC victory. But in the Miami to Nassau Race the boat was dismasted when an aluminum backstay block broke and he was out of the running.

Turner and the Bird Fly High

In June '69, *American Eagle* won the Annapolis to Newport Race and entered the Transatlantic Race from Newport to Ireland. At first the race committee was reluctant to allow her to participate in the race because of her light rig, her recent dismasting, her 20-feet of unsup-ported mast, and for other reasons of practical seamanship. Although all 12-Meters have strong hulls, built to Lloyd's scantling specifications, they are intended to sail match races in good weather off Newport and not to go transatlantic. Nevertheless, Bob Bavier and Dick Nye, Jr., took up Turner's cause and persuaded the race committee to let *Eagle* in the T. A.

Turner boasts, "When we came back for the '70 SORC we had the kinks out of the old Bird," and rightly so, for after setting a course record in the Venice Race, getting an eighth in the Lauderdale Race, and winning the last three races, Turner had won his second SORC championship. In the middle of the Circuit, Turner pulled off one of his biggest racing *coups* ever by flying to Sydney, Australia, stepping off the plane without sleep for the previous thirty-six hours, and sailing away on his 5.5-Meter. Five races later he had won the 5.5-Meter Gold Cup, one of the most prized trophies in the sailing world. In a period of one month, Turner had managed to polish off two of the toughest yachting events in the world.

Offshore, Turner has led a charmed life, winning not only in his early boats and in *Eagle,* but later in nearly any yacht he steps aboard. In 1973 he bought the One Ton racer *Lightnin'* and sailed her hard both in the United States and in Europe, placing second in the 1973 SORC, first in the Miami to Montego Bay Race, first in class in the Annapolis to Newport Race, first in the Scandinavian Skaw Race, and scoring good finishes in a number of other events. In 1973 he won the Martini and Rossi racing yachtsman of the year award, for the second time.

During a race, Turner is a walking, talking sideshow and his witty patter and determined sailing have won him a loyal band of avid young crew members. From the moment Turner casts off from the pier until the time he ties up again, whether four hours or four days duration, he is constantly talking, treating his crew to a running commentary on everything that happens during the race. His continuous monologe of tactical observations and free-associated ideas, thoughts and impressions sounds almost as if a loud speaker were wired up to the deepest recesses of his mind and broadcasting the raw material of his most personal thoughts. A naval history buff during his school days, Turner is especially fond of nautical simile, likening his position on the race course to famous naval engagements in history—all to the amazement and delight of his crew. Yet Ted's almost non-stop patter is by no means limited to clever remarks, poetry recitations, and line-by-line recounts of episodes from "McHale's Navy." Turner keeps a constant eye on the nitty-gritty of the race at hand: halyard tension, trim, sheeting angle, sail draft, and a hundred other fine points that affect his boat's optimum performance. Although his crews are always among the best of any fleet he keeps them on their toes with his constant monitoring system.

Almost to the man, the young crew who work the American ocean racing circuit profess great admiration for this colorful sportsman and they are a group that is generally reserved in their approbation. Thousands of yachtsmen around the world look up to Turner as the giant of ocean racing, a dashing and romantic figure to be emulated. The men who will be sailing with him on *Mariner* are all old *Eagle* and *Lightnin'* veterans who know Ted and how he sails. He was driven across oceans with most of them, and most would readily follow him to the ends of the earth. They have been dismasted together, run aground together, weathered gales together, been wet and miserable together, and gotten drunk and cried in their beer together. Rich, poor, executives, and dropouts—Turner's band of merry men is a motley gang who love racing and love Ted Turner. They will fight their guts out to get him across the finish line first.

Bob Bavier, a Yachtsman's Yachtsman

If there is any one individual who represents the American yachting Establishment, it is the 55-year-old Robert N. Bavier, Jr. He is probably the most prominent single yachtsman in the United States. Born into a yachting family and raised on a steady diet of sailing, he has lived yachting as completely as any man alive.

Since graduating from Williams College, Bob Bavier has worked for a single company all his life, the Yachting Publishing Corporation, where he talks and writes sailing eight hours a day. Through the years he has given generously of his time, not surprisingly, to yachting organizations such as the North American Yacht Racing Union, which he headed for five years. Bavier was personally responsible for extending NAYRU's domain to include ocean racing—one of the prime reasons why the sport has sky-rocketed in popularity in recent years. There is hardly a national offshore racing committee in which he is not an active, influential member. When American Onion Patch and Admiral's Cup teams are chosen, Bavier sits in on the selection. When the Martini & Rossi yachtsman of the year is selected, Bavier is the nominal head of the committee. The magazine he heads now sponsors the World Ocean Racing Championship. He is the current chairman of the NAYRU Appeals Committee, a member of the Racing Rules and Class Racing committees. He is also on the IYRU Permanent Committee and on the Rules Committee, and was instrumental in the founding of the international governing body of ocean racing—the Offshore Rating Council.

Bavier's involvement in sailing policy-making goes back to the late 1940's when NAYRU adopted their present rules. In 1948 he, Mike Vanderbilt, and other American representatives went to the International Yacht Racing Union in London to convince the Europeans to adopt the American rules for racing. Although they were not successful, Bavier and others kept returning to the IYRU annual meetings and pushing for the adoption of the NAYRU rules for worldwide use. Eventually, a number of yachting federations on the Continent started

Bob Bavier, skipper of "Courageous"

using the rules, then the English—who had been the holdouts all along—gradually adopted most of them. By 1958 yachtsmen all over the world were racing under the same right-of-way code. This universal adoption of the NAYRU rules was a strong encouragement to the growth of international racing both in one-design and ocean classes. The prime-mover throughout this period was Bob Bavier.

It is in the important area of racing rules that the *Courageous* helmsman is probably the most firmly grounded of all the men who will be competing at Newport. His continual involvement in the area since the late 1940's has made him an undisputable authority. Competitors will likely think twice before challenging his claim to right-of-way on the race course. In his entire racing history, he has never lost a protest.

A Member of the Establishment

In many sailing circles, the East Coast yachting Establishment is not thought of very highly, mostly because of its dominant position in the sport. Yachting first became popular on Long Island Sound and although it has relatively recently spread across the country, men from the East still generally remain in control. In many peoples' minds Bob has been stereotyped as one of the mossbacked Eastern set who relish their power and are loath to relinquish it. As far as Bavier is concerned, nothing could be further from the truth. He has risen in the ranks of yachting administration simply as a result of his unflinching and selfless dedication to the promotion of yacht racing. When something needed to be done, he was willing to offer his time and energy to see that it was accomplished and, of course, was never paid a dime for his time. Furthermore, it has been Bavier as much as anyone else, who has been responsible for getting new people from around the country into the top echelons of yachting government.

Bavier Has Early Racing Success

Bavier was born in 1919. His father, Robert N. Bavier, Sr., was one of the most outstanding yachtsmen in the country in the 1920's and '30's. Even in his later years, after World War II, he was a sharp sailor who could whip some of the finest yachtsmen on Long Island Sound. Bavier Sr. was of the species of rare individuals whose interests are as boundless as their enthusiasm and energy. He graduated from college with a degree in mechanical engineering, designed an ice truck that was extensively used, built a car from scratch, and seriously toyed with the idea of going into auto production. He was one of the first yachtsman to see the advantage of the Bermuda rig and in 1924 won the Bermuda Race in his *Memory*. Ironically, the CCA almost didn't allow him to compete because they considered the new rig unsafe. The

Bob Bavier at the helm of "Salty Goose" during the 1973 Admiral's Cup

senior Bavier was a genius at mechanical design and throughout the '20's and '30's made winches, lightweight blocks and other sailboat gear that was decades ahead of its time. In 1930, he started the family's America's Cup tradition by sailing in the afterguard on the Clinton Crane-designed *Weetamoe*. Bavier's racing career was highly successful, and he won races right up to his last NYYC cruise in his modified Fisher's Island 31.

Although Bob sailed with his father since childhood the senior Bavier never attempted to teach his son how to sail but rather allowed him to watch and learn by trial and error. Bob got his first boat at age eleven. On his first excursion as skipper he careened around New Rochelle Harbor, and collided with another boat, but by his teens Bob was winning a number of club and Long Island Sound championships. These were the years of his most ardent racing and his most numerous successes. When Bob returned from a race, his father would never explain his mistakes to him, but rather, he would ask what Bob thought he had done wrong. This Socratic method of instruction worked well and the young Bavier became a fine and confident skipper. While he attended Williams College, he won the famous McMillian Cup twice in a row, an outstanding accomplishment.

Bavier Defends the Cup in 1964

In the 1950's Bavier did exceedingly well with his 30-foot *Memory*, winning most of the races on Long Island Sound and the 1959 Block Island Race. In 1964, he reached the ultimate in yachting by successfully defending the America's Cup, after having won a far tougher contest against Bill Cox in one of the most talked-about boat-for-boat duels of modern times. Bob was a navigator aboard Ted Hood's *Robin* in 1970 when she won the Bermuda Race and placed second in class in 1972 in his own 40-foot *Witch*.

Bavier's approach to racing since his college days—with the single exception of the 1964 America's Cup season—has been quite relaxed. A family man with growing children and a wife, Charlotte, all of whom love to go boat racing, Bob has spent most of his time in low-key club races on Long Island Sound. With the exception of the one season that he campaigned his *Witch* most of Bob's sailing in the top levels of ocean racing has been in boats owned by other people. Although Bavier is a member of the Eastern yachting Establishment, he is not particularly wealthy. Certainly, he cannot afford to spend the extravagant sums of money others, such as Turner, plow into the sport. During the summer of 1973 Bob decided to once again take up small boat sailing to sharpen his feel for the tiller, so he bought a Soling and participated in some of the most competitive fleet racing in the nation.

For Bavier, yacht racing, both in the one-design classes and in ocean racing, is something to be intensely involved with when on the race course but not a full-time proposition. Although the very nature of his job requires that he talk yachting all day long, he has never made winning races his primary goal in life—except for his 1964 summer, when he devoted five months solely to making *Constellation* a winner. In 1974, Bavier can be counted upon to put in the same long hours all summer long to bring victory to *Courageous*.

Probably the most important aspect in Bavier's selection as the skipper of *Courageous* are his qualities of 12-Meter leadership. There is much more to being a good America's Cup skipper than merely being able to make boats go fast and knowing the racing rules. The skipper of an America's Cup boat must be a leader of men. He must be able to win the respect of his crew and induce them to work until they drop. He must have his syndicate's complete support and exhibit an ability to get things done by delegating responsibility to competent people. Bavier's ability to gain the respect and devotion of his associates and to successfully mediate among conflicts, is probably his most out-standing quality. His patrician poise and engaging demeanor make him a natural leader.

Gerry Driscoll and the "Intrepid"/West Syndicate

The 50-year-old Driscoll, like the other 1974 American helmsmen, grew up sailing. He has been a consistent winner on the West Coast and is a member of an elite core of older yachtsmen who win races year after year, despite tough, young competition. Driscoll's most out-standing victories have been in the highly competitive Star Class where he is a World Champion. He has won the famous Congressional Cup twice, in addition to many local championships.

Gerry first got a good taste of America's Cup action in 1964 when he worked in the cockpit of the old 12-Meter *Nereus* along with the skipper Briggs Cunningham. *Nereus* was the trial horse for *Constellation* and while Bavier was just getting her into the groove, Driscoll was coming down with an advanced case of 12-Meter fever. The helm of a Twelve is habit forming and Gerry was immediately hooked. Two years before, Driscoll had met Olin Stephens for the first time in the course of discussing an S&S-designed boat that Gerry was building. Not only did the two men share the same interests in boats, they were also both art connoisseurs and sports car buffs. The two men have been loyal friends ever since.

In 1967 Driscoll worked with Stephens on modifications of the nine-year-old *Columbia*. Owned by Californian Pat Dougan, the boat was supposed to be the "West Coast's" bid to defend the Cup. Once in Newport, a dispute over the crew broke out between Driscoll, who was slated to be on the helm, and the backers. As a result, Gerry

Gerry Driscoll checks the old "Intrepid" underbody

eventually gave up his position as skipper. Walking away from *Columbia* must have been a difficult decision for Driscoll, but he made it and there was probably no one at Newport that summer who wanted a chance at the defense more than Gerry.

Driscoll went on to design a 12-Meter for the 1970 match which only reached the tank testing stage. It might seem odd to some that a builder would try his hand at the intricate and sophisticated process of designing a Twelve, but builder Bill Luders had done the same thing in 1964 with *American Eagle* with good results. Driscoll was unable to round up the necessary financial backing for his 1970 defender and was forced to drop his plans. After the July trials in 1970, when *Valiant* had suffered repeated losses to *Intrepid,* Olin Stephens prevailed upon Driscoll to become a member of the *Valiant* afterguard as a tactician and Driscoll sailed with McCullough in the final, unsuccessful trials against Ficker in *Intrepid.*

In 1972, Gerry conceived the idea of replacing *Intrepid's* underbody with a new hull (retaining her original deck and rigging) for the 1974 challenge. This is essentially what Sir Frank Packer had done in 1967 when a new bottom was built for *Gretel* to take advantage of the "grandfather clause" that allowed all old boats to continue using the equipment they already had. Olin Stephens offered the opinion that if *Intrepid's* complete underbody was replaced, particularly in aluminum, she would probably be considered a new boat and therefore, would not be allowed to keep her lightweight titanium mast and rigging. However, the designer further stated that *Intrepid* could probably be altered enough in wood to be competitive with the new aluminum Twelves and still keep her light rigging. On the strength of that recommendation, Driscoll went about organizing a new West Coast effort behind *Intrepid.* The obvious advantage in using *Intrepid* would be that she was a known quantity and had been definitely a super-Twelve in wood. With some improvements, she could be even more competitive, and because she would only need modifications to her afterbody, she would be quite a bit cheaper than a new Twelve.

Probably the most noteworthy aspect of the *Intrepid*/West campaign is the fact that when the boat was modified in the winter of 1973-74 the Chance-designed underbody was completely torn away without Driscoll recording the boat's design features. Both Stephens and Driscoll felt that the 1970 modifications had made the boat slower than she was originally, so her new afterbody will be more along the lines of a restoration with some up-dating current with new thinking at S&S. Tests of the new design were carried out primarily at the sophisticated Lockheed test tank in San Diego. There, 12-Meter models are eight feet long instead of the three-foot models used at the Stevens Institute in Hoboken, New Jersey. Because the model is larger fewer scaling problems are supposed to be incurred. Video tape cameras were attached to the towing carriage so that the model could be closely watched as it was pulled down the 320-foot-long tank. It is reported that some minor discoveries were made during the testing of the *Intrepid* model at Lockheed and that these details were incorporated both in the modifications of *Intrepid* and into the Stephens-designed *Courageous.*

The biggest element that favors the *Intrepid*/West effort is time. Launched in late February, Driscoll and his crew had two months to tune up and train off San Diego before the boat was shipped to Newport. That was two months that *Mariner* and *Courageous* did not have to prepare. Although there is some division of opinion as to exactly how much time is needed to bring a Twelve to her maximum speed potential, there is no doubt that the extra time that *Intrepid*/West was able to train in Southern California will be a definite help. Theoretically, she will hit the starting line in Newport in near peak tune, with seasoned crew handling, whereas the two new American Twelves will still be making adjustments. Whether or not Driscoll and his men can maintain their initial edge over the new—and supposedly faster—aluminum boats, only time will tell.

Driscoll, like Bavier and Turner, is a remarkable helmsman. Like

Gerry Driscoll, "Intrepid's "skipper

"Intrepid" navigator Andy Radell, and fordeck boss Andy MacGowan with Bill Ficker

them he has been sailing all of his life and has demonstrated his ability in the top levels of competition. Like them he has served a long apprenticeship aboard Twelves. He is also a natural leader and has assembled a loyal cadre of young men who in every way rival the crews of the new boats.

9

Duel on the Design Board

When the *Courageous* syndicate announced in December 1973 that it was suspending operations for the 1974 defense two men, more than any others, were deeply disappointed. One, was Olin J. Stephens II and the other was Britton Chance Jr. Stephens, who had invested a good part of the last two year's of his life on the design, was understandably saddened. Chance was disgruntled because he had been robbed of his opportunity to duel with Stephens on his own ground.

"I wanted a clear shot at Olin," Brit Chance complained after the cancellation announcement. "I am disappointed . . . I was looking forward to the crunch . . . to the direct confrontation. Now, it is just going to fade away."

The most monumental design rivalry since Clinton Crane took on Starling Burgess in 1930 has developed between Chance and Stephens and the battlefield of the Twelves would be as good a place as any to square accounts. Chance does not merely want his design to defend the America's Cup, he wants it to vanquish Stephens in the process. Chance was not happy with the thought of only conquering the challenger, he wanted to dethrone the master of the design world at the same time. That is why the misfortunes of the *Courageous* syndicate threatened to cheat Chance of his showdown with Stephens.

At 65, Olin Stephens, president of Sparkman & Stephens Inc., has been the king of the yachting design hill for nearly two decades. His reputation and clients circle the globe and his influence is all-pervading. Stephens dominates the design world much as General Motors dominates the auto industry. More than being the racing world's most successful naval architect, Olin is also the holder of the America's Cup design mantle. It is this distinction which Chance covets most.

Although there is no such thing as an "official" America's Cup designer, over the past 90 years of Cup history it seems that one American designer seems to always dominate in each era. In the 1880's Edward Burgess' designs dominated in three Cup matches in a row.

After his death, Nathanael Herreshoff defeated all threats to his design superiority, both foreign and domestic, from 1893 until 1920, staving off six challengers in the process. After Captain Nat's retirement, Starling Burgess, son of Edward, inherited the invisible America's Cup design wand and created the next three defenders. In 1958 Olin Stephens' *Columbia* was selected to defend the America's Cup and he became only the fourth man in over 70 years to enter the hallowed ranks of the successful Cup designers. Stephens has worn his crown well since 1958.

In 1970 Brit Chance got his first opportunity to match wits with Stephens on the America's Cup course. By designing the modifications to *Intrepid,* and by virtue of her beating the new Stephens-designed *Valiant* and then going ahead to successfully resist the challenger, Chance had enhanced his reputation. Yet, his 1970 design victory with *Intrepid* was hollow. Afterall, the boat had been first designed by Sparkman & Stephens in 1966 and was generally considered to be a breakthrough boat. Brit had only modified the afterbody of a fast boat and could not claim full design credit. Worst of all for Brit's ego, many people in Newport said that his modifications had actually made *Intrepid* slower than she was in 1967.

Olin J. Stephens II Gets His Start

Olin Stephens had already been captivated by sailing and boat design when a case of jaundice forced him to withdraw from the Massachusetts Institute of Technology during his first semester in 1926. After recovering, the 19-year-old Stephens dove directly into design work, more eager to get on with the business of designing than to finish his college education. In the 1928 issue of "Yachting" magazine his first plans were published. Discussing his 6-Meter design in the article, Stephens said, "In any design the most important factors of speed seem to be long sailing lines and large sail area, with moderate displacement and small wetted surface. Then comes beauty, by which is meant clean, fair pleasing lines. Though *per se* beauty is not a factor of speed, the easiest boats to look at seem to be the easiest to drive." Over the years Stephens would turn out some of the most graceful lines ever produced for a sailboat and the picture in his mind's eye of what a sailing yacht should look like has become what generations of Americans have come to expect in aesthetic sailboat design.

Stephens' career really got started in 1928 when his father, Roderick Stephens, Sr., introduced Olin to Drake Sparkman, a young New York yacht broker who wanted to join forces with a designer. After seeing Olin's drawings, Sparkman offered him an informal partnership until 1929 when the young Stephens would turn twenty-one and formal papers could be drawn up.

Olin's first ocean racer was a 30-foot boat named *Kalmia* which Sparkman sold to Arthur Hatch and Stephens steered in a race from New London, Connecticut, to Gibson Island, Maryland, in the Chesapeake Bay. The famous schooner *Niña* won the fleet prize, but Olin won his class. This was a good start, yet it was not until later, when Rod Sr. put up $28,000 of his own money for a new design, that the Stephens name began to get around. The sport of ocean racing was still in its infancy, and many of the boats used were direct descendants of the Gloucester fishing schooners and other workboats with designs proven over the years in rough North Atlantic seas.

"Dorade" Launches Stephens' Career

Olin's first big ocean racing success was the 52-foot *Dorade,* a long, narrow boat with only a 10'3" beam, fine ends, and an easily driven hull shape. With Olin at the helm and both Rods, Sr. and Jr., in the crew, the yawl took second in Class B in the 1930 race to Bermuda. But it was not until the Transatlantic Race in 1931 that Olin Stephens became a household word among yachtsmen after winning that race two days ahead of the rest of the fleet. Then, with Rod Jr. at the helm, *Dorade* won the classic Fastnet Race. Upon the Stephens brothers' return to the United States, they were given a ticker tape parade down Broadway to City Hall, the only time such an honor has been accorded to yachtsmen for a sailing feat. Now the Stephens name was firmly established and the Sparkman and Stephens partnership was permanently cemented. After a year at Cornell University, Olin's younger brother, Rod, decided that he liked boat building and sailing much more than the confines of academic life and joined the S&S effort. He was a perfect complement to Olin and from the beginning, the two brothers made a tough-minded and expert team.

Throughout the 1930's Olin Stephens' reputation grew among the Long Island Sound sailing community. The success of *Stormy Weather,* for Philip LeBoutillier, and the victories of R. J. Schaefer's *Edlu* which won the 1934 Bermuda Race with Robert N. Bavier Sr. at the helm added to the S&S fame. Other Stephens Bermuda Race winners have included *Baruna, Gesture, Argyll, Finisterre* (the only boat to win the Bermuda Race three times), and more recently, *Noryema.* Other outstanding S&S-designs that have become world-famous ocean racers include: *Bolero, Kialoa, Dyna, Bay Bea, Aura, Charisma,* and many others. Nor has Stephens' design success been limited to ocean racers. He has designed everything from dinghies, to Lightning and Blue Jay class boats, to 100-footers. The success of his 6-Meter and 12-Meter boats has been steady since the late 1930's.

The Sparkman & Stephens design office is located at 79 Madison Avenue in Midtown Manhattan and in many ways the vast office there reflects the character of Olin himself; it is spartan and unassuming, with no frills or extravagance. Olin occupies the corner room looking out over Madison Avenue from the 12th floor. His room is furnished with an old wood desk, a wood table, and two or three wood chairs that seem to have been there since the company moved in during the late 1940's. The offices seem to symbolize a pre-World War II efficiency and frugality that many companies have long since forgotten.

All of his life Olin has been shy, soft spoken and modest. Olin always has been the reserved member of the team and Rod the more out-going, energetic, and physically dynamic. Rod was famous for years for feats of muscular prowess, such as going up halyards hand over hand or shinnying up a headstay to right a fouled spinnaker. Even today in his early 60's, Rod Stephens Jr. runs up the 12 flights of stairs to his office after lunch to keep in shape. Olin's dynamism, on the other hand, is demonstrated in the power of his ideas and insights into problems. When he discusses the intricacies of the IOR rating rule with a committee of the brightest young American designers, no one grasps concepts or the subtleties of a complex situation more quickly than Olin. His mind is as sharp and quick as ever.

Olin Stephens is a Renaissance man. He drives a sports car and follows grand prix racing. He is also a painter, and in fact, was pointed toward an artist's career as a young man before taking up boat design. He is a voluminous reader and can speak in depth on a wide range of subjects; his erudition goes far beyond boat design and matters of the sea. Stephens has a seemingly endless capacity to explain and re-explain the most simple concepts about yachting or yacht design—or the most complex—to anyone who asks, whether he is a customer willing to spend half a million dollars on a new boat or a Sunday afternoon gawker strolling along a Newport dock. His reserve of patience is almost endless.

In addition to being a yacht designer, the president of a small company, and a member of various committees in the yachting world, Stephens also runs what amounts to a school for naval architects. Many major yacht designers in the world have worked at S&S at one time or another, and every season young men from the United States and all over the world apply for work in his famous office to learn the ways of the master. It is not uncommon to see a Japanese, Dutch and an English team working side by side on a new boat designed for a German client. Ironically, some of Stephens' heaviest competition comes from former employees who strike out to make good on their own.

Brit Chance Challenges the Master

One of the first things that surprises many people about the designer of the *Mariner* syndicate's 12-Meter is the youth of her designer.

At 33 Britton Chance, Jr., is quite a young man to be designing a boat to defend the America's Cup. He seems all the younger to many people in American yachting, because they can remember when he came on the scene. They have watched his progress, and more important, the successes and failures of his boats. Most active and influential East Coast yachtsmen predate Chance and to some degree this has cast him in an awkward position. He is like the boy next door who has grown up.

Brit comes from a sailing family. His father is regarded by people who know him as an unquestioned genius. With a Ph.D. in physics, Britton Chance, Sr., forged a successful and affluent career in science. He had become a successful yachtsman by the time his son was born, and it was natural that Brit Jr. should be brought up around the water and yachts. While Chance Sr. was working at the M.I.T. radiation laboratory during World War II, Brit sailed in International 110 dinghies, and when the family went to Sweden after the war, at age 11 Brit started skippering the family's boat as they cruised the coast. Like many men who grow up in a sailing family, Brit's all-consuming interest in childhood was sailing. He was crewing on "E" scows at age nine. Later he skippered Moths and Penguins. He started ocean racing as a crew when he was 14, an activity that he has pursued intermittently ever since. At 15, he went to Sweden for the 125th anniversary of the Swedish Yacht Club in 1955. That was the year of the last great meter regatta and 8-Meters, 6-Meters, 5.5-Meters and many other meter boats were racing in connection with the club's celebration. This was the first time that Brit had seen keel boats for quite some time and he was enthralled by the beauty and grace of these lovely sailing machines. It was the ambience at the Swedish Yacht Club and the excitement of so many beautiful racing sailboats that caused him to enroll in the Westlawn design correspondence course. (One summer Brit even worked for Pierre DeSaix in the Stevens test tank.) But, Brit never finished the design course, nor did he finish college, dropping out of his physics and math classes at the University of Rochester during his junior year.

In January 1961, when Chance was 21-years-old, he made up his mind to go into yacht design and went to work for Ray Hunt, as a draftsman. Dissatisfied because he could not work under the direct tutelage of Hunt—versatile and highly creative designer of both power and sail boats—Chance quit and by September was working for Ted Hood in his two-man design department. At the time Hood had spent very little time in the tank, so it was natural for him to draw on Brit's limited testing experience during the crash program to design *Nefertiti*. During the weeks of December and early January both Hood and the young Chance spent evenings running the models of Ted's new 12-Meter down the long tub-like Steven's tank.

Britton Chance Jr., designer of "Mariner"

Chance Makes His Reputation in 5.5s

In February 1962 Chance had a falling out with Hood over the design credits for *Nefertiti* and left before the lines were completed. The following year Brit's first design was built, a 5.5-Meter boat named *Complex V*, for Brit's father who had won an Olympic gold medal in the Class in 1952. As in the Stephens' family, it was the father's confidence in his son's ability that launched his career. *Complex V* was third in the national championships that year and was second in the Seawanaka Cup eliminations. Brit sailed his second design, the 5.5-Meter *Charade*, in the 1964 Olympic trials and held the lead until the last race when he was narrowly beaten out by Don McNamara.

Throughout the early 1960's Brit built up valuable experience in meter boats. During the summer of 1961 he crewed on the 12-Meter *Columbia* as a spinnaker tender and during the 1962 America's Cup trials he crewed aboard Hovey's *Easterner*. From then on, Chance's love affair with the mighty Twelves seemed to grow each year.

A key break in Chance's career came in 1964 when he received a $10,000 grant from the "Twelve Meter Fund" established by Palmer

Sparkman and Bob Stone among other NYYC members. The aim of the grant was to encourage the study of 12-Meter design. For the next year and one-half Chance drew lines and made tank tests with the grant.

By 1967 Brit Chance's design reputation was made in the 5.5-Meter Class. That year his design won the world championship and until 1973 his boats won every year. It was also one of Chance's 5.5 designs that won the 1968 Olympic gold medal in Acapulco, Mexico. In 1967 Brit also designed his first cruising boat, a One Ton boat for a European client. Because of Brit's success in the 5.5-Meter Class and because the class was more popular in Europe, it was natural that his design reputation would grow faster on the Continent than in his native land.

During the late 1960's, Chance impressed both the French sailing family of Le Guillou and the Swiss boat builder, Herman Egger, who were all keenly interested in 5.5-Meter boats which ultimately led to his commission to design the 12-Meter *Chancegger.* The boat was built by Herman Egger and later the French designer André Mauric based his own America's Cup challenger, *France,* quite heavily on the Chance design. The irony was, of course, that in 1974, Chance's design would be a potential defender against a challenge from Bich, with Jean-Marie Le Guillou sailing *France.*

Chance Enters the 12-Meter Club

Before the construction of *Chancegger,* only five American designers had ever seen their 12-Meter dreams come to fruition—Olin Stephens, Bill Luders, Phil Rhodes, Ray Hunt and Ted Hood. With *Chancegger,* Chance joined that exclusive club in 1968 with the added momentum of having done the latest design. His gamble with the French boat paid off, and in 1969 Bill Strawbridge came to the Oyster Bay naval architect and asked him to re-design *Intrepid* so that she would be competitive with the latest brainchild of Olin Stephens in 1970.

Improving on the S&S-designed *Intrepid* was a formidable task. In 1967, she had proved greatly superior to both the 1964 *Constellation* and the challenger *Dame Pattie,* which was known to be faster even than *Gretel,* the fastest foreign 12-Meter built to that time. But, most difficult of all, the modified *Intrepid* would have to be faster than the newest Stephens boat and never before had any designer been able to beat a brand-new Stephens 12-Meter design.

Intrepid '70's tank tests indicated that she was faster than the 1967 *Intrepid* in higher wind strengths and one-tenth of a knot faster than the 1958 *Weatherly* in light air. One-tenth of a knot means 64.8 seconds on an America's Cup windward leg and that prediction seemed to be born out by the actual races with *Weatherly.* Pierre DeSaix indicated after the 1970 trials that the Chance-modified *Intrepid* had tank tested faster than the new Stephens-designed *Valiant.* DeSaix said that both *Valiant* and the Chance-modified *Intrepid* were faster than the 1967 *Intrepid.* With design reputations at stake, people divided into two camps, one holding that the original *Intrepid* was actually faster than either *Intrepid '70* or *Valiant* and the other contending that Chance had actually improved the speed of the old Stephens design.

Showdown in the Tank

In the fall of 1931, Stevens Institute of Technology professor Kenneth S. M. Davidson towed the first model down what has come to be the most famous test tank for racing yachts in the world. The tank used today at Stevens—in what is now called the Davidson Laboratory—is exactly the same one used in 1931, a 130-foot long, semicircular steel tub. The model is towed down the length of the tank attached to an "I" beam overhead. The object of Professor Davidson's towing tank is primarily to determine the resistance of a boat's hull to the water and thereby determine it's speed. The tank is also able to measure the model's side force (leeway), righting moment, and yawing moment, as it travels through the water.

In the first years of the tank's operation, crude scales were affixed to the models. As the little hull was pulled along by an electric motor the designer would walk beside the model watching the needle on the resistance scale. It was a crude system by today's standards, but Davidson proved early in the game that the results he was getting were accurate. One of Davidson's most enthusiastic supporters was the young designer Olin Stephens.

In 1937 both Stephens and Starling Burgess tank tested models for what would be ultimately chosen as Mike Vanderbilt's *Ranger.* On the race course, *Ranger* lived up to the tank predictions and sailed away from *Endeavour II,* as if she were one of the slowest "J" boats ever built. The success of the 1937 America's Cup defender seemed to confirm in the minds of many that the tank could be used to explore many different avenues of yacht design and thus speed the progress of the art by eliminating, in the tank, what might have taken years to discover by building and sailing a full sized yacht.

The Role of Pierre DeSaix

The man who has been running the Davidson Laboratory test tank since the advent of the 12-Meter challenges is Pierre DeSaix. It is with this energetic man that most of the secrets of the 1974 defenders reside. Because DeSaix is responsible for testing models of defenders for the

American designers, he is the only man in a position to know and compare the relative speeds of the American boats. Because of his unique position, DeSaix must be careful not to tell one designer what another is doing or how another designer's models have performed. Not surprisingly, both the American designers and DeSaix are most sensitive about this point. Because Brit Chance worked for DeSaix in the tank as an assistant while he was in college, many competing designers feel that DeSaix might inadvertently "spill" some vital information to his old friend. Both Chance and DeSaix vigorously deny that this would ever happen. DeSaix points out that if he were to leak information, designers would no longer use the Stevens Institute test tank. He asserts that the only instance of a slip in "security" at the laboratory occurred in 1958 when one designer happened to step into a room where the model of another designer was stored.

Yet, it seems unavoidable that rumors about one designer getting inside information about the progress of another's testing will persist. When America's designers are working in the tank, it is natural that they try to read DeSaix's expressions almost as hard as the data readout, looking for a raised eyebrow or some indication as to their boat's relative progress.

Since only a few designers in the world have been actively working on 12-Meters, there is very little information available for a newcomer to build upon; it is probably here that DeSaix offers the most help. In a number of cases, while a new designer is stumbling in the dark, DeSaix has pointed out speeds on a graph that a Twelve must attain to be competitive. This is done not to give anyone an edge, but simply to let a designer know that he is within a competitive range or that his design has a long way to go before it is built full size.

DeSaix has said of his special designer relationships, "It is particularly frustrating because we can only advise each designer in a general way, and can only work with him to the extent that we do not reveal in any way the problems or progress that the other designers are making on the same type of boat. True, we bring forth all the basic hydrodynamics knowledge we have to help each designer, but as far as particular shapes, it is up to the designer. This is frustrating as we often watch a designer make a serious mistake or miss an important point, and we cannot help him."

The Trial of Tank Testing

Basically, the test tank procedure works like this: A naval architect submits the lines drawings and all the important data about the new design to DeSaix. He turns the lines of the hull over to one of the model makers who works with the laboratory. About two weeks later, a four-foot, perfectly scaled ($.9'' = 1'$) model is returned to DeSaix for testing.

The models cost about $1,000 apiece and it is not unusual for a designer to have seven or eight models made—all with different underbody shapes—in preparation for one final design.

The model is attached to the towing carriage and then run down the tank at a wide range of speeds and heel angles. Wind speeds of from six to 30 knots are simulated and heel angles from just a few degrees to about 30 degrees are tested. Within those wide ranges of heel angle and speed, sensors attached to the towing carriage monitor the four following elements: 1) hull resistance, 2) stability, 3) side force on the hull, and 4) the location of the center of water force. The most important of these, of course, is hull resistance, followed by side force on the hull. The model with the least hull resistance as it goes through the water—everything else being equal—will be the fastest boat on the race course. Similarly, a boat might have the least hull resistance, yet be very susceptible to side force and make excessive leeway. A boat that slips to leeward more than a few degrees will be slower getting to a windward mark than one which has a bit more hull resistance yet can "go where it is pointed." The righting moment of the boat or its stability is a third important factor to the final speed made good

Bob McCullough, Olin Stephens and Pierre DeSaix watch the tank testing of "Valiant" in 1969

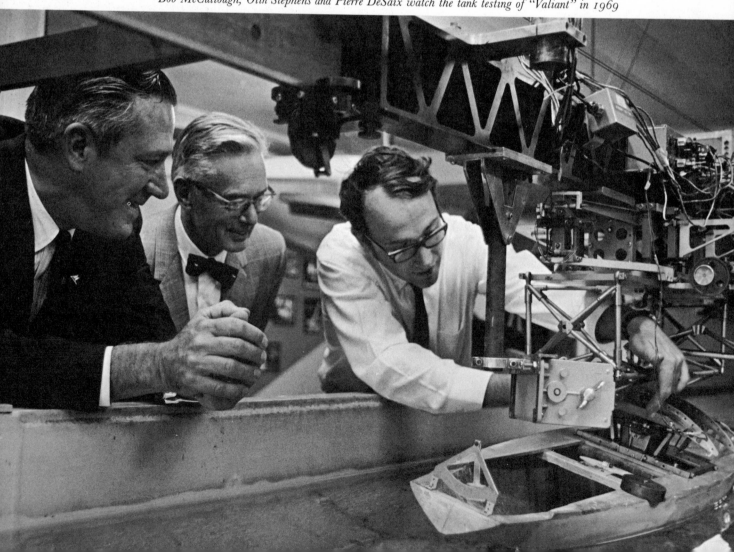

to windward and a factor that can be altered somewhat once the design is out of the tank.

Throughout the tank testing the designers are primarily concerned with the "velocity made good" (vmg) to windward characteristics, as well over half of the America's Cup race course is to weather. To win an America's Cup race the boat must be able to get to the windward mark first. Of course, reaching and running are also important, but to a lesser degree, as there are only two, relatively short reaches and one 4.5-mile downwind leg. A good America's Cup boat is one that is superior to windward and can hold its own on the off-the-wind legs.

The designer, then, must come up with a hull shape that is a compromise among all the trade-offs that exist. Resistance can be reduced by trimming away keel and underbody, but then directional stability is decreased and the chances of making more leeway are increased. Olin Stephens' addition of the trim tab on *Intrepid* in 1967 was found not to increase drag appreciably, but with the tab set four or five degrees to windward, a two degree reduction in leeway resulted. This is an example of an ideal improvement because definite benefits were obtained in one area without penalties in another. Stephens also considerably reduced *Intrepid's* wetted surface (skin area) by approximately 40 square feet by cutting away the conventional keel shape. This elimination of wetted area, i.e. drag, enhanced boat speed by reducing resistance.

Another resistance-causing factor is the quarterwave. This is the "second" wave that is created as any boat moves through the water. The first wave is, of course, the bow wave and the second appears

Threads attached to hull indicate flow over the bottom in tank tests

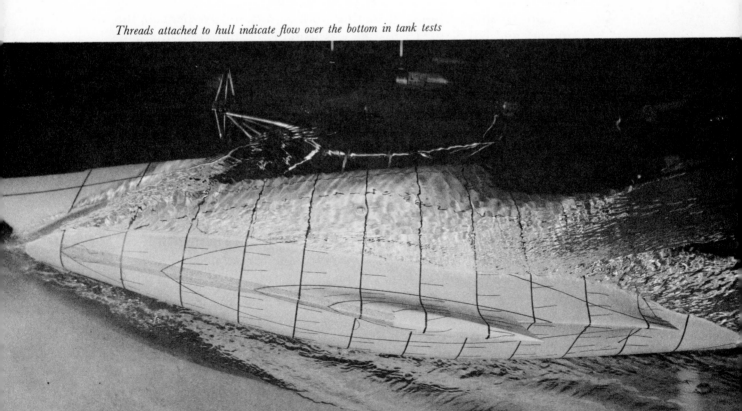

somewhere along the stern quarter-section of the boat. The higher the wave and the farther forward it is, the greater is the resistance and therefore the greater the drag. Although naval architects have long known that quarterwaves were undesirable, they did not know why they were caused. It was not until the mid-1960's that Pete DeSaix discovered that the quarterwaves were created by what is called "separation." DeSaix installed underwater viewing ports in the test tank so that the underbody could actually be observed and photographed as the models were towed down the tank. Short threads were attached over the entire body of the hull, so that the direction of flow over the hull surface could be determined. The surprising discovery was that just below the point on the hull where the quarterwaves appeared, the threads were pointing perpendicularly to the direction the boat was moving. This meant that water was no longer able to continue along the side of the underbody and had "separated" from the hull; instead of the water sliding by, it was actually being pulled along by the hull. This was the first time that it was known that the phenomenon of separation and quarterwaves were related.

Crudely speaking, the separation is caused by the traditional shapes designers have always given hulls. The bow is a point that divides the water and as the water travels aft along the underbody, it is naturally compressed tighter and tighter against the surface, as the beam of the boat becomes wider and wider. It is at or near the quarter section of the boat that designers begin to bring the waterline shape back in and there the flow begins to separate because it is no longer being compressed against the hull; in fact, pressure is being relieved. In essence, separation is caused by an abrupt change in the pressure gradient along the surface of the hull.

Brit Chance did some facinating work on pressure gradients in the summer and fall of 1973 while he was working on the *Mariner* design. He fed the measurements of *Intrepid, Chancegger* and his new 12-Meter into a computer at Grumman Aircraft Company, and it drew a picture of the different hulls, showing the pressure gradients along the surface. With this computer program, Chance for the first time was able to predict where the separation would occur by noting where the pressure gradient significantly changed. The location of the separation would be the location of the quarter wave. Using the computer allowed him to alter the lines, feed the new information into the calculator, and gradually work the area of dramatically changing pressure farther aft, thereby moving the quarterwave as far aft as possible without laborious tank work. The designs that looked good on paper were then incorporated in a tank model for testing to confirm the computer's predictions. By the end of November, Chance was confident that the computer had accurately predicted the points of separation.

In 1966, Stephens developed the design of a full afterbody to reduce the quarterwave and move it aft. This fullness of *Intrepid's* after

The quarterwave starts far aft on the 1970 "Intrepid" (top) and farther forward on the model of the 1967 "Intrepid" (bottom)

sections was called "a kicker" by Stephens, and as soon as she was launched, the clean quarterwave predicted in the tank was proved under actual sailing conditions. Her trim tab, kicker, and reduced wetted surface all contributed to make her a superior boat and something close to a breakthrough in 12-Meter design.

Design Progress is Slow

The most surprising thing of all about the 12-Meter Class, and about the test tank in particular, is that since the building of *Vim* in 1939, there has only been an improvement in speed made good to windward of $\frac{3}{4}$ of one knot. All of the time and money of all of the designers has only been able to increase boat speed a seemingly infinitesimal amount. Yet, these fractions of a knot of speed when multiplied by the 24.3-mile America's cup course result in differences of two or more minutes at the finish line.

Since 1958, the major changes on Twelves that have resulted from the tank include: 1) the reduction of keel area, 2) the addition of a kicker and an improved waterline exit, 3) a general lengthening of the waterline, 4) movement of the center of buoyancy aft, and 5) a "V" shape on the bottom of the keel. Overall speeds have improved about

¾ of one knot over most of the wind ranges except in light conditions where there has been very little progress since *Weatherly*.

Conceivably, a breakthrough 12-Meter design might be in store for the 1974 match because of the advent of aluminum construction. Because aluminum hulls can be built lighter than wood hulls, 4,000 pounds of weight is saved and can be moved to the keel. This transfer in weight creates approximately a four-percent increase in stability, a greater righting moment, and a slightly lower center of gravity. The slight difference in stability means that the aluminum boats will stand up straighter than their wood sisters, present more sail area to the wind, and possibly point a bit higher. The total effect should be a dramatic increase in speed for the 12-Meters. No one is willing to say exactly how fast the new aluminum boats will be, but something near a tenth of a knot is possible.

The tank testing programs carried on by both Stephens and Chance for their 1974 boats were prolonged affairs lasting about 18 months. During that time the two American syndicates spent over $100,000 apiece in their tank programs. Both designers tested about eight different models and as many as 13 modifications were made to each model. This means that each designer explored nearly 80 different hull shapes. At a cost of $1,500 per day for the services of the test tank and the laboratory's related services, it does not take long to run up an exorbitant testing bill. In addition to the normal testing procedures in the Davidson smooth water tank, tests were run in 1973 in the Stevens rough water tank.

Olin Stephens spent quite a bit of time in the large swimming-pool size rough water tank, making sure that the designs that looked fast in smooth water tests also performed well in the sea conditions that are likely to be encountered off Newport.

Recent studies have proved that the short chop created by the spectator fleet around the America's Cup buoy has a definite effect on the 12-Meters, and some designs are more susceptible than others to adverse conditions. DeSaix points to the 1964 English challenger *Sovereign* as an example of a boat that tested well in the smooth water tank but performed miserably at sea. DeSaix speculates that the reason she was so disappointing on the race course was that when her hull was forced to punch through the short chop, it actually incurred nearly twice the drag that it might have experienced in smooth water.

What is a 12-Meter?

The term 12-Meter refers to the formula to which the America's Cup boats are designed. Boats in the class are designed in such a way that when measurements of their various speed-producing factors (such as length, sail area, stability, and freeboard) are cranked through a simple formula, the result does not exceed "12 meters." Of course all measurements are metric. (Measurements could also be taken in feet and inches and the result would be "39.37 feet.") The formula is:

$$\frac{L + 2d + \sqrt{Sa} - F}{2.37} = \text{Rating (12 meters)}$$

"L" stands for the length, yet the number is neither the overall length or the waterline length but rather a number affected by other measurements taken in a prescribed manner using the load waterline as a starting point. Generally speaking, however, "L" will vary in proportion to the lengthening or shortening of the waterline length. The "d" stands for the difference between the skin girth and the chain girth measurements. The "chain girth" is a straight line from the beam to the keel, and "skin girth" is the distance along the surface of the hull as seen in a cut-away section. "Sa" represents sail area and the square root of the figure is calculated to convert the number into linear measurement. "F" equals freeboard, the distance from the waterline to the tip of the shear. "2.37" is an arbitrary figure used to produce the 12-Meter equation.

In yacht design perhaps the most important single factor is length, as boat speed to windward is closely related to the square root of the waterline length in feet. Consequently, the longer a designer can stretch a 12-Meter's waterline, the better; this is the reason that there has been a gradual lengthening of waterlines since 1958. Yet designers cannot get a longer waterline without paying for this increase in speed-making potential elsewhere in the formula; usually it comes from the sail area. With the increase in measured waterline length over the years has come a reduction in sail area. This trade-off has enhanced performance in wind conditions above 13 knots, but in light air the boats suffer because then they need all the sail area possible.

Many aspects of the 12-Meter are controlled by governing class rules which set arbitrary limits (such as masts being limited to 82 feet above the deck) or prohibit some measurements to exceed a percentage of other measurements. (For example, the draft of a 12-Meter is limited to a depth of .16 l.w.l. plus 1.64 feet, without severe penalty. This means for a 45-foot waterline the draft cannot exceed eight feet ten inches. The rule also dictates minimum beam, 11.80 feet, and a number of other critical aspects of 12-Meter design. The height of the jib halyard is specified at 75 percent of the mast height and even the crown of the deck is limited to $\frac{1}{20}$th of the maximum beam.) The idea behind these and many other limitations on design is to simply prevent too much diversity in hull and rig. Standardization enhances the prospects of good racing since the likelihood of one boat being vastly superior to another is reduced.

On the America's Cup course the idea of formula racing helps both the challenger and defender in as much as they both know approxi-

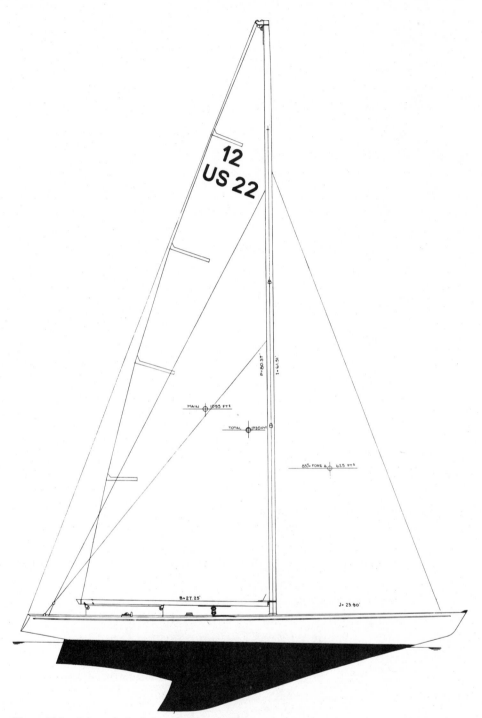

"Intrepid '70" is typical of the modern 12-Meters

mately what kind of boat the opposition will be producing and that any divergence from the norm will be minor. Yet, despite the fact that both challenger and defender are of very similar design in three out of the last five challenges, the defending boat has been markedly superior. In the other two cases (involving the two *Gretels*) the foreign boats were only marginally faster. It is precisely because there is so little creative latitude allowed that the designers spend so much time tank testing. They must insure that there is not one square foot of surface area that can't be eliminated or one inch of length that can't be added or subtracted without affecting performance.

This is also the reason that the sailmakers feel that it is with their craft that real breakthroughs in 12-Meter speed can be found. Every little detail that is not specified by the rule is taken advantage of by either reducing weight or windage, or by producing some other favorable modification.

In 1970 these were the major measurements of the two America's Cup boats:

	Intrepid	*Gretel II*
Length overall	64'5"	62'
Length waterline	47'	46'
Beam	12'3"	12'
Draft	9'2"	9'
Displacement	65,000 lb.	60,000 lb.
Sail area	1,750 sq. ft.	1,750 sq. ft.

The End of the Twelves

The end of the 12-Meter Class is at hand. In 1973 the NYYC fathers asked both Chance and Stephens to come up with recommendations for a new type of boat for contesting the America's Cup. Both designers have agreed in principal that another boat suitable for America's Cup matches can be found. Consequently, the prospects are good that 1974 will be the last year for the Twelves.

The reasons for the club's interest in discarding the Twelves involve practical economics. A Twelve is only used for one thing—the America's Cup. Between Cup years the boats are hauled out and stored because they are not competitive in any other kind of racing. Off the America's Cup course they are little more than expensive white elephants. It has become too difficult for the club, as well as potential challenging yacht clubs, to raise the vast sums of money that are needed to build boats for a single seven-race series. It would be far easier to raise the money involved for Cup contenders if the boats could also be used for ocean racing.

It seems likely that the two American designers will recommend

that Cup boats in the future be built to a given rating that will fall somewhere between 47 and 55 feet, under the International Rating Rule. Further, there would also be a number of restrictions written into the conditions requiring that the boats conform in a number of areas to insure that they be somewhat similar in boat speed. Conceivably, centerboards would be disallowed, all winches would be required to be on deck, sloop rigs would be mandatory, etc. The general thrust would undoubtedly be to produce boats that would be designed to a relatively narrow range and still be good ocean racing boats. The American ocean racer *Running Tide,* which is 61 feet long, has often been suggested as a good size ocean racer for America's Cup competition.

The end of the 12-Meter era?

10

Power for the Glory

There is no other racing sailboat quite as fascinating as a 12-Meter. They have a beauty and grace all their own and they have captured the imagination of yachtsmen since they were first built in England at the beginning of the 20th century. Because of their awe-inspiring size and because they are the boat of the America's Cup, they are dreamed about by yachtsmen everywhere. Just as with all sail boats, Twelves get their power by harnessing the invisible force of the wind and transferring it, as if by magic, into energy through their enormous sail plan. The tremendous horsepower needed to push the 65,000-pound Twelves at speeds up to 12 knots comes from a rig that is as old as the class itself and which is rigidly controlled by the class rules.

Mainsail—The primary driving force for Twelves comes from their massive mainsails. Usually around 1,100-square feet in size, modern mains usually measure about 79 feet along the luff and about 27 feet along the foot. The aspect ratio of conventional mains is about 3:1 (three feet on the hoist for every one along the foot). The Australian challenger *Southern Cross* has a main with a very short base—just over 20 feet, giving the main a 4:1 aspect ratio. Although a high-aspect ratio main is more efficient than a lower aspect ratio of equal area, what is given away on the foot cannot be gained on the hoist because 12-Meter masts are limited to 82 feet, therefore the higher the aspect ratio, the lower the sail area.

Genoa—The 12-Meter rule states that the hoist of the headsail can be no higher than 75 percent of the height of the mast. Since the mast height is limited to 82 feet and most are built to the maximum, 12-Meters' have genoas with hoists about 61.5 feet off the deck. There is no requirement about the length of the base of the foretriangle (a triangle formed by the mast, deck and jibstay) so the jibstay can be placed as far forward as the designer desires. Usually, a Twelve's "J" measurement (distance from the mast to the tack of the sail on the bow) is from 22 to 25 feet. Some boats, such as *Nefertiti* and *Heritage*,

The origin of 12-Meter power

had longer "J's" but they did not seem to be particularly effective. The class rule prohibits the genoa from extending more than $15\frac{1}{2}$ feet abaft the mast. Normally, there is about 740 square feet of sail area in the foretriangle and about 476 square feet of genoa area abaft the mast. This adds up to a genoa of around, 1,200-square feet, giving a 12-Meter about 2,300-square feet of total sail area. But because the rule only measures 85 percent of the foretriangle, the total "rated" sail area is usually around 1,750 square feet.

Spinnakers—Spinnakers cannot be hoisted higher than the genoa and are limited to a maximum size along the foot and leech. The history of 12-Meter spinnakers has not been a very distinguished one with more losses being attributed to incorrect spinnaker selection than any other sail on the boat. It is a cardinal rule in 12-Meter racing that large spinnakers are not effective and small "chutes" are used for the most part.

A typical racing Twelve sail inventory consists of about 20 to 30 sails including two or three mainsails, a full range of spinnakers in different weight cloth, two light floaters, genoas of varying weight material, and a few staysails. A suit of sails for an America's Cup summer is usually a $40,000 proposition.

To the above list of sails can be added a few new ones for 1974 as syndicates are bound to try starcut close reaching spinnakers, various types of "blooper" spinnakers set to leeward of the primary spinnaker, and even mainsails made out of Kevlar, a new DuPont organic fiber that has high strength and low weight.

Ted Hood: Power Broker

For the most part, designers have drawn a "standard" sail plan and turned over the problem of making the sails and producing the power to the sailmaker. Early in the development of 12-Meters for America's Cup defense, one man—Frederick ("Ted") Hood—quickly demonstrated that he could produce sails that were the equal if not superior to any in the United States. Since the early 1960's Hood sails have been almost standard equipment on American defenders and Ted Hood's role in producing the power to stoke the mighty Twelves has been unrivaled.

It seems strange that in a country with so many sailmakers that one man has been able to maintain a monopoly on 12-Meter sails. The story of Ted Hood's rise is an important one, because each America's Cup summer much of the burden of fending off the challenger rests on his shoulders. To him has fallen the responsibility, almost by default, of single-handedly designing, cutting and creating the 12-Meter sails.

Hood opened up shop in 1950 and in 1954 got started on the road to his America's Cup dominance when he made a suit of sails for Lee

Ted Hood, the sailmaker for the Twelves

Loomis' yacht *Good News.* These sails were among some of the first that Hood had ever made for a big, ocean-going boat. It turned out that he couldn't have been picked by a better customer. Loomis was from Oyster Bay, a member of the NYYC and the Loomis family was at the core of the New York yachting Establishment. *Good News* did well and Loomis spread the word about the Marblehead, Massachusetts sailmaker.

When Capt. John Matthews, also from Oyster Bay, considered campaigning his 12-Meter *Vim* in the 1958 trials he went to Loomis for advice. One of the first things that the yachting sage recommended was that Ted Hood make his sails. Capt. Matthews gave Hood the order and Ted spent August and September of 1957 testing out sails on *Vim* and *Gleem.* Although *Vim* did not win the 1958 trials, Hood's reputation was made due to the good showing of the old boat.

One of the reasons for Hood's initial success among the 12-Meter syndicates was his early acceptance of a new material—Dacron. When DuPont first came out with the material in the early 1950's most of the sailing community was hesitant to try it, except Ted Hood. He learned how to work with the material and got a jump on the rest of the industry. Hood also made his own cloth, unheard of for sail-makers up to that time. Ted's father was a successful entrepreneur in the textile industry and in 1952 Steadman ("the professor") Hood gave his son a set of looms on which to weave the Dacron filaments to his own specifications. It was largely because of his father, and his father's resources, that Ted got into the weaving business which would ultimately become one of the defender's trump cards. Since the 1958 match, every American 12-Meter syndicate has used at least one suit of Hood sails.

The Secret of Hood's Success

Hood feels that the phenomenal success of his 12-Meter sails is due to the fact that they do not blow out of shape after being used. Sail shape is the single most important aspect of a sail and if shape is lost because of stretching, then power and speed are reduced. Most fabrics start stretching, according to Hood, in a matter of 10 to 15 minutes in fresh winds. This stretch is because of "cold flow." (When Dacron, a synthetic filament is pulled for a short duration, it does not stretch; however, when it is put under tension for a prolonged period of time "cold flow" takes place and the filaments begin to elongate. Dacron elongation can be as much as 10 percent.)

Hood attributes the long life of his sails to his careful selection of polyester fibers, with certain twist characteristics, and to the tight weaving done on his own looms. Further, his fabric does not undergo a heavy resin finish, which tends to break down over a period of time. These three relatively simple elements—fiber selection, weaving and finishing—are the most important reasons why Hood cloth is less stretchy and has seemed to hold its shape better through the years on the America's Cup course. It is because of this stretch factor that many sailmakers are experimenting with the low-stretch ($4\frac{1}{2}$%) Kevlar fibers.

Kevlar—the New Super Fabric

In 1973 a new DuPont fiber was released in limited quantities to a few sources for testing purposes. Originally known as Fiber B during its developmental stages, the new organic fiber was first developed by the DuPont Chemical Company for use in automobile tires to replace the fiberglass or steel wire imbedded in the rubber for added strength. The new fibers were twice as strong as fiberglass and half the weight. The two sailmaking firms that picked-up quickly on Kevlar were John Marshall's North Sails loft in Stratford, Conn. and Hood Sails.

The possible advantages of Kevlar are that it has more strength and less stretch for its weight than conventional polyester yarns. The undesirable aspects of Kevlar are that it is brittle and it chafes easily. Conceivably, a Kevlar main could be as light as 5.5 ounces per square yard, which would save weight aloft without giving up the non-stretch characteristics so important in sails. Theoretically, a Kevlar 5.5 ounce main will hold its shape as well as a 7.5 ounce Dacron main. More likely, in 1974 the Kevlar sails will be of about the same weight as the Dacron, but far less stretchy.

The Sailmaker's Showdown

Probably the biggest single push by a competing sailmaker since 1958 when Hood took on Ratsey (Ratsey & Lapthorn sails were used on *Columbia*) is developing in 1974 from North Sails. The North company, like Hood, has lofts around the country and world and one of these lofts will be leading the charge against Ted Hood's dominance in America's Cup action. Although Lowell North has been involved in 12-Meter sails through his work during the 1964 and 1967 challenges, the main 1974 thrust is coming from the young man who runs the North Stratford, Conn. loft—John Marshall. This Olympic bronze medalist has been competing with Hood in the lucrative offshore market during the last two years, and has succeeded in being the first loft in some time to slightly loosen Hood's hold on the ocean racing fraternity.

The 30-year-old Marshall contends that 12-Meter sails are relatively poorly developed because, historically, sails for this class are only built every three years or whenever there is an America's Cup challenge. During the intervening years, sails for Twelves are simply not made in the United States because there is no demand. Consequently, Marshall contends, the development of Star Class sails or Lightning Class sails is much farther advanced than those sails which are used in defense of the America's Cup. There have been five challengers in Twelves and there have been five summers when Hood and other sailmakers intensively tried to develop sails, but since 1958 the progress in sail development in other classes has been far greater. John maintains that the sails are as important to the ultimate speed of the defenders as the hull itself. He sights as proof the fact that older 5.5-Meter boats are often able to beat new designs simply because their sails have been perfected and are producing their maximum power potential.

Marshall, who has been sailing since childhood, gained his reputation in one-design classes and during the last few years has been ocean racing. In 1972 he won an Olympic bronze medal in Dragons. Lowell North, a life-long friend of Gerry Driscoll will be aboard *Intrepid* and Marshall will be in the cockpit as the tactician and an alternate helmsman. North sails will be used on *Intrepid* and this boat will be a vehicle to show the potential of John's new sails, much the same as *Vim* demonstrated Hood's ability in 1958. Marshall considers his experience in making one-design sails a definite asset in his clash with Hood. Never-

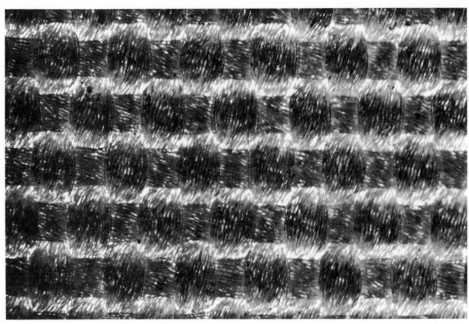

A microscopic view of Hood mainsail cloth

theless, Marshall is realistic enough to realize that Hood has over five summers of experience behind him and that it will be nearly impossible to catch up with the master in just one summer.

John has tried to close the technological gap between himself and Hood somewhat by being the first sailmaker to experiment with Kevlar mainsails. In August 1973, he used a Kevlar mainsail on the ocean racing yacht *Charisma* during a race across the English Channel. Halfway through the race the mainsail ripped from the leach nearly to the luff in one of the lower panels. The sail was reefed down and made it the final 100 miles of the race without further mishap. The experiment showed that there was still much to be learned about working with the new material. A rip in the mainsail of a 12-Meter would almost automatically cause a race to be lost.

John Marshall will also be leading the charge for the cloth manufacturer Howe & Bainbridge. There are predominately four important weavers of polyester yarns in the United States for yacht sail cloth: Howe & Bainbridge, Watts, Aquino, and Hood. Since Hood has also dominated in the offshore racing market in the East, the other manufacturers have been unable to puncture a large part of the big-boat fleet. A victory for Howe & Bainbridge on the all-important battle ground of the America's Cup, although it would mean peanuts in actual cloth sold, would be well worth the effort just to open up a kink in Ted Hood's armor.

Rig and Mast Shapes

The mast is strictly specified by the 12-Meter rule and there is very little room for variation. In addition to being no higher than 82 feet, the masts can weigh no less than 1,000 pounds including all fittings, cleats, spinnaker pole track, masthead fittings and related gear. Further, according to the rule, masts must have a dimension of 14-inches fore and aft to a point 30 feet off the deck where they can start tapering to diameter of about 5½ inches at the masthead. At the deck the width of the mast is about 9½ inches. The center of gravity is required to be at a point exactly 38 percent of the mast height.

In 1970 the main differences in the masts were the expensive titanium tapered top sections on the American boats and the double rows of vortex generators on the Australian mast. The titanium was used on the American boats to reduce weight aloft and thereby increase the boat's righting moment. The vortex generators or turbulence inducers, as they are sometimes called, are designed to disturb the boundary layer of air flowing over the mast to create a more favorable pressure differential for better mainsail efficiency.

As titanium and all exotic materials have been excluded for the

John Marshall, sailmaker and alternate "Intrepid" helmsman

1974 match (except for the old boats) the tops of all spars will be tapered aluminum. Early pictures of the Australian mast show it to be of a "D" shape. This is an attempt at a better aereodynamic form than the more rectangular shaped masts which have been used in the past.

The American masts were extruded by Alcoa in Pittsburgh and are not too different from what they have been in previous years. Because of the extremely high costs involved in having a different shaped die made, the Americans employed the same die that was used in 1970, although modifications may have been made after the extruding was completed. Three masts will be made for each boat, at a cost of about $40,000 per set. The American masts are in three sections whereas the Aussie mast is in one piece, a slight advantage for the potential challengers.

Other 12-Meter "Go Fast" Features

A 12-Meter is a 60- to 70-foot boat weighing between 55,000 and 65,000 pounds and designed to do one thing—win four races off Newport, Rhode Island in September. Everything about a Twelve is directed to that. On deck, there is no other yacht quite like a Twelve. It is the last word in yacht race thinking. In the cockpit, the new Twelves have twin steering wheels, port and starboard. This was an innovation introduced by Alan Payne on *Gretel II*. The twin wheels allow the helmsman to get far to leeward or to windward to see the luff of the genoa when sailing to weather and it also allows him to look on the other side of the genoa when approaching turning marks.

Forward of the cockpit is the tailers platform and the large coffee grinder winch drums. In 1970, *Valiant* had her drums below deck, thus having the ultimate in clean topsides. However, there is debate as to whether or not the slight amount of weight which is lowered and the very little bit of windage that is reduced is worth what is lost in crew eye contact.

The sheeting drums are connected below deck with a custom-made grinding system that allows four men to crank eight handles simultaneously driving one drum. Australian Payne first designed the cross-link for *Gretel* in 1962. The S&S-designed *Intrepid* was the first Twelve to have grinders below in 1967. The winch mechanisms used on the American boats are for the most part, made by the Barient Company, a leading American winch manufacturer, and are specifically designed for the unique problems encountered in America's Cup racing. Like everything else on the boat, the winches are designed to win four races. Basically, each drum is connected to grinding handles just below. The light-weight units have three gear rations. The first gear ratio (about 1:1) will allow the drum to be turned very fast for bringing in the

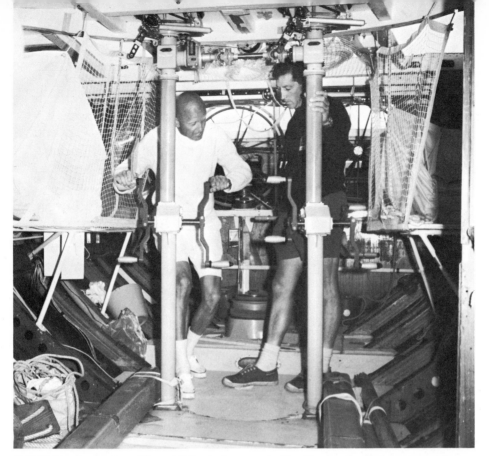

Bill Ficker demonstrates "Intrepid's" winch system to Jim Hardy after their 1970 match

sheet just as the boat is past head to wind and there is no strain on the sail. Second gear is the intermediate range, designed to give power to the effort of pulling the tremendous genoa in against the wind, and third gear is a high ratio of turns of the handle to actual inches of sheet taken in. This gear is used for the last 18 inches of sail trim that is the most difficult to sheet home. The high ratio (on the order of 24:1) is a necessity as each revolution of the handle turns the drum a fraction of a foot. In light air one man can easily handle the cranking operations with his partner only helping with the third gear operation. In moderate and heavy airs the crew will switch on the cross-connect system which links up both sets of grinders and allows four men to sweat home the genoa in short order no matter what the wind speed.

The procedure is usually to have one man slowly grind in the slack as the boat is coming about, then start grinding furiously when the boat is heading into the wind and the genoa has luffed with air on the backside (called "the break"). Then, two men spin the handles as fast as they can to take in the sheet while there is no load on the sail. When the wind fills the genoa, the connecting switch is thrown, and two more men add their muscle to the effort of sheeting in the sail.

The key word on the deck of every Twelve is efficiency, and the sail handling by the boats involved in the America's Cup in 1974 will be flawless by August. After months of intensive practice, those five crews will be the best yacht racing, sail-handling crews in the world. And, they'll let you know it.

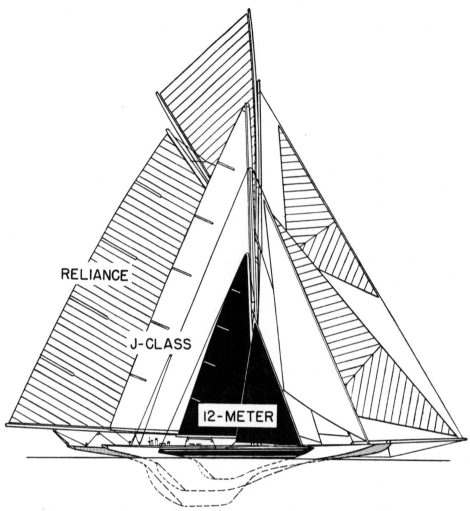

A comparison of sail plans of America's Cup yachts

11

Tactics of Victory

The first tactic of all usually occurs long before the matches even begin—the tactic of preparation. Traditionally, new American boats are launched in April or May and practice until the preliminary America's Cup selection trials in June. While the Americans are tuning up against each other, the challenger is being hoisted aboard a freighter for shipment to Newport. In 1970, for example, the eventual challenger *Gretel II* was on a slow freighter steaming from Sydney to Providence with 10 stops in between. She left on June 10th and arrived on August 11th—thereby losing the two most important months of preparation just before the match races.

Until 1974, the Americans had always been the best prepared to do battle and the challengers usually arrived in Newport with too little, too late. This year, challenger Bond intends to deviate from history. He purposely had his boat launched by early December 1973 so that he would have plenty of time to test her against *Gretel I* and *Gretel II*, change the new boat if need be, and train his crew. By the time Bond arrives in Newport he will be better prepared than any modern challenger. Once in America, the Australians will continue their tuning and crew drills to be as ready as possible for the challenge. In contrast, it is the Americans this time who were slow to prepare and it remains to be seen if they can catch up.

Psychological Tactics

Bill Ficker, skipper of *Intrepid,* showed in 1970 that he was a master of psychological gamesmanship. Although he was starting out with a three-year-old boat sailed by the greenest crew in Newport, and designed by the youngest and least known of the three designers represented, the Californian quickly managed to overcome these and other seeming drawbacks. Ficker wanted his operation not only to be an

Out of phase, "Intrepid" crosses "Dame Pattie's" stern

efficient and smooth-running team but also to have the appearance of being efficient and smooth running. A veteran of many high-pressure one-design and ocean racing sailing meets, Ficker was aware of the importance of not only being completely in control of one's self and boat, but of also making sure that the competitors were aware of that competence. Top flight international yachting competitors are cool-headed, relaxed and organized—all elements that win races and demoralize the opposition. All during the summer at Newport, Ficker exuded those qualities and made sure his crew did as well.

Ficker instilled in his crew the importance of maintaining a facade of confidence, win or lose. His calm, self-assured intensity was imparted to the crew early in the season, even though things were not going particularly well. *Intrepid* lost five out of eight races in the June series against *Valiant*, the boat that would ultimately be her chief competitor. Yet this record did not seem to phase the *Intrepid* crew, and in the July trials they won every race except one and were well on their way to selection. *Intrepid* entered the final trials as the "boat to beat," a distinction that Ficker feels is psychologically advantageous on the race course.

Bill's subtle psychological warfare would start at 10 o'clock every morning during the summer. *Intrepid* left the dock on or before the hour for a full day of drill out on Block Island Sound or at the mouth of Narragansett Bay. The strict departure time insured that all the crew completed their duties on schedule. It never went unnoticed by the rival skippers who were also trying to get their boats out on the Sound for practice but couldn't manage to leave the dock because of some overlooked detail. Ficker's organization not only helped the whole *Intrepid* effort; it also had a subtle domoralizing effect on the opposition and contributed to the "boat-to-beat" mentality.

At precisely three o'clock each afternoon, *Intrepid* would stop her sailhandling practice and come into port. Five hours of drill was enough for any crew and enough of the day was still left to accomplish the hundreds of details necessary to ready the boat for the next day's activities. In addition, the crew would work hard toward a set goal; for they knew that at precisely a certain time each day, it would all be over. Furthermore, the land support faction of the syndicate knew exactly when to expect the boat to arrive at the dock and would be there to expedite sail repairs, gear changes and anything else that needed immediate attention. Even the cook at the syndicate house knew exactly when to have the meal prepared.

The effect of *Intrepid's* 3 o'clock "quiting time" on the crews of the other boats still out practicing was also important. Because the opposition got started later in the morning, they had to stay out later in the afternoon. When the other crews saw the *Intrepid* gang going in "early" they began to wonder why they had to work so late, and their own performance started to become sluggish. Again, the "boat-to-beat" concept was further reinforced.

Another important aspect of the psychological strategy of the America's Cup, as in any important sailing meet, is having a crew that can accept defeat without losing morale. The crew must neither become demoralized, nor, more importantly, must they appear to be demoralized to their opponents. There are bound to be some defeats through a 12-Meter summer. In fact, in only one year—in 1967 when *Intrepid* was the only new boat and markedly faster than the older contenders—has the ultimate defender been obvious from the start. When the winning crew arrives back at the dock and finds "beaten" competitors, they experience a psychological lift. Instead, if they find a crew that has just lost a race in high spirits and confident of winning the next, the "mental" win is neutralized. Hangdog looks and expressions of defeat only bolster the opposition. All of this is basic psychology and is well understood by most teams going to Newport. Both 1974 skippers, Bob Bavier and Ted Turner, assert that a few defeats will not be allowed to demoralize their crews. "Over the years," Ted Turner says, "I've lost many more races than I've won. My crew has been through defeat many times and they know how to bounce right back."

One of the best psychological warfare campaigns took place in 1970 when "Ficker is Quicker" buttons, ribbons, and bumper stickers appeared around Newport at mid-summer. The rhyme was fun to say and caught on, and soon people who didn't even know Ficker or *Intrepid* were wearing the encouraging slogan. Curiously, the phrase had been coined by the irrepressible Ted Turner one afternoon at cocktail hour. Steve Van Dyck heard it, immediately realized its psychological value, and had the pins made up. The *Valiant* syndicate quickly followed with a *"Go Valiant"* set of bumper stickers but this only acknowledged the impact of the Ficker slogan all the more. The buttons came out at a time when few people were really sure which boat was really quicker and left them with a subconscious bias that was difficult to overcome. Although the net effect of the "Ficker is Quicker" slogan on Morgan, McCullough, and ultimately, on the Australians is impossible to determine, it certainly didn't do Ficker any harm.

In 1964, the popularity of the expression, "Beat the Bird," had proved psychologically effective in urging the crew of *Constellation* to triumph over *American Eagle*. "Beat the Bird" was repeated all over Newport and was a good psychological ploy for the boat that had been consistently losing but was felt by many to have winning capabilities. Although the slogan acknowledged that the "Bird" was the boat to beat, it also gave the *Constellation* gang cause to rally and had a detrimental effect on the *American Eagle* crew who knew that much of Newport supported the come-from-behind boat.

The fact that a challenger has never won the America's Cup is, of course, the biggest psychological factor of all. With each passing and unsuccessful foreign challenge, its impact increases. Some of the richest men in the world have gone after this coveted prize with the most clever naval architects in the world, yet out of 21 challenges, only one boat

Block Island Sound is the site of the America's Cup match

has even been able to win two races! This is the biggest "psych" of all, and it hangs over Newport like a summer high. Even the most determined contender can never completely repress the knowledge that for 104 years the New York Yacht Club has been invincible in its defense.

Pre-Race Tactical Preparation

It goes without saying that the more one team knows about the behavior of the other, the better. Historically, the 12-Meter crews have closely watched their opposition during a race for hints about their coming maneuvers. When beating to windward, members of both afterguards carefully scrutinize the opposing crew for signs of their preparing to tack. Twelve-Meter crews go to great pains to avoid signalling a tack before it is made, but an experienced observer can usually detect some tell-tale give-away. Even though the crew might be motionless, a member of the afterguard will inevitably put his hand on the main sheet or take his binoculars off, or the skipper himself will change his position slightly to get ready to tack. Even on the modern Twelves, with most of the crewmen below deck, the practiced eye can usually detect intimations of a soon-to-be-executed maneuver. Good detective work before the final showdown can reveal tacking clues.

Quite a bit of pre-race observation is also involved in finding out what weight sails the opposition has aboard and what the different sails look like. When one boat hoists her genoa, the other boat then knows what weight cloth she will be using during the race. Actually, there are not many times when one crew's selection of a sail will come as a surprise to the other, but in a few cases, knowledge of the enemy's sail inventory can help. More important is which weight spinnaker they choose, and for this reason most 12-Meter syndicates order all of their spinnakers in white. The light, half-ounce spinnaker must be indistinguishable from the one-and-a-half ounce chute. The beautiful spinnaker that the French used in 1970 with the large, colorful crest was surprising. Though visually impressive, it alerted the Australians to exactly what weight cloth the French had chosen; all summer the Australians and the Americans had been carefully noting what chutes the French team had been hoisting in various wind strengths, and their notes proved valuable when it came time to race.

Knowledge of the Rules

Though usually taken for granted, the skippers' complete understanding of the complex International Yacht Racing Rules is obviously of prime importance. The helmsmen must have not only a letter-perfect command of what they say, but also a lightning ability to apply them in any situation that may suddenly occur. This is particularly critical during the start because a number of the rules change after the gun goes off. In the 1970 trials George Hinman, a member of the international rule-making board, may have had an upper hand at the starts because of his complete mastery of the rules. In contrast, Martin Visser, the man at the Australian helm for a number of the starts in the 1970 America's Cup match, cost the challenger one race through his misinterpretation of the rules. Probably the most outstanding example of a man who knew the racing rules, but not quite well enough, was T. O. M. Sopwith. Had he hoisted his protest flag immediately (instead of half an hour later) after Vanderbilt failed to respond to his luff (and not protested a pre-start port-starboard incident) the race committee most assuredly would have awarded him a third race in the 1934 challenge. Sopwith could well have sailed home with the America's Cup, save for his tardy protest flag. The rules clearly read that the flag will be flown at the first opportunity after the infraction.

Some Starting Tactics

The most basic starting tactic is to cross the starting line sometime after the starting gun and as far ahead of the opposition as possible.

"Ahead" does not necessarily mean to windward; it may mean a safe leeward position, where the leeward boat is ahead of the windward one and therefore has clear air. Winning the start might also mean crossing the starting line slightly behind but on the windward quarter of the other boat. If a wind shift is expected, that will also determine the best starting position.

A boat's speed will largely determine what starting strategy the skipper will choose. If one boat is clearly faster than the other, she is wise to stay away from her opponent and cross the starting line at about the same time as the other boat, maintaining clear air. Bavier used this approach in 1964 against *Sovereign* when it became obvious that his *Constellation* was much faster. The American helmsman simply wanted to stay away from the challenger to keep from being fouled— the only possible way Bavier figured he could lose. *Constellation's* superior boat speed soon took care of the challenger. Bus Mosbacher used the same tactic in 1967 when *Intrepid* was clearly faster than *Dame Pattie*. In both cases the challengers, Peter Scott and Jock Sturrock obliged the defenders and did not go after them to grapple for control at the start.

Although a winning starting tactic for the faster boat may be to start behind his opponent, this is definitely not a good strategy for the slower boat. She must start first, as far ahead of her opponent as possible. An aggressively sailed slow boat will try to wipe-off the fast boat at either end of the line (by forcing the other boat on the wrong side of the mark) or she will try to force the other boat over the starting line early. A slower boat is more likely to initiate the famous circling maneuver; if she can slip on to the faster boat's tail, she can control her.

Mosbacher, in a controlling position, forced Sturrock over the line early in the first race of 1962 when *Weatherly* was the slower boat. Traditionally, the challengers have not been very aggressive at starting except in 1970—when they had a faster boat—the single time that they probably would have been better served by only going for good, clear-air starts.

Being first over the line after the gun is important in fleet racing, but in match racing it makes little difference when the boats cross the line. In one of the 1970 races Hardy had slipped behind Ficker and was driving him away from the line in a controlling position, but he threw it all away when he left his opponent too soon to go for the line. He had not timed his move properly and *Gretel II,* arriving early at the line, had to kill way. Ficker, on the other hand, made a perfectly timed start and smashed by *Gretel* with full way on. Because *Gretel II* was as fast as *Intrepid,* it would have been better for Hardy to have waited for the gun before going for the line.

Another factor which may determine who wins the start is whether one end of the starting line is favored over the other. If one end is favored by more than a few degrees, other factors being equal, it may be worthwhile for a boat to start at that end and thereby gain precious yards to windward on the other boat. The New York Yacht Club race committee prides itself on setting starting lines that are as square to the wind as possible, but if the air is "fluky" the line may unavoidably favor one end over the other.

The Tailing Game

Undoubtedly, the best advantage in the pre-start maneuvers will go to the boat that can get on the other's tail. Mosbacher admirably demonstrated this point during the 1958 American trials when he was sailing the slower *Vim*. Bus would fall approximately one-half a length behind his opponent and then drive the other boat away from the

"Constellation" and "American Eagle" (21) locked in the circling maneuver

starting line by using racing rule 41. Rule 41 states, "A yacht which is either tacking or jibing shall keep clear of a yacht on a tack." When the lead boat wanted to tack or jibe around to head for the starting line, Mosbacher needed only to head *Vim* up or bare her off and hail "Don't tack" or "Don't jibe." Since *Vim* was on a tack, the other boat had to keep clear and because *Vim* was so close behind, her opponent could not tack or jibe and still remain clear. That allowed *Vim,* the controlling boat, to go for the line whenever she pleased.

There is one way that the lead boat can squirm out from under the control of the trailing boat. If she comes head to wind (or if heading off the wind, if she sheets in and luffs dead downwind), she can thereby force the other boat to either sail by or luff with her. If the trailing boat chooses to luff, the lead boat then needs only to tack or jibe away from her tormentor. But generally, the trailing position is a powerful controlling position, and skippers will jockey continually to get on the other's transom.

In 1964, Bob Bavier used the circling maneuver that results from this jockeying for position to his own advantage. When sailing by his opponent, he had his crew give the appearance that they were not ready to respond to an attack. The English skipper, Scott, lulled into thinking that the defenders were not yet ready to do battle was caught by surprise and *Constellation* got the controlling position.

George Hinman on Starting Tactics

In 1970, George Hinman steered *Weatherly,* one of the oldest of the modern Twelves, as a trial horse for *Valiant.* Later the selection committee asked *Weatherly* to compete in the trials so that each of the three hot contenders could have a race each day. Hinman couldn't have been more pleased and relished the opportunity to take on the younger skippers in their new boats and show them exactly what he could do even with an old war horse. Using old sails and a "pick-up" crew of young Long Island smallboat sailors, Hinman proceeded to dazzle the opposition with his aggressive starting and racing tactics. In the 13 races in which *Weatherly* competed, Hinman won nearly all of the starts, seven of them decisively.

Although *Weatherly* actually won only three of the 13 trial races conducted by the NYYC selection committee, she showed what an older, slower boat could do when aggressively handled. Hinman grabbed the starts (and the headlines in the next morning's papers) with his dashing tactics. By August the other boats had improved and *Weatherly* was polished off both at the starts and at the finish line by the other three boats, but the summer had been an exciting one.

Recently, George Hinman said the following about starts:

"The fascinating thing about match-race starting is that you can't go in with a definite plan and expect to execute it precisely. Rather, you must wait for the opposition to leave an opening, and until that happens you can't follow any organized plan. I do believe because of the short windward leg (the weather leg is now 4.5 miles but used to be 8 miles) that there is some merit in starting at the windward end of the line. I know that certain skippers, Bill Ficker for example, are inclined to start at that point. So if you're starting against someone with that philosophy you try to do one of two things: you either try to get there yourself, or you try to squeeze him to the other side of the committee boat. Only one boat can get in the advantageous position.

"How do you get to the windward end? Usually, you are circling before the start or going back and forth. It all depends on what the helmsmen do in the last minute which determines who will get the start. This business of going around in circles ten minutes ahead is unproductive because it is only the last minute that counts. Circling is really meaningless and wears the crew down.

"If someone gets on your stern going away from the line you are in trouble. You should never go beyond the triangle which is made up of both ends of the line and a "V" in the middle. If you stay in that "V" and then someone gets on your tail, you just sit up into the wind, and what can they do? You can sit there for five minutes and eventually one has to peel off on the wind one way, and one the other. As long as you are in that "V" you can, in theory, get an even start. If the man behind lets you sit on the line too long, almost until the gun goes, then you've got him. As you peel off he has got to be underneath you. His only defense is to come up along side of you and then at the gun one goes one way and one the other.

"The man who breaks from the rounding situation and goes for the line at precisely the right time to cross just after the gun is the man who wins the start. If he is too early then the man behind is in the controlling situation and should win the start. Whoever is in the right place in that last whirl in the last minute before the gun will be the man who gets the start. That's why I can't see starting the circling ten minutes before; there is simply no way you can tell who will be in the right place at the gun. That's one reason why the skippers are so nervous before the start, they know it can be a toss up. Of course, even good skippers are nervous before any big start . . . you never get over it."

Ted Turner on Starting Tactics

Mariner helmsman Ted Turner gives his views on starting:

"Every start has to be looked at individually. There is no way you can tell in advance what is going to happen. We'll be aggressive at the starts; particularly in the beginning until we determine whether or not we have a leg up on the opposition. We're going to try to win the starts not just go for clear air . . . at least not at the beginning.

"All that circling doesn't really accomplish one hell of a lot unless the other guy is unsure of himself. All that circling really does is give the spectators something to watch. Ultimately the sailing characteristics of our boat will determine our strategy. If our boat can point higher we'll try to start to weather of them. If we find that we aren't a good pointer but can foot fast, we will probably want to be to leeward. It all depends on the boat. If we're clearly superior to the other boat, we may just go for clear air and not bother to fiddle around with any of these maneuvers.

"When Mosbacher sailed *Intrepid,* a boat that was definitely faster than *Dame Pattie,* he just went for clear air. When he sailed *Vim,* a slower boat, he had to try to hammer the guy at the start so he could get on top.

"Our tactics will depend on the characteristics of the boat and upon what opportunities present themselves at the start. We'll do it exactly the way a bullfighter does with a bull. The first thing he does when he goes out there is test the bull out. Then he determines how he is going to fight the bull by the bull's personality. We'll go out there and do some early sparring to see how they react. We will have no plan of attack but rather will wait for opportunity. If you have a plan of attack, you're in bad shape.

"We'll probably start against Bavier 30 times during the summer and if we had a certain plan we followed each time we'd be cooked. It's just like chess. If you play with a guy who's only got one plan, after four or five games you know it and can combat it and the guy's up the creek. I am, basically, on the starts an opportunist, just the way I play chess. I don't really have a plan and I normally wait for the guy to make a mistake. The dangerous thing about the circling maneuver is that it's almost a toss up who will win, it's a 50–50 sort of thing. Yet, if we find that we can turn faster than the other boat and accelerate faster, then we have an advantage and I might use it. For example, if I had been steering *Gretel II* against *Intrepid,* I'd want to circle because *Intrepid* was slower at accelerating.

"If my boat accelerates slower, I'll try not to allow myself to be trapped like that and come in on a screaming reach with a full bore of steam from a long way away. Then Bavier will have a choice: he can either get on my stern and try to mess me up or he can get in front of me. I'll kill time away from the line, well beyond the committee boat until about five minutes before the gun and have a timed start. With four minutes to go, for example, I might sheet in and go for the favored end of the starting line. If the line is great and perfectly square then it doesn't matter where you start, except it's safer to hit the line in the middle because if you're early you can go down or you can kill speed by luffing up. If you are going for the committee boat end of the line and your opposition is coming up close-hauled, he can cut you off at the committee boat if you're early.

"There are so many starting possibilities that they can't all be mentioned. Each has a defense and whether a boat is ahead or behind to windward or to leeward, there are some good offensive and defensive strategies for each position. It's not like checkers where there are only four possible squares where a man can move to at any one time. The positions that the boats can find themselves in at any one time are infinite.

"If my boat is a shade slower I'm in serious trouble. The first thing I'll try to do is get the boat faster. As far as tactics go, I'll have to go for a clearly superior start, which means I'll try to get the opponent behind me and to leeward or in front of me and over before the gun. If I'm slower, I've got to beat him badly at the start . . . or foul him out, although I don't like fouling people out at the start. The ideal situation is to have a boat that is slightly faster; then I won't be too worried.

"*Gretel II* is a good example of a faster boat that lost. All you have to do is to be one percent faster and you should have it made. The *Gretel II* guys didn't know that they were faster and they didn't have a whole summer to race. *Gretel II* was on a ship from June 10 until August 11 and they didn't have a chance to find out how fast they really were. They didn't have time to get confidence in themselves. If they had the summer to race there would have been time to get confidence and they would have won the America's Cup.

"Time was the key. A bull fighter and a bull only fight for 15 minutes

George Hinman stares down the opposition

and they never let a bull fight twice because a bull would win if it knew at the beginning what it knows at the end. That was true of *Gretel II*. The only reason why the Americans win when they have a slower boat is because the foreigners are not really ready. That's the bad thing about letting them have these trials. They are going to get tuned up, they're going to get their confidence up, they'll be prepared."

Action at the Committee Boat

As in 1970, the prospects are good that the committee boat end of the line will be the site of the hot and close action at the start. By the very nature of the starboard "right-of-way" rule, the windward end of the line is favored and that is where the committee boat is anchored. In other words, a boat starting at the committee boat will be to weather of the other boat, whether the other boat is just to leeward of her or all the way down the line.

During the starting maneuvers, a boat that is being tailed will often try to seek refuge behind the committee boat. Bob Bavier points out

The committee boat is often used as a buffer in starting tactics

in his book "Sailing to Win" that a boat that is being tailed ". . . can then tack or jibe around the committee boat even though closely pursued, because the tailing boat cannot cut the corner to block her from doing so. It is for this reason that one often sees in match racing the two boats circling tightly around the committee boat."

Constellation used this tactic successfully in a close contest with *American Eagle.* Bill Cox had fallen in close on Bavier's stern. Bavier headed for the committee boat on port tack, then hardened up just as he was passing to leeward of her. Cox hardened up to pass to windward of the committee boat so that he would be on *Connie's* stern when both boats were past the committee, but Bavier used the buffer of the committee boat to jibe around and head back toward the line, thus shaking his cover.

Tactics After the Start

The object, of course, is to be first to the windward mark and be there as far ahead of the other boat as possible. Twelve-Meter skippers imagine two fences running down the course on the two lay lines (imaginary lines along which the boats can reach the mark without tacking) to the windward mark. The first boat to reach one of these lay lines can often be the first boat to the weather mark.

Here is where the classic match racing tactic of "covering" first comes into play. The boat ahead will usually cover by staying between the opposition and the mark, while the boat behind tries to break the cover by getting out of phase with (getting on the opposite tack) the boat ahead or by driving off to one side of the course or the other in hopes of a wind shift. If a wind shift is expected—in the afternoon near the Point Judith side of Block Island Sound there is often a shift that favors the port tack—the boat behind will usually drive off to the side where she expects the header. If the header comes, the boats will tack and the one closer to the new wind will have a better slant to the mark. If the boats are of equal speed, the one that has a better slant should be faster. If one boat is slower, yet has a better slant, she might be able to equalize the speed difference.

There are, though, some exceptions to the covering rule. One rarely tacks into light air to cover, because this kills boat speed and may allow the other boat to slip ahead. Often, too, the lead boat may relinquish her cover to tack to a favored side of the course. Bill Ficker successfully employed this tactic against the faster *Gretel II* in 1970. When slightly ahead on the windward leg, he would give up covering Hardy and gamble on a favorable shift that could put him even farther ahead at the windward mark. The distance he gained was essential to the 1970 *Intrepid* victory.

In those situations where a skipper chooses to cover his opponent

Covering is a basic match racing tactic

for a substantial period of time, the blanketed boat's key strategy is to get clear air at all costs. Furious tacking duels are not uncommon, with the boat astern trying to break free and the boat ahead striving mightily to keep her opponent in bad air.

Tactics Off the Wind

There will probably be more action on the two reaching legs of the America's Cup course than ever seen before. Traditionally, the two reaches, which comprise the second and third legs of the course, have been veritable "parades." Usually, the boat which rounds the weather mark first is the first to the leeward mark, although the gap between the boats may have changed somewhat. A spinnaker foul-up at the weather mark can dramatically reduce a boat's lead, but due to the extensive sail-handling experience of the crews, such a mistake is a rarity. The usual minor difference between the two boats' spinnaker handling will be in the time it takes each to set their chutes and get them drawing. A more quickly set spinnaker can mean a few seconds gain.

The second mark of the course is called the "jibe mark" because the boats jibe around it. Twelve-Meter crews generally have jibing techniques down pat and sloppy work is uncommon—particularly on the part of the American teams. The important tactical situation at the jibe mark, as well as the leeward mark, is the inside overlap. If a boat is able to establish an overlap within two boat lengths of a mark, the lead boat must give him room to get around the buoy. Obviously, if a boat can establish that overlap before the jibe mark, he will be in a commanding position after the rounding, probably being able to blanket the leeward boat and sail by him.

On the downwind legs, the crews usually hoist small spinnakers in light to moderate air, reserving their large chutes for higher winds in a fairly calm sea. This seems contrary to common sense, but there is a good reason. Air is easily spilled from the big 12-Meter spinnaker and they can only be used when there is a fresh, off-shore breeze and the skippers are sure that the chutes will stay full.

One of the few times on the America's Cup course that the boat behind has the advantage is in running before the wind. Twelves can pick up about a full knot in boat speed by heading up as little as ten degrees from the dead downwind course, resulting in important jibing duels on the downwind leg. Although the boat behind can never really keep the leading boat in her wind shadow for a prolonged period of time, she can momentarily slow the leader down as she passes astern. If the boat behind can do this often enough, she will grind the leader down. Again, the cardinal tactic in force is for the leading boat to cover the boat behind by always staying between her and the mark. When the boat behind jibes to port, the one ahead must also jibe to port or risk losing his leading position.

The boat that rounds the leeward mark first has a tremendous advantage. Because boats go faster on the wind than they do dead downwind, the boat that rounds first can go nearly twice as fast as her opponent which is still floating down to the mark under spinnaker. Rounding the leeward mark first is, in fact, even more important than winning the start. The boat that can round first with a margin of 30 seconds will be almost unbeatable on the last leg.

As the boats round the leeward mark, they will note the signals on the committee boat to see if the course to the windward mark has been altered. It is changed when there is a windshift to insure three windward legs. On this leg, the boat behind might try a different genoa and different tactics in order to get through. Since there are three windward legs the skippers get to know the tactics that will be employed by each other in response to certain maneuvers.

Crew Selection

Crew selection is one of the most important tactical decisions of all. It is, of course, a decision made far in advance of the match. Although the challengers generally have fine crews, the defending crewmen have always seemed to have an edge when it comes to sail-handling expertise. The biggest single reason for this is probably that the Americans spend three solid months in practice and experience heavy competition for the right to defend. In addition, as previously mentioned, it is not uncommon for American defenders to have a trial horse, utilizing a reserve crew. The American skippers quite often have the opportunity to pick from among over 20 men working both the main contender and the warm-up boat, whereas the challengers have often had to select their 11 men from the outset and stick with them. On rare occasions the skipper of the boat selected to defend has asked a crewmember of another American boat to join his crew for the final showdown, as in 1958 when Briggs Cunningham asked Vic Romagna aboard to execute his innovative spinnaker-handling techniques.

"Valiant" was the first boat to have genoa sheeting drums below deck

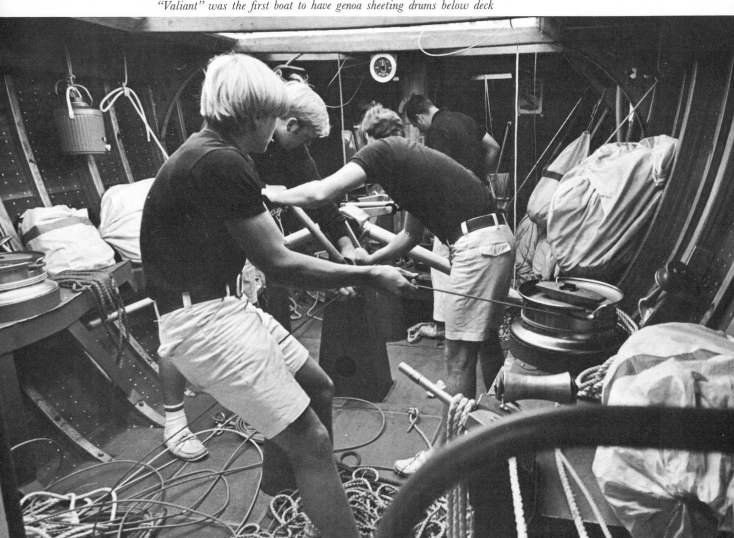

After knowledge of good racing tactics and procedures and physical strength, probably the most important attribute of a 12-Meter crewman is compatibility. Every crewman must be a good shipmate, both aboard the Twelve and ashore and must be able to get along easily with his fellow crewmen. This single quality ranks highest on nearly every 12-Meter skipper's list, after basic sailing experience. The individual crewmen must be team players. Even though each may be a champion in his own right, there is only room for one skipper aboard an America's Cup boat. To have even a hesitation in response to a sail-handling order is to risk defeat.

The crewmen must also be dedicated competitors. Dedicated enough to give up four months of their life to toil through a summer of drills and sail handling evolutions, many of which are below deck. The young men must be determined to do one thing for their 12-Meter summer—give 100 percent of their effort for the team. Because of the prestige of the America's Cup and the honor usually associated with being a part of the defense, American syndicates usually get the kind of men they need.

Bus Mosbacher has likened the 11-man America's Cup team to that of a football team. Just as a football team must get in shape, practice, work together, so the 12-Meter team must have split-second timing, an intuitive knowledge of what the man next to him is doing

The "Intrepid" crew celebrate after winning the 1970 match. The final tactic

and a readiness to accept orders without question. There is no room for the lone wolf, the know-it-all, or the temperamental individualist; all must be willing to subordinate themselves to the team. A good crewman can joke and take jokes, and he accepts criticism in the spirit in which it is given.

The regimen of the American crews is famous, and perhaps a bit out-dated. Some syndicates have even been known to set "hours" by which time the crewmen have to be in bed at the syndicate's house in Newport. This is to discourage carousing in the lively night spots. On this point Bill Ficker says, "I would like individuals who have adequate maturity to know what their responsibilities are. After all, the crew is just as concerned about what my habits are as I am about theirs. I don't think they would be very happy with me if I responded to their tremendous efforts on the boat by being out until all hours in the morning before a race carousing and drinking. There has to be a mutual respect for efforts involved."

"Basically you should always try to select crew members who know at least as much as you do but whose behavior patterns permit them to adjust to the style with which the skipper approaches the effort. I generally like young crewmen with as much experience as possible but who have not submitted to the too-familiar pattern of becoming so-called "experts" or become inflexible. I think also that the younger sailors are never satisfied with just winning, but have the spirit of gamesmanship which makes them want to destroy their competition. The younger crew also seems to be more resilient in coming back from a loss in order to fashion a win."

The 1970 NYYC America's Cup selection committee

PHOTO CREDITS:

Peter Barlow—i, 10, 102, 105, 113, 122, 138, 178, 189; **Robert Carrick**—171; **Bruce Crabtree**—157; **Geoffrey F. Hammond**—134, 147, 149, 158, 159, 160; **H. H. Harris**—68; **John T. Hopf**—5, 7, 92, 94, 192, 196, 199, 206; **Lois J. Kennedy**—137; **Kai Kruger**—119; **Edwin Levick**—64; **Denis Merlin**—98–99, 126; **Fusanori Nakajima**—76, 110–111; **David Rosenfeld**—114; **Morris Rosenfeld & Sons**—viii, 3, 24, 27, 34, 35, 37, 42, 46, 50, 53, 54, 60, 61, 62–63, 65, 66, 89, 141; **Stanley Rosenfeld**—70, 74, 78, 79, 81, 86, 88, 97, 100, 103, 104, 106, 107, 108, 125, 127, 131, 153, 166, 170, 180, 187, 202, 204, 208, 209, 210; **Western Australian Newspapers, Ltd.**—116; **Hugh D. Whall**—145.

Quotation of Bob Bavier on page 205 from his book "Sailing to Win" by permission of Dodd, Mead Inc, New York; Quotation of Bill Ficker on page 210 by permission of Sea Publications, Los Angeles. Picture on page 94 held in copyright by John T. Hopf.

AMERICA'S CUP
1851 to 1970

DATE	CHALLENGING CLUB	CHALLENGING VESSEL AND SKIPPER	TONS L.O.A. L.W.L. SAIL AREA	DESIGNER BUILDER	OWNER(S)
1870	Royal Thames Yacht Club	*Cambria* J. Tannock	228 T. 108' 98' 8,602 sq. ft.	Michael Ratsey Michael Ratsey	James Ashbury
1871	Royal Harwich Yacht Club	*Livonia* J. R. Woods	280 T. 127' 106' 18,153 sq. ft.	Michael Ratsey Michael Ratsey	James Ashbury
1876	Royal Canadian Yacht Club	*Countess of Dufferin* J. E. Ellsworth	138 T. 107' 95' 12,000 sq. ft.	Alex. Cuthbert Alex. Cuthbert	Major Charles Gifford and Syndicate
1881	Bay of Quinte Yacht Club	*Atalanta* Alex. Cuthbert	84 T. 70' 64' ?	Alex. Cuthbert Alex. Cuthbert	Alexander Cuthbert
1885	Royal Yacht Squadron	*Genesta* John Carter	80 T. 96' 81' 7,150 sq. ft.	J. Beavor-Webb D. & W. Henderson & Co.	Sir Richard Sutton
1886	Royal Northern Yacht Club	*Galatea* Dan Bradford	171 T. 103' 87' 7,505 sq. ft.	J. Beavor-Webb J. Reed & Son	Lt. William Henn, R.N.
1887	Royal Clyde Yacht Club	*Thistle* John Barr	138 T. 109' 87' 8,968 sq. ft.	Geo. L. Watson D. & W. Henderson & Co.	James Bell and Syndicate
1893	Royal Yacht Squadron	*Valkyrie II* Willaim Cranfield	94 T. 117' 86' 10,042 sq. ft.	Geo. L. Watson D. & W. Henderson & Co.	The Earl of Dunraven
1895	Royal Yacht Squadron	*Valkyrie III* William Cranfield	101 T. 129' 89' 13,028 sq. ft.	Geo. L. Watson D. & W. Henderson & Co.	The Earl of Dunraven Lord Lonsdale Lord Wolverton Capt. Harry McCalmont
1899	Royal Ulster Yacht Club	*Shamrock* "Archie" Hogarth	135 T. 128' 90' 13,492 sq. ft.	William Fife, Jr. J. I. Thorneycroft	Sir Thomas Lipton
1901	Royal Ulster Yacht Club	*Shamrock II* Edward A. Sycamore	129 T. 137' 89' 14,027 sq. ft.	Geo. L. Watson (1st Tank Tests) Wm. Denny & Bros.	Sir Thomas Lipton
1903	Royal Ulster Yacht Club	*Shamrock III* Robert Wringe	139 T. 134' 90' 14,154 sq. ft.	William Fife, Jr. Wm. Denny & Bros.	Sir Thomas Lipton
1920	Royal Ulster Yacht Club	*Shamrock IV* William P. Burton	97 T. 110' 75' 10,459 sq. ft.	C. E. Nicholson Camper & Nicholson Ltd.	Sir Thomas Lipton
1930	Royal Ulster Yacht Club	*Shamrock V* Ernest Heard	134 T. 119' 81' 7,540 sq. ft.	C. E. Nicholson Camper & Nicholson Ltd.	Sir Thomas Lipton
1934	Royal Yacht Squadron	*Endeavour* T. O. M. Sopwith	143 T. 130' 83' 7,561 sq. ft.	C. E. Nicholson Camper & Nicholson Ltd.	T. O. M. Sopwith
1937	Royal Yacht Squadron	*Endeavour II* T. O. M. Sopwith	163 T. 136' 87' 7,543 sq. ft.	C. E. Nicholson Camper & Nicholson Ltd.	T. O. M. Sopwith
1958	Royal Yacht Squadron	*Sceptre* Lt. Comdr. Graham Mann, R.N.	25 T. 69' 47' 1,819 sq. ft.	David Boyd Alex Robertson and Sons Ltd.	Hugh L. Goodson and Syndicate
1962	Royal Sydney Yacht Squadron	*Gretel* Alexander Sturrock	29 T. 70' 45' 1,854 sq. ft.	Alan Payne Lars Halvorsen Sons, Pty. Ltd.	Sir Frank Packer and Syndicate
1964	Royal Thames Yacht Club	*Sovereign* Peter Scott	25 T. 69' 49' 1,876 sq. ft.	David Boyd Alex Robertson and Sons Ltd.	James A. J. Boyden
1967	Royal Sydney Yacht Squadron	*Dame Pattie* Alexander Sturrock	29 T. 65' 2" 46' 11" 1,795 sq. ft.	Warwick Hood William Barnett	Emil Christensen and group of 15 commercial firms.
1970	Royal Sydney Yacht Club	*Gretel II* Jim Hardy	30 T. 62' 46' 1,750 sq. ft.	Alan Payne W. H. Barnett	Sir Frank Packer

DEFENDING VESSEL AND SKIPPER	TONS L.O.A. L.W.L. SAIL AREA	DESIGNER BUILDER	OWNER(S)	U. S. CONTENDERS ELIMINATED IN TRIALS
Magic Andrew Comstock	112 T. 84′ 79′ 1,680 sq. ft. Lowers Only	R. F. Loper T. Byerly & Son	Franklin Osgood	
Columbia Nelson Comstock	230 T. 108′ 96′ ?	J. B. Van Deusen J. B. Van Deusen	Franklin Osgood	
Sappho Sam Greenwood	310 T. 135′ 119′ 9,060 sq. ft.	C. & R. Poillon C. & R. Poillon	Colonel W. P. Douglas	
Madeleine Josephus Williams	152 T. 106′ 95′ 17,231 sq. ft.	David Kirby David Kirby	John S. Dickerson	Elimination Trials began in 1881
Mischief Nathaniel Clock	79 T. 67′ 61′ ?	A. Cary Smith Harlan and Hollingsworth	Joseph R. Busk	*Pocahontas* *Gracie* *Hildegard*
Puritan Aubrey Crocker	140 T. 94′ 81′ 7,982 sq. ft.	Edward Burgess George Lawley and Son	J. Malcolm Forbes General Charles J. Paine and Syndicate.	*Priscilla* *Gracie* *Bedouin*
Mayflower Martin V. B. Stone	172 T. 100′ 86′ 8,500 sq. ft.	Edward Burgess George Lawley and Son	General Charles J. Paine	*Atlantic* *Puritan* *Priscilla*
Volunteer Henry C. Haff	209 T. 107′ 86′ 9,271 sq. ft.	Edward Burgess Pusey & Jones Shipbuilding Co.	General Charles J. Paine	*Mayflower*
Vigilant William Hansen	96 T. 124′ 86′ 11,242 sq. ft.	N. G. Herreshoff Herreshoff Mfg. Co.	C. Oliver Iselin and Syndicate	*Pilgrim* *Colonia* *Jubilee*
Defender Henry C. Haff	100 T. 123′ 89′ 12,602 sq. ft.	N. G. Herreshoff Herreshoff Mfg. Co.	William K. Vanderbilt C. Oliver Iselin E. D. Morgan	*Vigilant*
Columbia Charles Barr	102 T. 131′ 90′ 13,135 sq. ft.	N. G. Herreshoff Herreshoff Mfg. Co.	J. P. Morgan C. Oliver Iselin E. D. Morgan	*Defender*
Columbia Charles Barr	102 T. 131′ 90′ 13,135 sq. ft.	N. G. Herreshoff Herreshoff Mfg. Co.	J. P. Morgan E. D. Morgan	*Constitution* *Independence*
Reliance Charles Barr	140 T. 144′ 90′ 16,160 sq. ft.	N. G. Herreshoff Herreshoff Mfg. Co.	C. Oliver Iselin and Syndicate	*Columbia* *Constitution*
Resolute Charles Francis Adams, II	99 T. 106′ 75′ 8,775 sq. ft.	N. G. Herreshoff Herreshoff Mfg. Co.	Henry Walters and Syndicate	*Vanitie* *Defiance* Launched 1914. Not active 1920.
Enterprise Harold S. Vanderbilt	128 T. 121′ 80′ 7,583 sq. ft.	W. Starling Burgess Herreshoff Mfg. Co.	Winthrop W. Aldrich and Syndicate	*Weetamoe* *Yankee* *Whirlwind*
Rainbow Harold S. Vanderbilt	141 T. 127′ 82′ 7,572 sq. ft.	W. Starling Burgess Herreshoff Mfg. Co.	Harold S. Vanderbilt and Syndicate	*Yankee* *Weetamoe* *Vanitie*
Ranger Harold S. Vanderbilt	166 T. 135′ 87′ 7,546 sq. ft.	W. Starling Burgess and Olin J. Stephens Bath Iron Works	Harold S. Vanderbilt	*Yankee* *Rainbow*
Columbia Briggs S. Cunningham	28 T. 70′ 46′ 1,817 sq. ft.	Sparkman & Stephens Nevins Yacht Yard	Henry Sears and Syndicate	*Vim* *Weatherly* *Easterner*
Weatherly Emil Mosbacher, Jr.	30 T. 67′ 47′ 1,845 sq. ft.	Philip L. Rhodes Luders Marine Const. Co.	Henry D. Mercer Arnold D. Frese Cornelius S. Walsh	*Nefertiti* *Columbia* *Easterner*
Constellation Robert N. Bavier, Jr. Eric Ridder	35 T. 68′ 45′ 1,818 sq. ft.	Sparkman & Stephens Minneford Yacht Yard	Walter S. Gubelmann Eric Ridder and Syndicate	*American Eagle* *Columbia* *Nefertiti* *Easterner*
Intrepid Emil Mosbacher, Jr.	30 T. 64′ 45′ 6″ 1,850 sq. ft.	Sparkman & Stephens Minneford Yacht Yard	Intrepid Syndicate	*American Eagle* *Columbia* *Constellation*
Intrepid William Ficker	32 T. 64′ 5″ 47′ 1,750 sq. ft.	Sparkman & Stephens Britton Chance, Jr. Minneford's Shipyard	Intrepid Syndicate	*Valiant* *Heritage* *Weatherly*

RECORD OF THE AMERICA'S CUP MATCHES

Date	Name	Allows	Elapsed Time	Corrected Time	Wins By
		M.S.	H.M.S.	H.M.S.	M.S.
Aug. 22, 1851	America	—	10.37.00	10.37.00	8.00
	Aurora	—	10.45.00	10.45.00	
Aug. 8, 1870	Magic	14.7	4.07.54	3.58.21.2	39.17.7
	Cambria	—	4.34.57	4.37.38.9	
Oct. 16, 1871	Columbia	1.41	6.17.42	6.19.41	27.04
	Livonia	—	6.43.00	6.46.45	
Oct. 18, 1871	Columbia	6.10½	3.01.33½	3.07.41¾	10.33¾
	Livonia	—	3.06.49½	3.18.15½	
Oct. 19, 1871	Livonia	—	3.53.05	4.02.25	15.10
	Columbia	4.23	4.12.38	4.17.35	
Oct. 21, 1871	Sappho	—	5.33.24	5.36.02	33.21
	Livonia	2.07	6.04.38	6.09.23	
Oct. 23, 1871	Sappho	1.09	4.38.05	4.46.17	25.27
	Livonia	—	5.04.41	5.11.44	
Aug. 11, 1876	Madeleine	1.01	5.24.55	5.23.54	10.59
	Countess of Dufferin	—	5.34.53	5.34.53	
Aug. 12, 1876	Madeleine	1.01	7.19.47	7.18.46	27.14
	Countess of Dufferin	—	7.46.00	7.46.00	
Nov. 9, 1881	Mischief	—	4.17.09	4.17.06	28.20¼
	Atalanta	2.55¼	4.48.24½	4.45.29¼	
Nov. 10, 1881	Mischief	—	4.54.53	4.54.53	38.54
	Atalanta	2.55	5.36.52	5.33.47	
Sept. 14, 1885	Puritan	—	6.06.05	6.06.05	16.19
	Genesta	0.28	6.22.52	6.22.24	
Sept. 16, 1885	Puritan	—	5.03.14	5.03.14	1.38
	Genesta	0.28	5.05.20	5.04.52	
Sept. 9, 1886	Mayflower	—	5.26.41	5.26.41	12.02
	Galatea	0.38	5.39.21	5.38.43	
Sept. 11, 1886	Mayflower	—	6.49.00	6.49.00	29.09
	Galatea	0.39	7.18.48	7.18.09	
Sept. 27, 1887	Volunteer	—	4.53.18	4.53.18	19.23¾
	Thistle	0.05	5.12.46¾	5.12.41¾	
Sept. 30, 1887	Volunteer	—	5.42.56¼	5.42.56¾	11.48¾
	Thistle	0.06	5.54.51	5.54.45	
Oct. 7, 1893	Vigilant	—	4.05.47	4.05.47	5.48
	Valkyrie II	1.48	4.13.23	4.11.35	
Oct. 9, 1893	Vigilant	—	3.25.01	3.25.01	10.35
	Valkyrie II	1.48	3.37.24	3.35.36	
Oct. 13, 1893	Vigilant	—	3.24.39	3.24.39	.40
	Valkyrie II	1.33	3.26.52	3.25.19	
Sept. 7, 1895	Defender	0.29	5.00.24	4.59.55	8.49
	Valkyrie III	—	5.08.44	5.08.44	
Sept. 10, 1895	†Valkyrie III	—	3.55.09	3.55.09	.47
	Defender	0.29	3.56.25	3.55.56	
Sept. 12, 1895	Defender	0.29	4.44.12	4.43.43	
	‡ Valkyrie III	—	Did not finish		
Oct. 16, 1899	Columbia	—	4.53.53	4.53.53	10.08
	Shamrock	0.06	5.04.07	5.04.01	
Oct. 17, 1899	Columbia	—	3.37.00	3.37.00	
	@ Shamrock	0.06	Did not finish		
Oct. 20, 1899	Columbia	0.16	3.88.25	3.38.09	6.34
	Shamrock	—	3.44.43	3.44.43	
Sept. 28, 1901	Columbia	0.43	4.31.07	4.30.24	1.20
	Shamrock II	—	4.31.44	4.31.44	

Date	Name	Allows	Elapsed Time	Corrected Time	Wins By
Oct. 3, 1901	Columbia	0.43	3.13.18	3.12.35	3.35
	Shamrock II	—	3.16.10	3.16.10	
Oct. 4, 1901	Columbia	0.43	4.33.40	4.32.57	.41
	Shamrock II	—	4.33.38	4.33.38	
Aug. 22, 1903	Reliance	—	3.32.17	3.32.17	7.03
	Shamrock III	1.57	3.41.17	3.39.20	
Aug. 25, 1903	Reliance	—	3.14.54	3.14.54	1.19
	Shamrock III	1.57	3.18.10	3.16.12	
Sept. 3, 1903	Reliance	—	4.28.00	4.28.00	
	Shamrock III	1.57	Did not finish		
July 15, 1920	Shamrock IV	6.42	4.24.58	4.24.58	
	*Resolute	—	Did not finish		
July 20, 1920	Shamrock IV	7.01	5.33.18	5.22.18	2.26
	Resolute	—	5.31.45	5.24.44	
July 21, 1920	Resolute	—	4.03.06	3.56.05	7.01
	Shamrock IV	7.01	4.03.06	4.03.06	
July 23, 1920	Resolute	—	3.37.52	3.31.12	9.58
	Shamrock IV	6.40	3.41.10	3.41.10	
July 27, 1920	Resolute	—	5.35.15	5.28.35	19.45
	Shamrock IV	6.40	5.48.20	5.48.20	
Sept. 13, 1930	Enterprise	—	4.03.48		2.52
	Shamrock V	—	4.06.40		
Sept. 15, 1930	Enterprise	—	4.00.44		9.34
	Shamrock V	—	4.10.18		
Sept. 17, 1930	Enterprise	—	3.54.16		
	††Shamrock V	—	Did not finish		
Sept. 18, 1930	Enterprise	—	3.10.13		5.44
	Shamrock V	—	3.15.57		
Sept. 17, 1934	Endeavour	—	3.43.44		2.09
	Rainbow	—	3.45.53		
Sept. 18, 1934	Endeavour	—	3.09.01		.51
	Rainbow	—	3.09.52		
Sept. 20, 1934	Rainbow	—	4.35.34		3.26
	Endeavour	—	4.39.00		
Sept. 22, 1934	Rainbow	—	3.15.38		1.15
	Endeavour	—	3.16.53		
Sept. 24, 1934	Rainbow	—	3.54.05		4.01
	Endeavour	—	3.58.06		
Sept. 25, 1934	Rainbow	—	3.40.05		.55
	Endeavour	—	3.41.00		
July 31, 1937	Ranger	—	4.41.15		17.05
	Endeavour II	—	4.58.20		
Aug. 2, 1937	Ranger	—	3.41.33		18.32
	Endeavour II	—	4.00.05		
Aug. 4, 1937	Ranger	—	3.54.30		4.27
	Endeavour II	—	3.58.57		
Aug. 5, 1937	Ranger	—	3.07.49		3.37
	Endeavour II	—	3.11.26		
Sept. 20, 1958	Columbia	—	5.13.56		7.44
	Sceptre	—	5.21.40		
Sept. 22, 1958	Columbia	—	Time Limit Expired		
	Sceptre	—			
Sept. 24, 1958	Columbia	—	3.17.43		11.42
	Sceptre	—	3.29.25		
Sept. 25, 1958	Columbia	—	3.09.07		8.20
	Sceptre	—	3.17.27		

Date	Name	Allows	Elapsed Time	Corrected Time	Wins By
Sept. 26, 1958	Columbia	—	3.04.12		6.52
	Sceptre	—	3.11.04		
Sept. 15, 1962	Weatherly	—	3.13.57		3.43
	Gretel	—	3.17.40		
Sept. 18, 1962	Gretel	—	2.46.58		00.47
	Weatherly	—	2.47.45		
Sept. 20, 1962	Weatherly	—	4.21.16		8.40
	Gretel	—	4.29.56		
Sept. 22, 1962	Weatherly	—	3.22.28		00.26
	Gretel	—	3.22.54		
Sept. 25, 1962	Weatherly	—	3.16.17		3.40
	Gretel	—	3.19.57		
Sept. 15, 1964	Constellation	—	3.30.41		5.34
	Sovereign	—	3.36.15		
Sept. 17, 1964	Constellation	—	3.46.48		20.24
	Sovereign	—	4.17.12		
Sept. 19, 1964	Constellation	—	3.38.07		6.33
	Sovereign	—	3.44.40		
Sept. 21, 1964	Constellation	—	4.12.27		15.40
	Sovereign	—	4.28.07		
Sept. 12, 1967	Intrepid	—	3.25.03		5.58
	Dame Pattie	—	4.31.01		
Sept. 13, 1967	Intrepid	—	3.29.21		3.36
	Dame Pattie	—	3.32.57		
Sept. 14, 1967	Intrepid	—	3.20.14		4.41
	Dame Pattie	—	3.24.55		
Sept. 18, 1967	Intrepid	—	3.27.39		3.35
	Dame Pattie	—	3.31.14		
Sept. 15, 1970	Intrepid	—	3.26.03		5.52
	Gretel II	—	3.31.55		
Sept. 20, 1970	**Gretel II	—	4.37.03		1.07
	Intrepid	—	4.38.10		
Sept. 22, 1970	Intrepid	—	3.24.34		1.18
	Gretel II	—	3.25.87		
Sept. 24, 1970	Gretel II	—	3.23.38		1.02
	Intrepid	—	3.24.88		
Sept. 28, 1970	Intrepid	—	4.28.92		1.44
	Gretel II	—	4.30.37		

†Disqualified for fouling Defender.
‡Withdrew on crossing the line.
@Carried away topmast and withdrew.
††Parted main halyard at masthead sheave-withdrew.
*Throat halyard rendered on winch drum-withdrew.
**GRETEL II was disqualified for a foul after the starting signal and the race was awarded to INTREPID.